A Trapper's Legacy

A Trapper's Legacy

By
Carl Schels

ICS Books, Inc.
Merrillville, Indiana

A Trapper's Legacy

Published by:
ICS Books, Inc.
1000 E. 80th Place
Merrillville, IN. 46410

Distributed by:
Stackpole Books
Cameron and Kelker Streets
Harrisburg, PA. 17105

Library of Congress Cataloging in Publication Data
Schels, Carl.
     A trapper's legacy.

     Trapping--Minnesota. I. Title.
SK283.6.U6S34 1984   639'.11'09774   83-26496
ISBN 0-934802-12-2

PUBLISHER'S PREFACE

Carl Schels was a young man when the great depression struck. Raised in the city he found himself homeless with no job prospects. Having an innate love for the wilderness, he decided to make a living from the land. But, like so many with this dream, the practical aspects proved overwelming. He had no experience, no equipment, no concept of the techniques required to survive.

Carl Schels did turn to the woods for a living and this is the story of that experience.

Publishers like to turn out literary works of art. The temptation to edit journals is extreme and seldom is a journal published without considerable alterations. However, doing so eliminates its usefulness as original source material. Fortunately, this manuscript remains unaltered. The Swedish vernacular and unpolished style of the author does not destract from his story, but rather, lends authenticity to the events that occured. The author has been honest in the description of his emotions and actions which he took during this time, and for this he is to be commended.

Carl Schels

A Trapper's Legacy

I lost my job as a factory worker in the 30's in Chicago. The depression was in evidence all about me and therefore, with the enthusiasm of youth, I started on my way up to the northwoods thinking that here would be my opportunity to make a fortune, little realizing that a city boy does not always find it easy to survive in the rigorous life of a woodsman. Through bitter experiences, through perseverance and what amounted to pioneering in the twentieth century, I was able to make a living. However, the comparison of life in the 30's compared with the things we did in the later years is almost a revelation and many of the things accomplished then could not have been done now.

The work in the woods includes the actual fundamentals like sawmill logging, living with wildlife, trapping, eating what was available, the hardships of winter, many times without shelter, makes this story almost unbelievable when we think in terms of the 1960's in a civilized, modern world.

I started out in an old Model T Ford and found a job on a mink farm where I stayed two years working only for my board. The mink farmer was a bachelor and a very strange person. My job was to feed the mink and it was customary in those days to find an old horse, shoot him and feed the meat to the mink. The mink ration contained oatmeal which was purchased in 100 lb. bags and that meant that my breakfast for two years was oatmeal every morning. Even after all that oatmeal every morning, I still like it to this day. The horsemeat was ground up, mixed with carrots and other mink cereals and made into small meatballs and fed to the mink. For the first year I never left the property of this farmer. He started me clearing land, cutting down rather large trees with a four foot crosscut saw, then cutting it into firewood. The mink farmer was truly what one would call a first class slave driver. The first year there I never left his property. He would go to town once a week, all dressed up, smoking his cigar, driving a Model T truck. There was three-fourths of the 40 acres still in woods. So, he started me clearing land cutting down the larger trees and then cutting this into firewood. In the middle of the summer, in July and August, this can become a tough job for a young fellow who was a "greenhorn." A narrow stairway led to an attic where the roof, all rough wood, no ceiling, was so low it would touch my head. There was a single steel cot and this became my sleeping quarters. I must say it was hot in the summer and cold in the winter.

The Mink Farm

Many things happened while I was with the mink farmer. The second spring I was there, there was a forest fire nearby. The mink have a peculiar nature after they are bred. The females, if something comes along that scares them while they carry their young, will kill their young and eat them as soon as they are born. Now this is what happened to two-thirds of the bred females - they killed their young. The mink farmer said to me, "You must have made some unnecessary noise like shooting the shotgun or something while I was in town and I hold you responsible for the loss of those mink." They were worth $2,000. I told him about the fire and that I was not to blame. He was always right nor could I tell him anything. He would say, "You take orders from me - you are working for me." And also, the orders were that I was not to touch anything that did not belong to me. Then, I used to think, he is only giving me my board. Realizing how hard the times were it meant a lot in those days to a lot of people to have a place to sleep and something to eat. I could also say, the reason I stayed there was because I did not know any better. However, this was part of my beginning of life that at that time I did not know or think about.

My disposition, by nature, was to crave the intangible parts of life - always looking for new adventure, then going to the extremes to find out about them. Prohibition was in effect. There were plenty of moonshiners around. One day a fellow came around in the afternoon when the mink farmer had gone to town. He was a big man, lived about four miles from us. He had been drinking whiskey but he was not drunk. Being confined and not seeing anybody we soon got going on a long conversation. He said, "You know, this guy you are working for, well, he isn't much good. You know what happened to all those other fellows who worked for him? They all got sent back to Chicago." I asked how this could happen. "Well," he said, "you know this mink farmer doesn't ever want to pay anybody. He knows some people in Chicago. They would know of some young fellows who did not have a job and were down and out. They would write to the mink farmer and send him the names of these young men. He would write them telling them what a nice place he had. He would make it sound very romantic, promising some wages and saying that they could learn to trap and make extra money that way. He would send them a train ticket and soon he would have help." He told me he knew of three fellows that were sent back. He said the sheriff in town was a good friend of his and told him what happened. He said, "The mink farmer is a good politician and he pays me a little for the things I do for him. So, I help him out. You know what he did to those fellows?" By this time this was getting very interesting to me. Being somewhat spellbound I said I sure would like to know. "Well," he said, "when he finds out that some of these fellows can't do all the work he accuses them of stealing something from him. Then the sheriff would come out to arrest them and take them to a town ten miles away. He bought them a ticket and saw they got on the train to go back to Chicago." And, so that went. He warned me, "You'd better watch out about this." I told him I wasn't worried. I was a good worker and he didn't want to get rid of me. However, I was getting very tired of the job and no pay. We were both very happy there talking things over. Then he said "How much will you take for your Model T Ford?" It had no battery, the tires were old, it wasn't much good and it didn't run. He said, "That's OK - I'll give you twenty gallons of whiskey." I heard it was worth $3.00 a gallon. So I said, "You can have it." He came over with his team and pulled it home.

Well, things started to happen fast when the mink farmer came back and found out about my visitor. His name was Mike. He said, "I don't want that drunk around here." Then I told him of the deal I made with him trading the Model T for 20 gallons of whiskey. He said, "How could you do this on my time, don't you know I am paying you?" He meant he fed me. Then I finally got up a little nerve for the first time and said, calling him by his last name, "You are doing a lot of things that are not right. Tomorrow I'm going to quit." "Oh, no," he said, "You can't do that. I haven't got anybody to help me." So, thinking out loud I did say I would stay with him two more weeks, and so I did. The next day in the afternoon I walked a half mile over to a farmer. His kids were all grown up and had left home. He had a team of horses and a half dozen cows. The old fellow never got really sober. He had a little shack away from the house and he said I could have that to stay in. He found out I would work for my board and he gladly would have me come over there. So it all worked out very good. I had Mike bring the 20 gallons of whiskey over to the farmer. It was in two barrels. This of course was a mistake. When the old farmer found out that I had all that whiskey he constantly wanted a pint. I made a hole in the shack, the one that was to be my home - where I would sleep, and here I hid the whiskey.

My two weeks would soon be up at the mink farmer. I looked ahead to being free and now that these people were friendly there was always new hope. The environment, responsibility and hardships I had while with the mink farmer certainly were gradually forcing me on my own. This was good for later in my life I found that I was able to go on my own.

It had been a practice for the mink farmer to pick up the skim milk for his pigs from the farmer where I now worked. In the meantime I had a chance to talk to an elderly woman who lived up the road on a hill. She could have been a widow, I never saw a man around. Well, I had a habit all my life of talking too much and this was one day I also talked too much. It was about the mink farmer. The people around here didn't like him - they had it in for him, and drove seventy some ducks he had up the river while he was in town one day and stole them. This woman told the mink farmer that I was talking about him and later I found out that she was called the newspaper of this certain river. No doubt she made it very interesting for the mink farmer. When he came over at his regular time for his skim milk he was mad and highly insulting. I came walking through the yard by the house. Here is where the argument started. First he said, ''I want you to stop telling these lies around here about me. ''Standing about five feet away from him I said that I was telling no more lies about him than he was about me. He started hitting me. I never was much of a fighter. It happened that I had a ring on my finger, by hitting back and forth, this ring cut a hole in his lip. This started heavy bleeding so he stopped fighting and held his hand over his mouth. Then he said, ''I know you've got all that whiskey. I am going to report you to the prohibition agents if you don't pack up right now and get out of the country.'' Finally after all this commotion the words just seemed to pop right out of my mouth and I said, ''The only way you can get me out of here is to kill me and carry out my dead body.'' Nothing ever happened about this. He quit coming for the milk and I didn't see him again for a long time.

To get accustomed to my new surroundings was one thing I will always remember. This was milking cows. There was a time when I left a good home because I didn't want to milk cows. Also here I would like to point out the reason. I did not go back home, which was in a warm climate, because when I left there on a

6

freight train we had what was called good times. Now in the 1930's we had bad times; I was too proud to go home so I stuck it out. However, my thoughts did wander back home especially when I had to milk cows. This old-time Kentucky farmer up here in Northern Wisconsin was a smart cookie. When milking time came he was never around, probably sleeping somewhere on the hillside underneath some trees. As I mentioned before he could consume more of the moonshine liquor than many other men that had the same habit. He had a reputation that he never got what is called sober. Like the saying goes, "One can get used to many things, and so I did get used to milking cows.There were times when this chore got heavy- this was haying and threshing time. There was a good team and I used to like to drive them. I got along good in this line. Then I was doing all the cutting of the grass, raking and shocking same. Then came the time when it was hauled and placed in the barn. Threshing time came and one farmer would help the other. One farmer had considerable acreage and the threshing machine would be set up near the barn. Three or four wagons would haul to keep things going—had a so-called hayrack - this will hold considerable grain. The grain is in bundles and schocked up piles in the field. The driver stays on the wagon to place the load while two men throw up these bundles. Now on this certain day, I was hauling with out team. The horseflies were very bad that day - it was hot. The wagon had a high extension in front built out of wood. There I placed the lines. The wagon was about one-third loaded, the horses could not stand the flies anymore and started to run. I did manage to get up to the front to get hold of the lines. However there was one mistake. A crossbar that holds up the wagon and slips on to the very end in front, was too loose. Moving considerably more back and forth on the runway it slipped off and this in turn let the tongue fall down to the ground. This tongue was about 10 to 11 feet long. Going at this speed when the tongue dug in, the wagon had to raise up. This means that the wagon is raising 10 feet or so up in the air, by this time releasing the team completely from the wagon. First my head, then the back of my neck hit the extended wood frame and I was knocked unconscious. I flew to the ground all curled up. I am happy to say that I got only sore and stiff out of the deal and no broken bones. Very few people had insurance those days. This soreness lasted about a month and I got over it. Like the fellow said, I never made any complaints. There was one thing that burned me up about those Kentucky farmers - the lady would never make or cook a meal for Sunday dinner. Where I came from Sunday dinner would be the best in the week. She would say, "Today we don't work anyway." Boy, I used to think that was terrible.

There was another thing that happened toward early fall. The son-in-law, a fairly big moonshiner, came to set up his still back on the farm by a side hill. This hill is rather high, heavily wooded and runs for miles to the south. While this mash

7

was fermenting the yellow jackets came for a drink, falling in by the hundred. When it was ready there would be the mash left. The cows are crazy for mash and it seems they did waddle coming home for milking at night.

No doubt someone will think that by now my memory must have failed me. Many times we hear the saying that all things work together for good. Let me say right here and now - you'd better believe this for it is as true as the day is long. While I am writing here about my experiences at present,many years have passed, one thing followed another that certainly by now, when I am able to look back, did work together for good. Let me explain it this way. Like a large cable holding up the span of a bridge, each strand of cable forms the strength needed. So, each trial, success or failure that comes along in life seems to form another strand which in turn should mean strength. When our thoughts are compelled with faith this of course means complete trust or confidence and this to me has always meant new hope and it keeps on going until we come to the last strand which should give us sufficient strength to abolish all fear.

Now to go on, I found when late fall came somehow I could feel that I was not welcome anymore. Several times I heard mention that one of the boys and maybe one of the girls would be coming home (they were working out) so they needed the shack or the little house that I was using for my home. One thing that bothered me was to be a burden to somebody else when I would have to think that I was not welcome. So one day the son-in-law approached me and said, ''I've got a forty up on a lake.'' Folks, let me say this was a large springfed beautiful lake.''There is a shack on it so why don't you go up there and stay. You can clean up some lake frontage there and I will pay you.'' This was really something - here the first time in my life doing my own cooking, washing dishes, etc. I had to get hold of enough money to buy food. Certainly it wasn't long before those things came, one thing after another. There was a good road into the place. It was somewhat isolated in many respects. it was two miles through solid woods to where a family was living. In those days people were hard to get acquainted with. These people had a large family and were poor. Mostly all natives had deer meat most of the time and also muskrats salted down. I learned that one party would have as many as 150 muskrats all pickled away in a large stone 20-gallon jar. This was a good old Swede logger who had an Indian woman. This Indian woman really knew how to fix that wild stuff. There was another large lake several miles east from where I was and that is where the Swede lived. Before I go on here I do want to tell you that this man was the first to build a jammer for loading logs. This consisted of two trees, mostly spruce was used, 30 to 36 feet high placed in an A frame unit. Two of these long logs were made into one unit with a crossbar. They were peeled and when dry

8

would not be so heavy. A large bottom about 8 feet wide and 12 feet long was hinged on to this A frame. When moving it up a logging road this bottom could be set down. A pole two-thirds up would hold the A frame in a balanced position in order to move. There was one block fastened at the very top and a cable running through and down to another block or sleeve. This bottom block was fastened solid. The cable from the top came down through the bottom. Some cables were 100 feet long. A team of horses would then pull on the end of this cable. To explain further, the other end of the cable that came down from the top of the A frame had a V-like parting. This would be made out of smaller chains with a hook like a fishhook made from 1-1/4 inch thick iron. There was also a ring on this hook. A 12 foot rope would be fastened on this ring. Two lumberjacks would hook each one on his end of a log. When the team went ahead the log would go up. Of course, in those days all logs were hauled on a sleigh, of prize winning loads of 10,000 feet of logs on a sleigh, four horses pulling. There are many things that could be said about those old time logging days. The so-called jammer that I tried to describe here was used for 40 to 50 years and is still being used in certain places. The boys have their loading equipment mounted on their trucks nowadays - it only takes one man to operate and it is nothing for this man to load 60 to 80 cords in one day. Most of these hauls are ten or more miles from the railroad siding. The A frame jammer did its work, (the one the Swede invented). Before that jammer was used, logs were rolled up by a single light chain. This was placed in position to balance the log going all the way up the skids by a lumberjack who was called a cant hook man. Oxen or horses were used to pull across from the load. Many times they were placed on railroad cars - open cars - high up. The fellow on the top was called the top loader and he was the highest paid man, besides the boss, of course, on the job. Some did get killed. When danger came some jumped. However they were very tricky. I think the Frenchmen made the best top loaders. A lot depended on the cant hook man. He had to be fast and to learn to release that log fast to keep it going straight.

To get back to my new living quarters by the lake. Everybody called these little houses shacks - nobody was insulted. There is so much comfort in these shacks until the bedbugs take over. Well, this one didn't have any bedbugs. It was 12 x 12 feet, 10 feet high in front and 8 feet in the back, and had two little windows called barn sash. There were many of these used in those days. It was rather dark in the place when the door was closed. Of course it was never closed in summer - there was no screen door. One got so used to flies that their singing and buzzing was company to your ear. Of course, a lot of lazy bachelors did let all the dirty dishes stand until there were no more dishes but there never were many in the beginning. It is surprising how little a person needs in order to survive. The table and bench were homemade - a few poles and a few boards. And those homemade barrel stoves out of a 50 gallon drum, when too much hardwood is placed in, give so much heat they can run you out of the shack in 20 below zero weather. It is not so bad if you can sleep on a bottom bunk. Now, the bed was in the shack when I came. Never did like them and didn't have enough brains to make another. The biggest fault was it was too big. It took one-third of the room in the shack. Double bunk beds were made out of rough 2 x 4's. There was a very small wood cookstove. It being late in fall that meant I would have to have a supply of firewood. There was a cedar swamp nearby and one could carry the cedar out on his shoulder. This wood is very light - 8' lengths would handle very well. This was no problem. This makes fine kindling wood and burns fast. You can also burn a shack down in a hurry - it draws sparks out of any little crack in a stove. If it got going too fast I would throw water on it - this gives a fine aroma for your living quarters. Well, the first winter there I must say I had the finest choice of hardwood. Not far away was a hillside grown up about fifty percent in ironwood. In this country they don't grow large. I cut everyone of those ironwood and managed to get them to the shack. Did you ever burn ironwood? You would know then that I am telling the truth - if you got a six inch chunk there would be coals in the stove in the morning.

One day a young fellow, fair size, came walking by the shack with a 22 rifle. He was very friendly and asked me if I was going to live here. I told him that I may have to ask my relative in Chicago for a little money so I could get by for the winter. This now is my first winter. After talking a while he said, "Why don't you go with me? I've got a trail through the woods going north about three miles. We've got a farm over there and we can give you some potatoes." "This would be fine," I said. So away we went. There was virgin timber back there, mostly hardwood, maple and hemlock and there was a partly established trail going through there - if you were careful you could find it. This was the first time that I had a chance to make a hike like that through timber. I never knew before such timber existed. We have to remember that I am still a greenhorn. We came out of the woods and then there were open fields. We had another half mile to go. The house was built into a hill, a two-story house. To this day I have my respect for the people I met there. His father and mother were past middle age. They had lived there many years. There were two grown-up girls away working. The family was religious. The mother was a sincere Christian. I was to stay for supper and also for the night. Being carefree in those days it did not take me long to make a decision. That evening I told these people my life history. They had a piano and the mother played a few religious songs. That evening I can remember well. There were prayers at mealtime. After all I told those people no doubt they felt sorry for me. Then they said, "Why don't you come over and help us cut our winter wood?" This was all done by hand in those days. I knew how to pull a crosscut saw and I was strong. So a deal was made to help one week and they would give me all the potatoes and rutabaga I needed for the winter. And, she said, "I want to loan you a couple of blankets for I know you don't have enough bedding." And so it went.

One thing missing in my shack was a root cellar. So I cut a good sized hole in the middle of the floor in the shack and dug a fair sized hole a few steps down and this answered the purpose to keep my potatoes and rutabaga from freezing. That was important. I needed a few dollars for a grub stake so I wrote my uncle in Chicago and told him what happened - how I moved up here to this lake, into this shack, and how I am now on my own. I wanted to get some flour, kerosene, matches, sugar and the few things one needs. Of course, I knew my uncle very well - he had a shoe shop there and managed to get by. It wasn't long before I got the $30.00 I asked for. This I would have to pay back when I could. Then I remember walking up a railroad track to the nearest town - around 8 miles away. Included on my grocery list was some rice and most important cinnamon. This I could not forget, for before I bought it I asked the storekeeper how much a small can would be. He said, "Ten cents." I took it as cinnamon on rice was a luxury to me in those days and I had a craving for this and was something that I could cook. Before I got back I had some new experiences. I was carrying 50 lbs. of flour on my back using binder twine for strapping like one would use on a packsack. This kept cutting into my flesh where the load bearing would carry the most part of the weight. This left marks on me for some time and it did hurt. After that trip, which was a day's trip, I could sleep. Back in this woods here where the road comes in it is very narrow. No snow plowing is or was ever done. It means breaking a trail through snow. At that time very few people had snowshoes. Now we were coming close to the end of 1933. On Sundays I would go over to the people that gave me the potatoes and other things. These were the only folks I associated with since I had been here. The solitude through the winter months never bothered me. Everything I had was to be saved - the food I had to buy - a box of 5¢ matches would last two years. The kerosene lamp was always lighted with paper out of the barrel stove. In the wintertime the fire coals were always there. After supper the lamp was blown out to save kerosene. By then I would manage to have a nice bed of coals so the damper could be open. This way it would not smoke and the light coming from the open door one could see enough even to move around in the shack. The stillness of the night, the solitude and the sense of security would bring peace of mind, in fact, it seems that I was unconcerned about anything. One could say I was hibernating.

I had ordered some small traps from Montgomery Ward for weasel and mink and for muskrat in the spring. When I think back - how ignorant I was on my first

11

trapping expedition. I heard a little about it. One could take a stove pipe or birch bark that one can make round. The weasel likes to run through things, then camouflage the trap. One can catch them this way and with bait. Weasels brought 35c to 50c, mink $4.00 to $7.00 and muskrat average size 65c. I knew practically nothing about trapping. Having nothing else to do I tramped the woods all day. One can see the tracks of the animals - then the thing is to be able to recognize them. However, if one works at it long enough once in a while you catch something. Weasel were plentiful so I got a number of them and two mink all winter. Muskrats are easier to catch so I got about eighteen of them when the ice started to go out. If one learns the hard way it usually stays with a person. Not realizing that, I would go to extremes concerning trapping and go way off somewhere out of civilization and take a chance of losing my life. Further let me state, not to get ahead of my story, that if one trapped fifty years, everyday you would learn something new. You know when you have made a good set to catch a beaver, say under the ice, and when you come along on an open water trap set for an otter and your trap was snapped but no otter. Then you adjust and re-adjust. You learn many things about nature. Your every move can correspond in a fashion that in a rhythm-like way can occupy a feeling of being close to nature. You can walk through the woods looking straight ahead, say a partridge or something is moving 20 feet behind to one side, 30 feet over. All at once you turn fast and look and you see the object moving. This may sound very odd but it has happened to me.

Finally the snow disappeared and spring was here. There was a fine natural spring straight down from the shack on an old railroad grade - it never froze over in the winter and here is where I got my water. I started to clear some land around the lake shore mostly brushing out what one calls the underbrush, leaving the larger trees stand. My rate of pay was $1.00 a day. The saddest part was I did not know that I had to take whiskey for pay. After I had worked thirty days and asked for my pay, then I found out. The owner, who was one of the second largest moonshiners from a town about 40 miles away, came in the summertime about every two weeks. "Well", he said, "you should not mind about the whiskey. Soon fishermen will come in and you can get 15c a drink (which was a small whiskey glass) or sell it two drinks for a quarter or $1.00 a pint." Well, it did happen the fishermen came starting the first day of the season. There was a good place to land their boats. A few old boats were here belonging to someone that would come fishing occasionally. I soon got permission to rent out these boats when not in use. This was a good all-around fishing lake including muskie. There were also some lumberjacks around and, of course, they were the best customers for the whiskey. A man nearing the seventy mark, who had never married and who had been a lumberjack all his life, came to see me. He loved to fish for muskie. There was a sawmill town not too far away south of here and he would sell the muskie to a boarding house there by the pound. Of course you can guess they did not overpay him. It was a little extra whiskey money for him. I don't believe that there were many of the old-time lumberjacks that did not drink. Many of them never married. This fellow owned 40 acres about three miles away on a fine small spring-fed lake. He had it for years. There were many fellows shacking throughout this area. If one stays in a place long enough then in time one finds out many things.

People like to talk about people. Certainly in those days the thing people had was a lot of time on their hands. There was a lot of lake frontage to clear out. One day I asked the old timer, let's call him John, "Why don't you come and stay with me?" We would manage, for after all he knew more than I did. he said he liked the idea of making his home with me. The next day he came - all he had was a small suitcase. Many people would have no suit, say for Sunday. one got so used to everyday work clothes that one felt very much out of place if you had good clothes on. I think one of the hardest jobs for a bachelor those days was to wash his clothes. Coming back to my new boarder - that was an expression very much in use then - a new boarder. Food was considered a very important value. Money was hard to earn, well, there was no job so there was little money around. However, money had considerable more value then than it has now. I paid $20.00 for the Model T Ford I came up with from Chicago in 1930 and it ran real good. So a boarder then just meant another person. It was a good thing when John came to live with me. He loved to fish - we had plenty of that. Oh, yes, he did bring a double barreled shotgun with slugs, the one you can kill a deer with. So then there was venison stew. In fact, I remember we would have more meat on our plate than potatoes. Down at the lake there was a very small pothole - there was a big log tree length dividing the pothole from the lake. John saw a couple of muskies playing, chasing one another. When one came near the log by the pothole he jumped right over and couldn't get out. John shot him with the old double barrel. He was a big one. When we had a large fish i would fillet them. John had a way all his own of fishing muskies. He never owned a rod or reel. He would not have used it if he had one. He fished from the back of an old flat bottom wooden boat (most of them were homemade - this one had a square back). He would stand on the back end having about 100 feet of line, using a daredevil or bucktail for bait and he would toss this out and when pulling in, using both hands, the line would curl up in a perfectly round circle so when it was thrown out again it would not get tangled. Well, John, I believe, was the champion muskie fisherman in his day for in that year he caught 36 out of one lake and two from another lake. Most of them he sold to the boarding house. One could say John was in good shape, for this meant about 12 miles of walking in a day. If it got too late he stayed at the boarding house overnight.

I believed John when he told me things that happened to him while fishing. One day, a Sunday, he lost a muskie and most of the line with it while fishing near an island. Those spots are easy for a fisherman to remember. Well, that took care of the fishing for that day. This meant five miles of walking back to the shack for John was the kind of fellow who did not have a lot of extra baits and lines. It always took a little time to organize another fishing rig. John, being such an ambitious fisherman, managed to be ready by the next Sunday. Here is what happened. He went back fishing near that island again when he hooked something. He pulled and pulled (those old timers used heavy lines) and saw a bunch of weeds coming up . Then he saw a line wrapped all around the weeds - he recognized his line - then he could see a muskie wrapped in those weeds. He got hold of the muskie and managed to get him in the boat. The hook of the bait was caught on the edge of his mouth. As soon as John got hold of the bait the hook broke off. John told me that acid in the fish started to rust the hook and in a week's time it was practically off. This fish was still alive. I could easily believe about the acid of the fish rusting off a hook because many times large fish had been hooked and then got away with the bait. Very seldom are those fish found dead on shore.

By now we managed to get along real good. The newest thing was that I learned to make some homebrew beer. John got hold of a 20 gallon stone jar - this was where the fermenting took place. When ready it was bottled. One seems to get things even in a depression when there was little money to be made. There in the summer months there was always somebody around doing some fishing or loafing around. The spring hole, or rather our well, I should say, was a good place to keep the beer cold. It was sold for 10c a bottle. After all, it was prohibition. It was wild stuff. If one shook the bottle too much before opening you were lucky if you had half left. And so the time went on and fall came. John was a great hand at picking berries - raspberries were plentiful. Then I found out how to can them. Oh, I was a great guy thinking about food for the winter. Most of our extra money went for buying fruit jars. I canned over 100 jars of raspberries. This made a good combination with potato pancakes. In the meantime I had ordered a 25-20 model Remington rifle. This was always considered a violating gun. It had all the fire power needed but the main thing was it didn't make a lot of noise. I don't know why they quit making them - it only weighed five pounds. Out in the farm country and in the woods mostly everyone in those days got their deer meat. Some had it all year around. One bad thing that I always hated was the so-called professional violators that would kill a deer and just take the hind quarters. We never wasted anything. I

14

could never go for the liver, however, and that was left in the woods. I even canned the bones cut up. This made good soup. However, one time I made a mistake and washed the meat and then canned it. The meat itself has enough liquid in it. You cover the fruit jars with water and then boil for three hours and that is it. This type of canning will keep for two years. However, when I put in water that was bad. Well, we never used this canned meat until winter set in.

Having a few dollars by now one can get prosperous in a hurry and I always was a good spender. Well, I thought I should have some transportation even if I couldn't use it in the wintertime - a Model T Ford. It would be a great satisfaction having one. Well, Chicago was the best place to get one I thought. Not having seen my relative for over three years this would now be a big thing. John, my partner the lumberjack, was well able to take care of things while I was gone. I would have to hide one thing and that was the whiskey. I would leave him a gallon. I had about fifteen gallons in five gallon oak barrels. There were plenty of brush piles around here and when John was fishing I got rid of the whiskey. We had it in the shack down in the cellar hole. I explained everything to him and he was happy the way things were. One of the strongest impressions I made on him was that whatever he did to be sure not to burn the shack down. I would have to get up real early the next morning so by noon I could catch the Greyhound bus in the town. It was an eight mile hike. I always wore breeches with 10'' high top boots. This is the way I dressed for my trip to Chicago. I borrowed a pack sack from my Christian neighbor friends. Yes, I must take some canned deer meat to my uncle. Two quart jars wrapped up in good shape with a few pieces of cloth - that was it. I got off the Greyhound bus east of Lincoln Park, as my uncle lived on Fulton Street, and I had to walk all the way through Lincoln Park to get over west. All the way walking through the park I was worried about the cops on account of the deer meat I had in the knapsack. It shows. when one has a guilty conscience this always happens. "Well," my uncle said. "you got back." He had a big smile. Both he and his wife were glad to see me. For a treat they would have some of the canned deer meat I brought for supper. Here is what happened. I did not know that this was from the batch of meat I had washed when I canned it. I put a can on the stove and was all ready to heat the meat. The lid came off of the jar and there was a smell that would knock any average person out. Never could I forget that smell. They got it out of the house as quickly as they could. This made me feel very bad. It took me quite a while to find out why this batch spoiled. It was later when someone told me one day never to wash deer meat so then I knew how it got spoiled.

Well, I found a Model T Ford and after four days in the city this was all I could stand. It was Saturday morning when I started out. I had two victrolas and lots of records, some dishes and a couple good castiron frying pans. I was loaded down. I made it back late that night to the shack in Wisconsin. On the way home I would think about John how he might have managed to get along. He was as happy as I was when I got there. We sat up late that night telling each other all the things that happened. So the summer went fast and fall was here. This is the most busy time to get ready for the winter. Later on after I learned a lot about the life of a beaver I would compare myself to them for they really work hard. The whole family pitches in. You know, beavers mate for life. Every day I learned something more about shacking and cooking. The main thing now coming up was trapping. One waits until the fur is at least partly prime. You find this out when you skin the first rat. Inside the hide is supposed to be white. We always caught them too early for one is desperate for that money. So, the first skins would be half blue inside and sometimes even turn partly black. However, they sold fairly good, that is, the price wasn't too bad. All the skins we sent to Montgomery Ward and I did think they were very fair. Everyday, by now, the weather got colder so the fur got more prime. By now I had accumulated more traps including some larger size called No. 3 and a few No. 4. The No. 4 Newhouse trap was for wolf, coyotes, also beaver. It took all the strength I had to set one of those No. 4's and I had to use both of my feet in order to make it. So, like all the violating, it would start before season opened and when one is young you are not afraid doing what I might have considered a little violating. Of course what I didn't know was that there are other violators around and I am still a greenhorn. So, getting very bold setting out some 40 traps around the lake and over by a creek, I was exposing myself too much. I did consider myself lucky the way everything happened. John, being an old timer, saved me in a way. He said, "You'd better hide those hides for the game warden might come around." I took his advice. He had a 50 gallon steel barrel. I took it in the boat one-third around one side of the lake. There was a big spruce swamp very thick with trees. I carried the barrel back about 300 feet in there. I had a cover making it waterproof. I knew that I had around 65 muskrat skins in there. As I said, there were other violators around but I never saw them but they saw me. The way I exposed myself was going around on the edge of the lake looking where some old log was hanging in the water as this was always good for a good set. Most of the time one could see evidence of muskrat. The lake was 1½ miles wide. Someone reported me to the game warden. I did not know this, in fact, I never saw anyone around. So one morning, now being late in fall, I got up early in the morning like most every morning, especially when I was trapping. It was not daylight yet. I went down to the lake shore looking over a half dozen sets, water sets for muskrats. I got three rats and so I went back thinking about making breakfast. As I got within fifty feet of the shack it was just getting daylight, I saw a figure of a man walking hurriedly toward me. He grabbed the muskrats out of my hand and also a few traps. I stopped and he said, "You are

16

under arrest."He took me into the shack. It was a little chilly and John was standing hugging the cookstove, I could see that he had just got a fire going. What I did not know was that the warden had asked him a lot of questions before I came back, like, what did he do with all the furs, where do I put all the carcasses and how long have I been trapping. John told me later when he asked all the questions he kept saying, "I don't know, I don't know." So finally the warden said to him, "You don't know very much." John said, "Guess I don't." He threw a lot of questions to me, of course, what I did with the furs as that bothered him the most. He tore our beds apart. ransacked my suitcase, and taking the few rats I had and the few traps, he said,"Let's go." I knew John would get along. So we went.The warden had his car parked down this narrow one lane road which was the only way in around a curve. We knew he had sneaked in. Driving ten miles ·to his house he went and had breakfast. I sat in the car. He had told me that he would take me to the county seat where the courthouse was and put me there in jail. My whiskers were long - I don't know what the judge thought of me. After two days I had my hearing and this meant thirty days. I wasn't in there very long and the sheriff found work for me and one doesn't mind this for it meant to get out. I was there for twenty-seven days, three days off for good behavior. I don't know to this day how I got back to the shack, should say my home, for it was a good thirty miles away. Found everything OK there. John kept busy getting up wood for the winter. One of my main thoughts all this time was about the muskrat skins I had in that barrel down in the swamp. They would bring enough money to take care of us on groceries through the winter having all the wild meat and canned berries, wild rice, and we managed to get potatoes, carrots, rutabagas and cabbage for exchange of work. On five dollars a month we could live like kings. Everything since I came here had improved so much that one learned from day to day more how to help yourself.   The first chance I had I went down to the swamp to see if anything happened to the barrel. It was all there - this was an excellent hiding place, after all, it was our best place of security. Just a month before the game warden caught me a man was up from Chicago on vacation with the mink farmer. He knew my uncle, they were good friends. He told him to come over and see me, that I had a good place to fish.There were plenty of them. It was nothing to catch a half a water pail of them in three or four hours. He talked for an hour before he left and he seemed to be a regular guy - a good fellow. I did tell him I had some whiskey. He got very much concerned about this and said, "Oh, if you could give me a couple of gallons or kegs. Just think the price I can get for that in Chicago - $10.00 a gallon. But, I don't have that much money. Could you trust me?" One thing, when it came to trusting people I was a champion. Somehow I know I would be the last person on earth to lose faith in human nature. Now, after many years, I do find where I lost several thousand dollars because I was easy going. I don't even say that I am sorry for that. Well, I got those two barrels of whiskey for him. He is to give me one half of his $50.00 sales price. And then he left. He owned a small place out in the country forty miles from here and he owned a three family flat in Chicago, renting out two flats. He, being up in age, would come up here and stay for the summer. So he said when he came back he would see me and then pay me and I should forget about it until then. Those kind of deals in the depression days were good deals. Most persons think it is nice to have money coming, especially hard earned money, a dollar a day for a day's hard work. Even in my case when I worked for the owner here, the moonshiner, he never was around much but I always gave him a good day's work. Somehow I was very conscientious and people soon found that out. That way I never had any trouble. Now I lost my trapping license for a year so I had to be very cautious. In desperation one can get very bold so I sneaked around quite a bit, like on a good moonlight night working all night all around the edge of the lake setting muskrat traps. One would row quietly so as not to hit the oars on the side of the boat for at night this kind of a sound can carry a long distance. By now I had over one hundred good traps. Then, you can learn new tricks for making sets. The trap does not necessarily have to set in water. For what I did I always had plenty of carrots.   First I washed them for each set that is land set. I take a bite of carrot in my mouth, chew it up fine and put it back into my hands closing my hands and submerging them into the water so as to kill the scent. First I put a little grass over the trap and then carrots on the top. These sets worked good. An elder stick is used for it is easy to find just the right size, with the small point down with short knobs of limbs left on so the ring of the trap would slide down easily. To start out the chain is already tight. Ninety percent of the time the animals get caught with their front feet. They always go for the water and when this happens the weight of the trap will drown them. One thing that astounded me often is where I set out around one hundred traps and found all the sets again. When I thought how hard I worked for a dollar a day and had to take pay in whiskey. Then for a good muskrat skin one could get 65c and if anything can get into your blood, it is trapping.

The winters years ago were more severe. After the lake froze up and the water got colder, trapping was tough. January, February and March, I found out later, it did not even pay to try, not after one learned how to bootleg beaver. It took several years to find out about this. Many days I remember a snowstorm in progress - the more it was blowing the better I liked it. There is something about it, one moves more actively, I guess, to keep the blood warm. There is always more adventure, it seems, especially when hunting deer. When the meat supply started to get low I would wait for one of these stormy days. This one particular day was one of these days. It was about nine in the morning and I was walking back on an old logging road - I had the old standby, 25-20 rifle. It was always oiled up, good pump action. When placing one shell into the chamber it was good for four shots. Of course, it was loaded full but one never needed this, as 99% of the time one shot did the trick. Like I said, it was an extremely stormy day. You could see the old dry limbs falling from some of the trees with the exception of the aspen (so-called popple). They get so rotten dead that in a high wind they really come down. If you are in thick woods one has to watch not to get one on the head. If you are going against the wind, and this one does on a day like this, you can sneak up to deer. There was about six inches of snow so I walked over to where there was a large old pine tree on a side kill. I crawled over on the other side of this and sure enough there were the tracks. Two deer, good sized, had gotten out of there in a hurry. So Indian fashion I sneaked after them. With all that wind blowing that was very easy. Only going about a fourth of a mile here was a lot of balsam, a regular thicket, going down a hill. It was, in fact, a kettlehole. I thought here they may have stopped for when deer get in a place like that they feel protected. Being very careful I took my steps very slowly looking and looking. Here to my surprise stood a nice doe about three years old. She was looking the other way about 100 feet from me. I took a good aim and fired. She took off like a bullet, went about 50 feet and dropped. Then one cuts the throat right away and drains the blood as this makes better meat. So I started to cut it out and skin it right there. Some limbs were falling down behind me and it was blowing. If you get cold hands you can warm up in a hurry when handling the insides of a deer. I was thinking right along if the buck was along he may come back for it is in late fall and they are still running. Having the doe half skinned out I thought I heard a noise. I had the rifle handy leaning up within reach. I looked up toward the hillside and there came the buck walking down toward where I was. First he had his head toward the ground smelling, then he looked up right towards me, I shot. And here he came right toward me. I shot twice from the hip. When he got within 10 feet I got another shot, this broke his front leg. He stumbled hard right there in front of me, sliding about 12 feet. His head went under in a pinched-in fashion and he came to this sudden stop. One of the bullets had hit his heart, I found, when I skinned him out. Many times they run three to four hundred feet after they are shot through the heart. He had a fine rack of horns, only eight points, but it was perfect. I had it mounted and still have it to this day. They have very gentle eyes. So here were the buck and doe laying twelve feet apart. It all happened within 20 minutes when I fired the first shot. When violating one skins out the deer, that is, I used to do it that way, where I shot them, cut them up, into about twelve pieces. The small one could be carried out in one trip and the larger one in two trips. You have to have a good pack sack.

The solitude of the winter months can gather your thoughts in many directions. One finds, however, when you are on your own that experience counts the most. Freedom of thought to explore and doing things of accomplishment bring satisfaction and peace of mind. Peace of mind does not mean sleepless nights. At times the whistling sound on a windy stormy night, howling around the corners of the shack could remind you of the comfort to be had mostly all from wood. First of course, the wood burning in the barrel heater, the 2 x 4 framing and the boards nailed on this and some felt tarpaper to make the shack. There was another job that was inside work and that is the making of stretcher boards. Cedar works perfectly for this. This can be split by ax out of large cedar blocks. They must be the right length - muskrat, mink, weasel and otter each take a different type board - they can be made very fancy and also somewhat stylish. This also means that after the skins dry or tighten they can be removed. Early in the spring I did catch my first otter. There was a very small creek running into a lake. The water here was open most of the winter. There was spring hole. The otter know all of the places they can enter a lake in the winter. They are extensive travelers, they love to play, sliding down a steep bank. Then they squeal for it must in some way tickle them. They also mate for life and are very devoted. The otter I caught here was alive. It was swimming back and forth over old wood in the water. If I had not had the rifle along I would never have gotten this otter. I had to act fast - he was hissing at me with his mouth open. Practically sticking the barrel in his mouth I pulled the trigger. That was it - he bled the heaviest darkest red blood I ever saw. Now skinning an otter is the hardest of all animals. Trying not to cut the hide, I took my time and that was half a day. It took me just as long to make a board. After all, I was learning and besides they were valuable. It brought me $9.00 from Montgomery Ward. In those days it was a lot of money and to think what one could buy with it.

When one is living under the conditions I was, there was constantly some new adventure to explore. John and I were doing a lot of talking about beavers. Up to now I had never seen one. Beavers have their home locations so that they can survive. Sufficient water flow and food is a must. Their first choice of food is the poplar - they take the bark of them; their next choice are elders and willows, then white birch. In desperation, when confined under the ice all winter and some get caught short on food, especially the old bachelor beaver, they cut down anything. Later I found out about these bachelor beaver. They live mostly in banks, lakes or rivers. Sometimes they have some brush, large sticks and mud piled up at their entrance from the water side going in toward the land and would look for this to find their location, that is, in the winter time when everything is still frozen up. The ice is soon going out and I started scouting for beaver. You must remember this was the first set I ever made and as usual I was going through a lot of work. Lots of times you find beaver in a swampy location. The water where usually three to four dams are made is 200 to 400 feet and dams are up to one fourth of a mile apart depending on the lay of the land. The first dam would have to take into consideration the depth of the water and to know how to engineer the depth of the water. The second dam downstream is made so as to support the bottom of the first dam. Of course, the first is the largest of all the dams, that is, for one colony which also means one house. The third is smaller and so on down, they would get smaller and at times look very cute like a toy. But believe me, a dam can be large. I have seen them one fourth mile long, not so high, depending on the lay of the land and then I have seen them so wide they could have been started 1000 years ago, built on and on and all grown up in grass so one could drive a jeep across, about 14 feet high and about 100 feet long between two high rock walls. This is a sight. The small logs are placed straight up and down by the hundreds and are woven together with a lot of mud. At times grass starts to grow so they are very strong. Through the summer months they keep repairing the dams. Here are their living quarters, usually the house not being very far away from the dam. However, I have seen where the house would be three-quarters of a mile up. They manage to get around under the ice a long way. I do think they have their spots where they can come up for air. I did learn that each one has his own feeding place under the ice, also that they can go a mile up the river, that is, in the winter where there would be a dam. I would dig a trench six inches deep so the water can run through. There a hole is cut just large enough to get in on the side of the dam upstream. Then a trap is set about six inches deep. There is usually mud on the bottom and that is very soft so one has to submerge sticks and chunks of wood to get a solid bottom. After the trap is placed it is covered with mud. Water escaping from this little ditch will show up on the water level entrance in their house. The first thing they will do is come down to examine the dam. They are very cautious when approaching something out of the ordinary. So, it does happen that one will not always get a beaver for they will shove sticks and whatever they get hold of ahead of them. And, so you hike from one of fifteen miles or more to a place where there is a colony of beaver and then you find a stick instead of a beaver. Now I am speaking of trapping, as one might say in civilization, for I found out later that wilderness trapping is an entirely different story. Speaking of stories - here I am way ahead again - for I wanted to explain how I made my first beaver set. It is so easy to get carried away after many years and when one gets old then it is only like a dream. Well, here I was out in the open marsh. If there is a little

21

wind and zero weather one can feel it. I had a hatchet, ice chisel and pack sack. I cut short poplar limbs and fresh greens from small saplings for bait. I did not know then that all I had to do was get a dead tamarack pole, cut a hole in the ice at least two feet square, wire the trap on top ot the pole, wire the fresh popple sticks on top and shove the whole deal in on a 45 degree angle. That's it. The hole freezes up in a hurry. Of course, this I learned later. So what I did, I got four poles, the water was about 10 feet deep so the poles had to be about 12 feet long; the poles are nailed in a pattern like a chair, about 2 feet apart, then a shelf is placed on it and then set in the hole straight down. What a job - an hour's work. It paid off. A trapper will look over his trapline with great interest and, of course, some disappointment and expectation. This day after making this first beaver set with so much commotion and then finding a beaver, this was really something. Then there was another thing foolish or sad. When I got beaver I would carry them all the way home, and this could be quite a distance, instead of skinning them right there or at least in the vicinity where they are caught. This can become a chore, forty, fifty, seventy pounds in weight. One time I got an eighty pounder. The most I ever heard of in Wisconsin was ninety-two pounds. This one was legal and the boys who caught it had it mounted.

So here now is where my history begins. The money earned trapping beavers would not only go for groceries but it might also be used for buying land. One can become a fox in the woods when it comes to dodging the game warden, especially after being caught once. I would say I was a good runner, had plenty of wind, never smoked. Should the game warden in those days be chasing me I would run like a ghost and this happened several times. He never did catch me. However, other things happened that always became a challenge. John got to talking one evening about the time I got caught and had to go to jail. He said, ''I didn't want to tell you but I know this fellow who squealed on you last fall. He is a deputy game warden and he is the biggest violator in the country.'' To think that he should get away and I had to go to jail. Then he said, ''I know a lot of the old timers around. Why don't you get up a petition and have the people sign it that this fellow isn't fit for a deputy warden.''So this is how I got to write the game warden a letter. When one gets up in the air about something like I was, no doubt I used a little strong language and I told them about this petition deal.The answer came within two days.''He came in his car back here to our shack. I had just stepped out of the shack and here he was. It took me kind of my surprise as I did not think he would drive all the way back here about that letter. Well, as usual, this fellow had a temper and he had a peculiar way of showing it. At times he did seem friendly and then again it appeared like he felt like killing me. Now he was really mad. First he said, ''Did you write this letter?'' ''Yes,'' I said reluctantly. ''Why,'' he said, ''what do you mean about this

22

fellow - my deputy?'' I answered, ''We heard he should not be a warden.'' ''Why.'' he said, ''don't you know that every officer in this state automatically becomes a warden?'' This I didn't know. ''Why did you write me this letter,'' he said very angrily. Calling him by his first name I said, ''I am sorry for anything I said in that letter that is not true.'' ''You had better watch you step'' was his answer and he got in his car and left. I never realized at that time that the question about this letter would come up again six years later.

By now I was desperate to catch beaver since I had caught three. They are also very hard to skin. Once I read it would take an expert one hour for this job. Yes, it took me that long and longer but as the years went by I could make it in a half hour. I had a dollar watch in front of me all the time from start to finish so I would not start daydreaming. It takes a good knife. You have to have a whetstone along. If you sharpen the knife only once while doing this job you got a good knife. A violator, when trapping, is always happy when the snow is gone as it is so easy to follow one's tracks. Beavers stay prime until the last of May. In Minnesota the lakes are from 200 to 1400 feet in depth and the water stays cold until the last of June. However, if you are in northern Minnesota in the woods the last of June, the black flies would have eaten you up. You would have to come out a little earlier.

Having good luck with spring trapping is like saying I was getting on my feet. It seems that man, being a proud creature, gets independent in a hurry. On my part there was a lot of ignorance mixed in with pride, or, you might say, I didn't know any better. At a resort around a good fishing lake where one could have customers there was always something to fix up. We needed a dock for boats. There never was a dock, in fact, I was the only one who rented boats on this particular lake. By now I had accumulated five old boats. Notice I am saying that I am doing all these things. Now John has been with me almost a year, he was a big help all around. For pay I boarded him and he managed to get a drink of whiskey now and then. He was very happy, for it was much better than staying by himself. I did most of the cooking and we ate good. Then there was again the time for the first day of fishing season. We had what we called ''big shots'' coming in, two men, muskie fishermen. Most of them are good sports, meaning they spend a little money. This time of the year we saw to it that there was home brew. Our customers, when they left, always seemed to be very satisfied. John would be clearing lake frontage while I built a big root cellar. How foolish this was, it was a big job and all hard work. I was doing this on my own and that meant that I would get no pay. Just forty feet from the shack on a side hill facing the west was a cedar swamp and this was a natural place to do this. It seemed that everything I did I wanted to do big and this I paid dearly for many times. I could have won a prize on the root cellar. I dug all the dirt out with a long handled round point shovel - I was a fool for digging. Considerable dirt, mostly gravel had to be thrown up the hill. This I would have for the roof. A 12 x 10 room, I lined all four walls with cedar logs, put a cedar roof across same, and then covered it with four feet of dirt and gravel. This was the first thing I ever built by myself and even with all the hard work the accomplishment was a lot of satisfaction. The first time the owner came up I showed him this cellar. Just think, the owner getting a good root cellar for nothing. He thought it was fine - he didn't even thank me. Many things in those days were taken for granted. What he did say was, "You know, I've got wine at home in barrels. I would like to bring it up here." What could I say, "Good, bring it up anytime." I didn't know too much about this fellow who had the reputation of being the second largest moonshiner from this fairly large town. He had a large family. His brother was his right-hand man, was not married and much younger. I think he worked for him for wages as there were a lot of partnership deals in those days even in the logging business. I found out these fellows were tough. The young fellow had served time for knifing someone. These things one finds out. So about midsummer out of the blue sky, as the saying goes, they came along with a truckload of lumber. Not knowing what this was all about they put John and me both to work. The boss, referred to here also as the landowner, said, "We're going to build a shed back there for aging whiskey." About five hundred feet straight back from our shack was a perfect spot for this project. We had to clear out with a grubbing hoe what had to be moved, to level off the spot for this shed, otherwise there was a heavy thicket of woods. Several large trees close to the shed, which had a flat roof, would practically cover the roof. Black felt tar paper was used for the roof and all around the side walls making this kind of airtight; no windows, 2x4 rack on the inside wall all around, two feet high for placing twenty-five oak barrels on same. This was 1,000 gallons or more and that was considered a batch. They were hauled back on a wheelbarrow, one by one, from the still. Then there was a 50-gallon drum barrel stove placed in the center of the shed. The shed was then heated until it was very hot. It took 10 days to do the job. The called it aging the whiskey. John and I took turns doing the firing. There was a lock on the door and we had to lock it everytime. After all, this was at least $3,000 worth of merchandise. Our pay was still in whiskey. What did it really amount to; ten days $10.00, night firing was $10,00 and for this John and I got 7 gallons of whiskey together. Also, we had to cut and carry the wood from all directions. The wood for night firing, of course, we got in the daytime. After ten days, at 9:00 o'clock in the morning, the young fellow came. He brought a frying pan and molasses with him. Out of this he would make a paste-like form, heating it until it got light brown. The bungs on all kegs were in an upright position and were left lying loose on top while going through this heating process. He would put about ten tablespoons of this syrup in each barrel. After mixing it around with a broomstick he would look to see how much color it had which was also light brown. Then he would say, this is good. We can sell it for one-year old whiskey. They would come in for the loading up on a Saturday afternoon pulling out early Sunday morning with this batch. I must also mention that there were two five gallon kegs along on the load. The boss would take the load by himself. A thirty-eight pistol was beside him on the seat. One time later he told me how he got stopped. The officer weighed him up. The load was fully covered with a tarpaulin so he asked him what he was hauling. He said, "Whiskey, hell what do you think." This was settled for one of those five gallon kegs of whiskey and then I knew why he took them along. And there was never a dull moment. I did do some fishing and often when it was pouring rain. I would put on my swimming suit and would stand for hours on the back of a boat casting for muskie. I never did catch one but I did get some large pickerel. The summer months went by, John was picking berries again and I canned them, always thinking about winter. Then something else happened.

The Indians were picking wild rice. They would camp on the lake three miles from us. This was natural wild rice lake, I don't know how far they came or where they came from. They set up their teepees with old mattresses inside. When they pulled out and were done with their harvest they would leave the mattresses and no one ever picked them up. What a sight! Somehow they found out that we had whiskey. They would come after dark knocking at the door, sometimes at midnight, to trade wild rice for whiskey, a pint or a quart. They, I think, measured it from what they knew about weight. This was cleaned wild rice - they did this by wind. When they left we traded 160 pounds. This was a new addition to our diet. With a double boiler this would simmer all night long in the winter time on our heater, therefore there was always something ready for our breakfast. We did have more wild rice than we needed. By now, having a few extra dollars in my pocket, my mind started to wander and wind up in Chicago. That was it - a trip to Chicago. That was it - a trip to Chicago to sell some wild rice not only to pay for the trip but to make some money. What a dream! When one thinks everything is in one's favor, things start to happen. I took the Model T into a garage for a checkup. I told John of my plans of my trip. It was OK with him. He would take care of things like always. Taking a sack full of rice I started out early in the morning heading for the big city to surprise my uncle and relatives, for they did not know I was coming. They were always glad to see me and to hear of my new adventures. The next day I went down to the Merchandise Mart to sell the wild rice. What an idea I had, walking in there looking around. A man came up to me and I told him I would like to sell some wild rice. "How many truck loads do you have?", he asked. "Oh," I said, "I've only got one hundred pounds. Of course by this time I was beginning to catch on. I asked if he could tell me of a place where I might be able to get rid of some and he suggested I go over to the Morrison Hotel and see the head chef. "Thanks", I said. I asked if he knew what they were paying a pound. He told me twelve cents. Not knowing anything about the price I figured that must be all right. Then I went over to the hotel. I have never seen such a large kitchen and so many chefs. I got down on the lower floor and then had to go to the other end to get where the head chef was. I told them about the rice. "Oh," he said, "we use very little and we wouldn't want that much." So that was it. I always learned the hard way. I went back to Wisconsin bringing the rice with me. I went to a resort town where I found they were selling wild rice. I went to one store, they asked how much I had and they said they would take it. The price was 17c a pound, 5c more than in Chicago. After hauling it around like that I started thinking how dumb I was.

I was very happy to be back in the old shack where comfort and freedom created contentment, a state of mind that would drive one's spirit where one can feel the youth of life. And, being constantly in contact with nature one can feel the joy of being alive - to captivate such environment one also finds that at times one has to pay a price. Having only 8th grade schooling was good enough in a depression. What counted most was not how much you knew but how many things you could do, like building a little when you had only $5.00 and many other things. Elements of nature are many. To correspond in behavior the benefits are not oversight but an understanding. It is easy to become a prisoner in our own surroundings when fascinated with wrong notions where body and soul surrenders to the enemy. So while the days were young and adventure lay ahead, the span of time that has passed since I have been here has taught me many things.

Now winter was here again - by now I could do some legal trapping for a year had passed since my last arrest. Not saying that I was very honest about this for I soon found out there was more money in illegal trapping that legal. One thing is when you have a license you move and wander about in the woods more freely, of course, watching out carefully for the game warden. John had gone to stay with his brother for a couple of weeks. One day I was looking for new territory east of the shack. I was scouting along a river mostly for signs of fur bearing animals. There was something moving all the time. Being what I thought a trapper now, one moves about with considerable expectations. Being a still clear day from further east back in the swamp I heard the sound of an axe chopping. Now I had to go and see what was back there in those woods. A way back I ran into a freshly built logging road. In those day these were manmade. Here there were piles of pulp, balsam, spruce piled separately. Whatever the size of the tree it is then cut up in 100" lengths. This was all handled by hand. I had never seen anything like this before and it was most interesting. Going up the road I found a middle-aged fellow smoking a pipe, working away in what seemed to be a leisurely fashion not knowing then that this lumberjack had a way of doing things where every move counts. Walking over toward him, I said, "Hi." When we got talking I found him very friendly. I said, "How long have you been around here?" First he explained he had to build a place to stay in. "Up a-ways here", he said, "there is a highland running all around the north end of the swamp out to another main road. Why don't you come up and look at my little house?" "Good," I said, "I would really like to see it." On the way up, talking, he told me no one ever came around to see him. He would go down to a sawmill town once a month, there they had a store, and he would get what he needed. We started approaching high land and in the distance I could see his place. What a picture! Cutest little log house I ever saw. The floor was hewed out of small balsam poles all the same size. The roof was the same, round part of the poles facing inside, squared up on the roof part and then covered with tar paper felt. "You know," he said, "I only bought the paper, the two little windows and the hardware for the door. The thing cost me $6.65." I told him I had never heard of

$6.65 Shack

anything like that and I know he was telling me the truth. "How much land have you got here," I asked. "There are two 40's and I want to buy more," he said. I was listening. "How did you get the money to buy this land?" "Oh," he said, "I never got married. I've been working out west on a farm for many years and I saved my money. Things got kind of tough out there lately so I thought I would go home. My home is in the southern part of the state. I was hitchhiking out there on the railroad track going south when I could see all this pulp and along east of the track so I stopped down there by that Frenchman to find out who owns this land. Boy, that guy knows everything going on around here. He told me if you give me $25.00 I'll take you over to the courthouse - we can take care of it from there. Also, I want you to pay me for running the lines for you.'' They did all this. He said there was around $100.00 back taxes on a forty then, the owner wanted $5.00 for the quit claim deed, he would run the lines for him with a compass. In those days that was good enough. So, here was another guy like me, I thought. Then I told him I was trapping and when I got back this way I would come to see him again. When I think back at my life all those years, how things happened to fall in place - the ups and downs, there always seemed to be things that were needed - a place to sleep, something to eat and if I had a disaster, which happened more than once in my life, even then the provision was such so one could always keep going.

Now the next day something new happened. I left the shack about nine in the morning, had a short trap line and I thought I would get back by dinner. No one was at the shack. I got back around one o'clock. There were six inches of snow on the ground. The first thing I saw were truck tracks. They had turned around in front of the shack and headed back out again. Then I saw some man's tracks going around in back of the shack. There was a small window and this was completely broken out. Someone had crawled in through the window opening. I couldn't figure out what had happened. Then I walked around. They hadn't broken the lock on the door. I always locked it when I went away. Unlocking the door I noticed the bed legs. They were made out of 2 x 4's and were all sawed off and the whole double bed, also the top bunk had completely collapsed. Being highly sensitive to the kind of thing it made me feel very bad. Immediately I thought of my boss and his brother - they could have been drunk and were going to play a joke on me. They didn't know me yet. I just couldn't stand for anything like that. I ran out two miles as fast as I could to the nearest neighbor here in the woods. There was a field and these people lived near this road. I had never been there before. I walked up to the door and knocked. The missus and several children were standing by the door. I asked if they saw anyone coming out of that road. Yes she had - she mentioned my boss by name and said they just came out. That was it - who do they think they are - what a dirty trick! So instantly I made up my mind to move out of there. I was thinking of where I could go and thought of the logger I had met and I would go and see him. I knew he had room in his shack. I decided to go right away as it was about three o'clock in the afternoon. To his place, cutting straight through the woods the way the crow flies, was four miles. By now I had learned a lot about the woods, signs of how to find where the sun is on a real cloudy day - take the knife blade, (a trapper is never without a knife), stand the point on your fingernail, I always used the thumb, and as you turn it it will throw a shadow. Then when the shadow comes to the thinnest point that would be the direction of the sun. When you looked at you watch, say it was eleven or twelve noon, in the winter months this meant sun was in the south. Of course there are other signs but this one will not fail you. Going back to my new lumberjack friend, I was thinking just how he would act when I told him what I had in mind. I had considerable canned goods, a car (although I didn't run it in the winter), some tools, a phonograph, and maybe he would be glad to have me. He was down in the swamp working. He was surprised to see me. I came right out and told him what had happened to me. He, no doubt, had gone through the mill himself, being about 48 years old as one could see he was a very understanding person. "Yes," he said, "if you can't get along with those fellows anymore come over anytime." I thought I really was in trouble with the moving. There were four old boats, the other two boats didn't really belong to me. Herman was the first name of my new friend. I told him about all the stuff I had, including the boats. He said, "In two weeks I got a farmer coming up, he lived seven miles away, with his team. He has a great big sleigh and will haul several carloads of pulp out to the siding for me." This was a place made by the railroad company where pulp could be loaded by hand using pickeroons. One could drive up a gradual incline getting up to six feet high going straight ahead. When unloaded there, it came down again. An empty gondola car can be placed there on the right spot when ordered. This was also a spur where one track came in from another direction, meeting here. Herman was very fortunate to have this layout as he had only a mile to go to this landing with the sleigh. I knew the farmer would come soon but having all this on my mind I walked down to see him the next day to see if he would move my belongings. He was up in years in the sixties. He had lived in this country all his life, a nice old man, and he knew the lake I was on. He said he could move me on a Sunday and the charge was to be $8.00. No one knew except these two people that I was moving out from the old stamping ground. Yes, I would have to tell John, the old lumberjack who had made his home with me for quite a while. He will have to go back and stay with his brother, in fact, he was there on a visit with him now. To get more things off of my chest I wrote a letter to my boss and told him what had happened to my shack, I did call it my shack and I felt the same as if I owned it, the same day the fellows were up. After he got that letter the next day he came up in the truck, his brother was with him. They started to give me trouble as soon as they got here telling me they never did this cutting down the bed and all. He said, "You come down to the root cellar with us." The younger brother had one hand in his pocket and was walking behind me. I got to thinking how he had knifed a fellow. All three of us got into that root cellar, the young fellow still standing behind me and the boss standing in front of me cursing and hollering at me that I would accuse him of doing all that damage to the shack. He said, "You must be crazy." Well, I got myself together thinking in the meantime that they are trying to pull a bluff. I learned to know the guys rather well by now, they go to the extreme to make themselves believe they were right and at the same time make me believe that they didn't do it. The young fellow was still standing behind me and never moved. "So," I said, "if you guys didn't do it I apologize for what I said." Then the boss kept saying, "You know then we didn't do it." Knowing that I was going to move out anyway this gave me enough satisfaction right there. They did not know that I was getting out and I did not tell them. So then they left thinking they had everything squared up with me. This much I could gather from their action. No doubt they were drunk when they did this and felt foolish afterwards.

I was looking anxiously forward to the day when I could move. Herman also had told me if I had time I could help him cut some pulp. This was the first time a job was offered to me where I could expect some pay. So the time did come on a Sunday when I moved out away from the lake and over to a small logging operation. The sun was shining and in spite of that it was cold. That sleigh was a sight with four boats and most all of my other things in the boats, piled in two and two fashion the only way we could get everything on. I constantly took pictures of practically everything I thought had some importance. This was one picture I didn't get. There were, no doubt, many other things going around in my mind. I did have two and one-half years spent in this type of environment with all the freedom and adventure and these, were no doubt, the best two and one-half years of my life, up to then. There always had been a never ending stream of new things, learning more and more day by day. My partner, John, the old lumberjack who enjoyed himself so much, would also lose his home. Now, this place really was our old stamping grounds. This happened so suddenly so who can foretell the future. Believing that our days are numbered makes one also appreciate each day and be thankful for it. Most men get to understand that the relationship between nature and God is very close. Having had the privilege to experience this understanding gave me a goal to follow. So, when things start going wrong I just couldn't let myself be discouraged. This in my life has won me all my battles. I was very happy the day I was moving out to a new place where the environment was entirely different than what I was used to. First, I would not be the boss like I have been as this would not be my place but I knew that I would get used to it and get along. From my observation and acquaintanceship I have had with Herman so far he seemed to be an easygoing kind of person. It was a long sleigh and the farmer had placed a hayrack on it as he had part of a load of hay when he came. He would be here for several weeks to get some pulp hauled out. Well, speaking about the length of that sleigh, we had the Model T tied on the back of the sleigh so the whole deal looked more like a caravan. The old fellow had a big team, they could handle this load well. We got to Herman's in good time, about two in the afternoon. Yes, this was on a Sunday. Herman did not work on Sunday - as long as I knew him we never talked about religion. We carried the most important things into the house. I have to be careful here what I say. This fellow had high respect for the home he had made here, something that was his place, that was more than 99% wood and he had carried it all out of the swamp on his back. So he called it a house. We got in the canned goods -- food was always well taken care of in those days and there was no waste like now where a large percentage goes into the garbage can. Herman could appreciate some of my canned raspberries and wild rice. Certainly he would have something new to add to his menu. I learned to make good potato pancakes and with raspberries, that was a delicacy. I also learned to make bread. To me this was an art. I remember the first I had ever baked. It had a terrific wholesome flavor, was dark brown in color, long shaped narrow loaf but it was so hard that if one hit somebody over the head with it I know you could knock him out. One could always soak it in his coffee. Making a stew was simple and it was one of the main things in our diet. All the wild meat I ever used I would parboil first for about ten minutes. It is surprising all the stuff that boils off from this.Then after washing the kettle, back in it went, adding at times, wild rice, rutabagas, carrots, potatoes, peas and beans. We always managed to have four of these items.We were in the depression, yet we had everything we needed.When one heard where people had committed suicide by jumping out of a window, I always felt sad to think that people got so materialistic so as to lose all the basic things of life. It was never meant that way from the beginning. We were so busy everyday that the struggle and hardship we had was a challenge. So the attitude was one of great satisfaction which in turn would bring me contentment that money could not buy. Yes, there are many things in life that money cannot buy, yet, many struggle just for the dollar, having all they need and sometimes, as they say, one foot in the grave, and looking for more money. So I am poor, I thought, it was easy for me to overcome the thought of being poor for I would think it is better for me this way than to be a drunkard.

Now here I was in my new home. For the next two weeks I slept on the floor because the farmer who was to haul out the pulp would need the extra bunk. I placed an old mattress on the floor every night and threw it up on the top of the bunk every morning. So that also meant I had to be the first one up. This, you know, can become a routine, up at five o'clock in the morning in the wintertime. First thing was to look at the very small drum heater for there would not have been room for a big one. Most of the time there would be a few coals left. Having so much wood it was easy to start a fire. There wasn't a time walking in from the job for dinner when we wouldn't pull off some birchbark to get a good handful. So there was always plenty of that on hand near the cookstove where we had a regular place for it. This birchbark has been the main thing for the woodsman to make a fire in a hurry especially out in the open under bad weather conditions. No doubt the Indians always made good use of it. I wanted to make a birchbark canoe but it never happened. After I got the fire going, the place, being so small, heated up in a hurry. Then I started breakfast and the old fellow would go out and feed the horses. There was a variety of things for breakfast; oatmeal with toast and jam, pancakes and syrup and always coffee, canned milk (this we bought by the case) with rice with cinnamon and sugar, eggs with bacon and toast, French toast with jelly or syrup, scrambled eggs - and to this day I like this homecooking better than any restaurant. Oh, yes, we changed menus around and Herman liked my cooking. We became the best of friends. He washed dishes, I dried them. Sundays we washed our clothes. Most of the time Herman had a pipe in his mouth. His teeth showed considerably and after holding that pipe and smoking for years he wore a hole between two teeth.

So here I am starting what I could consider a new career at this time. To use my old expression, I was again a greenhorn at this. Working now for this man he showed me what had to be done. He gave me so much territory, it was called a strip, we marked, about 200 feet wide, 400 feet long, located along a road in the swamp. Where thirty or forty cords would grow to one acre was considered a good stand of so-called pulpwood. Even in those days the work was piecework, by the stick or by the cord, a solid cord being 4x4x8 feet. Now everybody for the last eighty years got paid for eight feet, however, the paper company wanted it 8 ft. 4 in. or 100 inches. This extra four inches amounts to many free cords for them in time. However no one cared up to this day. So I took the job by the stick. What I could carry out on my back and pile on the road, this was, of course, more money. The larger ones would be piled two or three sticks together, two feet back having a large chunk of wood underneath so it would be off of the ground. A skidding chain could be swung around that part. Then one had to brush clean a narrow trail big enough for one horse to go through to skid this out to the sleigh road. This they call skidding trails. The tools I needed were an ax, and a saw. In those days a saw was four feet long and was called a one-man saw, a measuring stick and a pickeroon. These we bought but the homemade ones out of an old ax were many times better, especially when one tool on one handle could do the work of two. This we had made by a blacksmith. He took a double bitted ax, cut one side and half way down on one side. The other half was gradually pointed and then slightly bent at the point. This was very handy knocking off limbs, using the ax side. This was very easily done in zero weather for when frozen they break like glass. Spruce is easier to work with as it is light in weight. It is also the highest priced pulp on the market for it makes the finest paper. The balsam has a lot of pitch and is heavy like lead. This you find out when you lift or drag it around with the pickeroon. Then there is always a chance of getting hurt. I was lucky. The closest I came was one day when I was using a double bitted ax. Swinging up over my head the ax got caught on a limb coming down. It started to spin in my hands. Losing part of my stroke the ax was turning real fast coming right for the side of my head by the temple so I could feel the wind going down. Had I been hit there just right, it could have meant death. One thing I learned then is to have everything clear on the side and above when chopping that way. A lone logger or one-horse logger would cut all year long in this highland swamp, meaning they had no water in them. Then where the sleigh road would go, they cut the stumps right level with the ground and this made a very good winter sleigh road. They would cut a whole forty acres, piling the pulp that they could carry out. Then late fall as the snow kept falling they had to tramp every inch by foot so it would freeze down. Sometimes this had to be done several times so it would hold up the horses and the sleigh. Whenever there were holes they filled these with any kind of wood, placing it in corduroy fashion. This man I am staying with now had done this. He had over $1,000. worth of pulp in the woods. By now I was learning a little bit about this timber business, how much pulp and cedar some of the so-called tax "forties" had on them. A big lumber company owner would go through a section of land and log only the choicest trees that were on high land. This stuff in the swamp was junk to them in those days. When they first started out they only took the virgin white pine, many having 1000 ft. scale in one tree and more. There was a time when they did not know that they could take one of the crosscut saws they had, turn it sideways to cut the tree down. They chopped them all down with an ax. Today this seems very strange to us for they did use this same saw to cut the tree up in log lengths. Now we know how long it took man to find out about the chain saw bucking all these millions of feet of timber with a crosscut saw all the years before. Then there was another strange thing. When they did go into the swamps to do some logging, that is, winter, logging, they used only oxen. It was quite some time before they found out they could use horses. And so time changes everything; not knowing then, but time was constantly working on me for another change.

The very first people I had met back by the lake, the ones that had helped me out with potatoes, etc., she, the missus must have heard about my moving here to this place. Winter had gone and it was early spring. She came to see us and had some religious literature she wanted to leave with us. I would say that this was a distance of seven miles. One thing that came to my mind was that I wanted to get a picture of Herman and myself so I asked her if she would take the picture and she did. It turned out real good. In those days I sent to LaCrosse to get all my pictures developed. Most of the time I had my camera ready, an old box camera, and it took good pictures. The missus headed back and we thanked her for coming down to see us. That was the only time she ever came. Now my spring trapping started - all for beaver. I did forget to say that while there at the lake this last summer a guide from a nearby town brought a fellow down, a guest from a large resort, for some fishing. This was the first time I met this guide and I remember while talking to me he gave me a Hershey bar. He knew I was doing some trapping and he also heard that I got caught. He told me, "Don't forget, if you ever get illegal beaver I'll help you get rid of them." He also gave me his name and told me where he lived. Knowing that I could get rid of the hides I went trapping. Herman didn't care what I did as long as I paid half of the groceries. What I had in the back of my mind was that I wanted to buy some of these tax forties as I learned that one can make some money there. I didn't have enough money yet to do this so the beaver trapping was important to me, not only for that reason, but it was a fascinating adventure. The money could be made fast. The last of April and May was the best time. There were a lot of beaver around. I don't know exactly when this outlaw beaver trapping started but it was not many years back. I got in on it when it was a big business. However, there were not too many fellows in on it. They got to be rugged individuals staying out in the woods never less than a week at a time. One needed only a packsack, a little food, about ten traps, a good hatchet and knife, some blankets, and matches. These were kept in a small glass jar so they would not get wet. Oh, yes, a one gallon pail for cooking. I managed to get around walking from one place to another, sleeping here and there on a foot thick pile of balsam boughs, most of the time in a very remote place and often out in the middle of a swamp. I had rubber hip boots and could walk in twenty inches of water. When the swamp was wet I would cut many small evergreen trees until the pile got three feet high for a place to sleep. Sometimes I got caught in some very bad weather. I remember when I had to walk a long way through the woods and I had both of my ears frozen. I had lost my cap so I tied my handkerchief, (I had one of those large red ones), over my ears. It was half snow and half rain and the wind was blowing. Not having any place to go so I had a roof over my head I started for home. If a man didn't know, as it was with me then, how to manage to get along in the woods, you found that you constantly had to keep on learning to find out little by little how you might be able to do it better. And this also means how to make better concealed effective sets for two reasons, one to catch more beaver and the other so the game warden couldn't find or see the set traps. Very seldom did beaver trappers get caught. A game warden would have to lose a lot of sleep for that. If the water in the river was high the only place one could cross was a beaver dam. At one time the wardens waited twelve days for me to come out as they heard I was in there. What happened was that I was afraid and I mistrusted this place. Later on I heard about this place. I knew that in some places too near civiliztion you could not start chopping, for the noise would carry a long way. I would take along a so-called Swede saw blade. Bending a small sapling 1½" thick in a bow to the correct length I would cut in 2'' on each end with the same blade which has a round hole, one inch from the end. Then when placing this in there I would drive a nail through so as to hit the hole on the blade. I had a saw which at times was a life saver. A trapper will work and move with caution. Here several miles up the river from where this dam was was one I was afraid to cross. I cut eight 8ft. 6 inch dry cedar poles (that is dead cedar), tied them together with rope and made a raft, got a long pole and was able to get across. I used rafts often to get to the beaver houses on a flowage. I made good on my trapping and when I got back to Herman in that little house of his I felt like a millionaire. Speaking of comfort, I had a bed to sleep in, a roof over my head, things to eat, even like potatoes and other foods one cannot carry out on a trapline. Now I had many things to do.The first thing was to get a battery for the Model T so that I could run it. After a beaver is skinned it is then nailed slightly in an oval shape form on a large white pine tree for drying. For transportation they are then rolled up. One can roll fifty tightly to make a large bundle for a packsack load (2 large packs.)

The next day I went to town, three miles up the railroad track. All hoboes and wandering lumberjacks walked the railroad tracks at that time. Many going a long distance rode the freight trains. If one could pay you got service. After I got the battery I hired a mechanic to haul me back out on the main road. Herman, in the meantime had cleaned out a road. It just happened a high ridge ran all the way out from his place. It was easy to follow, very few trees on it, and it made a good road. This then came out to the main road. I carried the battery in from there. In one way now we started to get modern. We pumped up the tires. Oh, yes, in those days everybody had a tire pump, placed the battery in the car-the sound of those Model T's seemed somehow pleasing to the ear. We had pulled this car in on the winter sleigh road. Herman had told me before he would make a road out. After I got rid of the skins I got an idea that I had to build it on his land. Going up a hill one hundred feet away from his house seemed we both thought, a good spot. There was another reason for making this. I would have a place to run the Model T under a roof. This took 2/3 of the size I would make, for the other part partitioned off was only for me to sleep in. It was about 16 feet long and 14 feet wide. It required digging out of the hillside six feet down on the back part toward the hill so as to be able to level this up. When it came to digging I was fast now. I had to get some dry cedar logs. Using about 6 to 8 inch size I would carry them out of the swamp. This took a week making the bottom part about 7 feet high. For the roof I took a strong pole for the ridge supported on each end with a part of a log, this having a solid foundation up from the gable ends. Then I would lay the ridge pole on the top of this. Everything I ever started to make I made what I called a Paul Bunyan style to make sure it would not break down. Now the roof. Not having any roof boards I made it from about four inch round balsam poles. These are very uniform and straight. I placed one tight to the other in an up and down position resting on top of the ridge pole, notching out some and then driving one 20-penny size nail through each one. This was all good. Taking a smaller bitted ax, which was very sharp, I cut off all the rougher spots to eliminate anything that would punch a hole in this light 15 lb. felt paper. I was often surprised at this so called felt which was never made for roofing. Being cheap or rather the only thing one could afford, thousands of people used this for roof paper and also nailed it on the sides mostly over rough boards to keep the wind out. I have seen where felt was good for ten years. Now with the felt on top of the carefully smoothed up poles this did a good job. I had a long old flat bottom boat, this was square, four feet wide, which I brought with me from the lake. When I turned this upside down it made the floor with the help of some patching.   I found a windshield from a Model T Ford coupe and this I placed into the log wall on the south side for a window. Then I placed a few shelves in there. When the partition

was in I had a room about 15 feet long and 5 feet wide and this fancy window. All in all it was a cozy place. I had a single folding cot for a bed. Now, I made one mistake. I did not peel the balsam poles. The grubs started working in the poles. They will work underneath the bark making runways the thickness of a pencil, some coming out to the surface here and there. Working mostly at night they can make quite a noise sounding like a bunch of small sawmills running loose. Believe it or not where the fine sawdust came out it would pile up six inches high. The place took me a month to build. It was worth it. Now Herman asked me if I wanted to cut some balsam and peel it. The peeled brought more money than the rough and there was a good market for it. Well, this was something new again. When the sap is in the trees that was considered the peeling season, from mid May until late August. Then the bark comes off easily. No other wood has pitch like balsam. Then, going to the extremes like always, when I started to peel this I didn't wear a shirt and carrying most of it out on my shoulder I developed a large callous on my right shoulder - the kind you get in the palm of your hand. And, there were hundreds of mosquitoes. One day a fellow was walking around here in the woods, a tourist from Chicago. No doubt he heard me working on the edge of the swamp. He had never seen such a sight as I was, no shirt, all those mosquitoes, coal black hands and shoulders from the pitch of the balsam. We talked some. Before he left he said, "You must be crazy doing this." I told him I didn't mind it ·

About fourteen miles southeast there were potato farmers. One day Herman asked me if I would go over and get a couple hundred pounds of potatoes. I said, OK and tried to get him to go along. Somehow he was very contented with his life and as long as I would manage to get groceries he never left the place. So I went over alone. I got to talking with a farmer, a friendly person over six feet tall and I told him what I was doing. "Oh," he said, "why don't you come over here next fall. We have beaver back there on our creek and we'd like to get rid of them as they keep damming the place, flooding all the timber and then the trees die." These people owned 2000 acres, and 1400 of this land was woods. They were the most industrious, kindest and honest people I had ever met. This, of course, I found out later. I tried to explain to him that it would be better for me if I had a place of my own to stay in. "Oh," he said, "you can stay with us. We go to Florida anyway in the winter to do potato farming there. We seed potatoes down below Miami. There is some frostproof country there. My wife would like to have somebody stay in the house to keep it heated so the flowers don't freeze." So I told him I would be happy to come and then I could trap. I told him the one thing a trapper looks for is new territory. When leaving I told them that I would be back in the fall. In the meantime I got a letter that my uncle wanted to come up from Chicago to see me. I wrote them at once and told them how to find me. I managed to find an old iron double bed with a cot. This would have to be set in the stall garage where I kept the Model T. It had no door so we would hang some old bed sheets up. I would have it ready when they came, two grown-ups, man and wife, and and eight year old boy. He could sleep in at Herman's when they came. They found me and were surprised what a layout we had. There was an old wood burning cookstove I brought from the lake and this we set outside under the trees, added two lengths of pipe and it worked. One thing that was bad for city folks was the mosquitoes. We had to keep a smudge going constantly. An old wash tub filled with good coals from a wood fire and covered with green grass or ferns will make a lot of smoke and is a big help in keeping mosquitoes away. They were a considerable nuisance when I was taking a bath. I had a fifty gallon drum setting up on a wooden pole frame affair. I had a faucet and by wiring a tin can punched full of holes to it I had a shower. I would fill it up partway with water from the pump in the morning, this would be cold, and by letting it stand all day it would be lukewarm. This worked good. My company stayed a week. They went fishing most of the time and seemed to enjoy everything with the exception of one thing. For the first time since I had built the new shack where they slept it got flooded with six inches of water overnight. It had a gravel floor and we had a heavy downpour raining all night. So the water came rushing off this hillside taking some dirt with it. They were surrounded by water and couldn't get up out of bed. We got poles in there to get a dry place for them to stand. When they left I told them they would have something to remember and they said they didn't think they would forget it for a while.

It was an early fall and the thought of buying the next forty acres of land was working on my mind. i looked it over several times and there was a lot of timber on it. So, I decided to go to town where the county seat was to find out about the details. I found out the back taxes were only $76.00 and $5.00 to pay to the original owners for a quit claim deed. This I did. Now I was a landowner. I told Herman and it was OK with him. He said, "I've got all the cutting I can handle now anyway." This forty acres was east from where I was staying now. Also, it went out to the main highway. Here was little clearing and immediately I decided to build a shack there. Not having far to walk, only a quarter mile, was a big help. So I started to level a spot the next day. Having had a little experience in building gave me considerable confidence. But when I got it done it did not turn out like I had expected. Leaving too many large holes in between the logs took much time to close up. Not only that, but it looked terrible. Closing up the holes is called chinking. Blue clay is used and this is found where there are frost holes by digging two feet deep for it. You can work this like putty. This then is placed to that all the holes are closed. The main thing was that it was warm. I found a small horseshoe, I nailed this on the door, and I callled the place "Finlander" shack. Then came the digging

Beaver Dam . . . See Beaver?

of a well. Working hard in three day's time I had a fine pump hooked up. I had to go down about twenty feet digging part way and driving a point the rest of the way. I made a good heavy cover out of planking. I used this pump several years and I wonder how long people used it after that. I had the privilege of getting so much fresh cool water for three day's work and an $8.00 investment for the point, pipe and pump. How much we take for granted in everyday life. Where we are not in bondage if we seek out the truth, to preserve one from despondency, we are within ourselves building a foundation of strength and hope. When busy and there are so many things to do, the days and weeks go fast.

Now the moving-I always hated that. This is the fourth time since arriving in Wisconsin. Some things I left at Herman's. He had so much pulp cut that he had his cousin, a young farm lad from downstate, come up and help him. I started to clear the brush around the shack. My thought was to keep it as it was and in years to come the price would go up. I was planning on trapping and going over to the potato farmer when winter came. Shortly after I had left Herman, (the cousin was now there with him) he got up one morning, made breakfast and when it was about ready he called Herman. Nothing happened so thinking he may be tired he let him sleep a little longer. He ate breakfast by himself and when he was finished he called Herman again - no answer. So he walked over and shook him and found that he was dead. This was a great shock to this young fellow. He managed to let his father know about it and they came and took him down south to his hometown. He had had a heart attack. I heard he had $800.00 in his pocket. What a short memory. I thought of Herman the day two years ago when he walked down that railroad track finding that timber. It was really on account of him that I had gotten a start at what I was doing. That night I was laying in my new shack trying to sleep, thinking about Herman. He had been like a brother to me. How suddenly his life had vanished. Was this imagination for it seemed only like a dream and then to think that he had just fallen asleep. Our hopes at times seem endless, to risk our life to conquer the ambition of our thoughts. Then finally I must have gone to sleep consoling myself knowing that Herman was a good honest fellow.

Being very restless I drove over to the farmer just to see what he was doing. These people had plenty of work. They had started to clear some land and never seemed to get time to work on it. So they made me a proposition telling me that if I finished clearing this forty they would sow it in rutabaga and I would get half the money the crop would bring. The stumps are dynamited several years ahead in early spring when there is some frost still in the ground in order to get the fullest strength in the explosion. These people had one of the largest iron wheel tractors that could be purchased at that time and this was used for tipping the stumps outward. The back had a large iron hook two feet in length shaped like a fishhook with a twelve foot one inch cable fastened to this. Most stumps when dynamited split in half or three or four parts. One part would be hooked on at a time to get them loose. It was a job carrying that hook around all day. This I did while the farmer's son drove the tractor. He was an easy going good-natured man. He was married, had two boys, six and eight years old. There were three houses on this farm, the old man and his wife occupied one, sons one, and the other was empty. On this land clearing deal the main thing my share of the work consisted of was with the large tipped over chunks of these stumps. These had to be pulled out the rest of the way for most of them were hanging somewhat. This team, one of the largest in the country, could handle the parts of split stumps. This I dragged together in a pile for burning and the smaller pieces were picked up by hand. I hired a man for a dollar a day to do that part. We only got part of the field cleared when we had to stop as they had other work to do and now that it was getting colder I wanted to start trapping. This work would be finished in the spring. There was deer hunting coming up and the season was always open for a week. This has been a big sport for me since I have been on my own out here in the sticks and I never missed a season. There were several good streams nearby sometimes winding a long ways through the forest and meadows where there was no habitation. This I always liked as when violating one has more room to hide. I had learned a great deal concerning the life of the beaver, that they would have their young in May and June nine weeks after they are bred. Even when one gets immune to something like trapping beaver, when they have their young it was a sad experience when skinning a female, cutting her open to find two to six young that were ready to be born. How dainty they looked with fur, feet, mouth and that tiny flat tail. Even one trying to be tough somehow I felt that it is wrong and what a shame they could not live. When I think back now ever since Wisconsin had an open beaver season it was always at this time of the year when they are bred. I guess it always has been from the beginning of time, life for life. The first winter the old ones stay until March or April or until the ice goes out, then they leave the young in the old house and the old ones find a new place. The young ones stay in the old house for years then they find a mate and the second year they then build a new place. The males have their territory and they fight off other males in the spring when they pair off. You can see what fights they must have had when catching some of these males in the spring. Some would have large cuts in different parts of their body. Near an old empty beaver house I saw a large beaver floating ten feet out in the flowage. I got him with a pole. He was in good shape and I could tell that he had been freshly killed. I could not believe that this could happen. When I skinned him out I could see a large cut in the back of his

40

neck. This doesn't happen very often. I think for all my trapping this was the only one I ever found like this. Beaver are highly alert to danger especially when there are bear around. When they go up in the woods, cutting down trees or carrying limbs and logs down their slide, they keep one beaver there to watch. Should he hear the least odd noise or smell an enemy then he slaps his tail hard into the water so it can be heard by the gang. Believe me, when they come down that trail they stop for nothing. If you were standing in the way they would knock you down. There is another sad thing I often found here, people trapping and not knowing how to drown the animal. Most of the time they would have a front foot missing. They heal perfectly and very smooth. One finds this condition mostly in beaver or muskrat, however, occasionally one finds it on a mink or otter. One day I saw unusual tracks in the snow heading down to the creek. Not far down I had a mink trap set near a hollow log. Here laid a mink near the trap, blood scattered around and not in the trap. Then I could see he had lost one front leg before ringing off the other front leg and then losing so much blood and being very cold that night, he got out of the trap and was lying there all curled up frozen. I caught many beaver and muskrat with one front leg off. One day I got a beaver with two front legs off, no stubs were left - were off even with his chest. How that beaver helped build that eight foot house and helped carry in the food for their winter supply, I don't know. This location was in the north side of a small twenty acre springfed lake. It is surprising the fine locations they have at times. One time I found a newly established colony. One can easily tell by the freshly cut wood in the dam, the shiny fresh mud on the house. Poplar trees where considerable water was backed up were still standing some two feet out in the water. They had not had enough time to cut them all down. One thing they love to do is cut, chewing the trees going around and around until they fall. They take out very large chips - they have four teeth, two on top and two on the bottom. They are like a chisel curving slightly round. These teeth marks are very plain to see on the stumps and trunks of trees. One can tell from this if it was a large or small beaver that did the work. I have seen many trees twelve inches across on the stump and up to sixteen inches in size. They tackle every tree in their vicinity and when a person has never seen this it is always astounding to see it the first time. There are places where it looks like a small logging operation. I have seen locations where for a half mile in length and four hundred feet back from the flowage every tree was cut. In the back where they left off cutting the line running up and down was as straight as though one had run it with a compass. Then in hilly country they would drag this material down and up, and down again before they got to the water. One would almost feel sorry for them. Of course where they would run out of aspen (so called poplar), and elder and willows, they would cut white birch. It had happened at times that beaver have been on the same location for fifty years, their food supply gets too far away and they would have to move out. There are always unforeseen things happening to a trapper. He finds a perfect location that has never been disturbed, usually an out-of-the-way place, and this was my luck. I had followed this river down through the woods. At times the going was very rough and I had to leave the river bottom and walk around high land. However, when I found this place I felt it was all worthwhile. It was about seven miles back to the farmer's house where I was now staying. I made four excellent sets on the dam which must have been 150 feet wide. I thought I would wait a week before going back there as I always had plenty other places to go to. Well, something new again had happened. One of those large whooping cranes got in one of the traps. No doubt flopping around it scared the beaver, so that meant fourteen miles of walking for nothing. In the meantime I got acquainted with a young fellow that I could trust. I was making money now and I would pay him well to take me up north where my friend the guide had drawn me a map. He knew every place in this neck of the woods and he also had the reputation of being the oldest guide around. He showed me the exact location and told me how to find the place. I asked the young fellow, after getting me up there 40 miles from here, if he would come back after me in ten days. He would pick me up at a certain spot on this road at a certain time. I made ten sandwiches, took ten chocolate bars, one pound of salt, three cans of pork and beans, bacon, butter, frying pan, pup tent, one blanket, six traps and my 25-20 gun. I walked most of the day to get where I was going to trap. I put the tent on an island in a swamp not far away from the beaver pond. The first evening I was near the pond at sundown, well before dark, and I counted twelve beavers swimming. I shot two for supper, the others disappeared. I took only the choice parts of meat for eating. I found out that the liver is a delicacy. First you parboil it and then fry it. It is so tender you can press it with your tongue. I got eighteen beaver before the ten days were up and I had to come out to catch my ride back. From this trip I learned a lot more about trapping, that is, that one has to move around.

I was getting more involved in what I could consider a business. To think that I now owned forty acres of fairly good timberland, had a comfortable shack on it, a Model T Ford, and traps, and now this coming summer I would get half profit on forty acres of rutabagas. I would lose out on the spring trapping for there was too much at stake. And I also knew that as soon as one could get on the field the work would have to start in order to have the field ready for plowing. This they did with a breaking plow. Part of it had been plowed. They had an outfit where up to three inch poplars were plowed right under - they claimed it put nitrogen in the soil besides getting rid of the popple. I hired three men to take care of my end of the deal. In those days there were good workers for one dollar a day. I got along good at the farmer's. Through the winter months when I did not trap all the time I would help the son with the chores. They had a half dozen cows so there was plenty of milk. They also had a flock of chickens. By doing this I got my board and I would eat with them. There is always some beaver trapping in late fall, violating, also muskrat, mink and otter. Then there is an open legal season on the above mentioned animals starting about the first of March and ending around the 15th of April.

There were a lot of lumberjacks drifting here and there, some very old, some younger and there were several large sawmills around and these operated their own logging camps. Some had a very bad reputation for poor pay. Here is the way it worked. The food was very poor so most of these fellows stayed only one week. Payday was once a month. All the men at the same mill were paid company money, money that could be used in the company store for goods or exchange otherwise. A drifting lumberjack didn't like that. Most of these fellows stopping there wanted to get a few square meals and then go somewhere else again. Some of these men had made these rounds quite often knowing every lumber camp in northern Wisconsin and the bordering states. There were then three crews, one coming, one was staying and one figured on going. When a place was not liked the few dollars they had coming meant nothing and they wouldn't stay a month just to get pay. It was claimed that some of these so called big outfits were making money. Going up the road to my place I met a fellow walking. He had a packsack; he was not very old. When I got to talking to him he said the last job he had in a camp was for second cook. I told him that I was a trapper and as soon as muskrat season opened I knew of a place ten miles east down on the Soo Line, a kind of a shallow good-sized lake with a swamp bordering around the edge of it. Not far from there was an old building left there years ago from a logging camp. It needed some work on it, patching here and there. Having all this in mind I said to this fellow, "Why don't you come on down with me and cook for me." He said he would like that. Having to wait two weeks for the season to open I got him to stay in my shack as it was empty. I was staying with the farmer. In the meantime I had ordered fifty of the smaller traps for muskrat from Sears. With my old ones I would have one hundred fifty or two hundred traps. I had this constant urge to do everything to the extreme. Many times I suffered for this. Violating the game laws in those days was a common practice. People hated the wardens so badly they would not even talk to them if they saw one on the street. There were some tough guys around that always talked of shooting the game warden. Some of those wardens did come close. One I remember, was so bad they left him for dead, however, he lived, but he was never able to serve as a warden. They would place sand and gravel in a warden's car and even shoot it full of holes when they found it parked on some side road where the warden had walked into some logging camp or up a stream to catch someone spearing fish in the spring of the year. These things never entered my mind. I wasn't looking for this kind of trouble. Another thing that was bad for the warden was they did much traveling around using snowshoes in the winter. They found where every still was located. These were the biggest enemies - the moonshiners - for they did not trust him. It being hard times people broke the law, mostly killing deer to get some meat. A complete lawlessness existed in northern Wisconsin in the 1930's.

At present I had some beaver traps setting on a dam at a location where there was about twenty acres of heavy timber standing on one side of the river. On a Sunday morning I walked two miles to get there, checking the traps, but nothing caught. So I left them there. The reason I mentioned this stand of timber was I walked around on the north side to get to the dam and then walked on the south side to come out. The game warden had walked the same way some ten minutes later, being then behind me. Then seeing my traps on the dam he took them along with him. He also walked out on the south side to come out over a hill where there was a small clearing and a bachelor lived there. I thought at the time when I came out I shouldn't walk past the fellow's place for when one is violating you are suspicious of everybody. Instead of having to crawl around in the woods where there is considerable underbrush one takes the easy way of walking and many times this is a short cut.   An old railroad grade leading out to an established gravel road was his way out. I never walked slowly in these days and making good time I got to where the Model T was parked in the woods so it could not be seen from the gravel road, not knowing then that the warden was behind me. I did not see his car, not even the fellow back there in this cabin in the clearing. I left and had many other places to go for at this time of the year I was rambling around in the woods looking for fur or locations one could come back to after the ice went out where it was too dangerous to trap now. Then too, the snow would be gone. The warden was trailing me. He stopped at the cabin and asked the man if he had seen anyone going by lately. He told warden I had just gone by a short time ago. This fellow had seen me down in the store and knew who I was. So that was it. The same game warden that had arrested me four years before had a hunch that I was violating right along. Now he knew that these were my traps and he was mad. Traveling around the way I did, he just couldn't keep up with me. The way things happened was like a miracle. The warden was watching in the woods near the dam for a week. This was a good place to hide. I got so busy with so many things that I didn't get to go back.

Visiting the lumberjack one morning up in my shack he said he talked to the section foreman who had charge on the Soo Line and he would take us down on the repair car so we could get all our groceries, bedding, traps and other needed materials. You could manage OK to fit this on such transportation that was run by an engine. You could hear them coming a long ways off with their "putt-putt" sound. He also told me he liked his drinks so bringing him a pint bottle made a big hit with him. We started a week earlier for we thought we would fix the place up and being way out there in the sticks could also start trapping a little early before season. It was always tempting to get started ahead of the game. Then having everything ready to go, our friend made a special trip for us to get us there. This was a big lift for us - things like that one can really appreciate. Hard times, it seemed, brought many people closer together. I never got back to look at the traps where the warden was waiting to catch me.

Well, here we were all organized for this spring trapping. Most of the lakes have an outlet. This is where the ice goes out first for there is some current water moving. I had rough walking to go down to the south end of that lake. I'd never been there before. To my surprise there was a beaver family there. The evidence showed this plainly so I made three good sets. Then I followed the river down several miles. There was considerable open water and this was encouraging for here one could make some muskrat and mink sets. Knowing and recognizing directions I knew how to get back without going the same way I came. You always find a better way. There are times when you can get badly fooled running into swamps and potholes and a lot of underbrush and creeks one may not be able to cross. So there were times when I had to back track. On this day the going was good and I knew it had to be in a northwesterly direction to come out on the Soo Line railroad and get back before dark. My cook had a lot of time on his hands - he would make a good meal for supper. Our light was a kerosene lamp. Before going to bed I worked, sanding down muskrat stretchers. One never thought anything of going to bed early. It just seemed to come natural. After being out here eight days, season on muskrat and mink had been open three days, things started to happen. I went out early to a nearby pothole to see if I had caught anything - had several sets there for beaver. Yes, I had one big beaver. Got back and was anxious to show it to my cook. "Oh," he said, "I would be afraid to keep them around here." I thought it was strange for him to talk like that. What made me take his advice, like something told me to, I don't know. I took the beaver, walked back 100 feet from the shack and threw it behind a brush pile - there was three inches of snow on the ground. I had three muskrats to skin out. I had a regular hanger for skinning. I hung a muskrat on it hanging it up on the door frame where the sun was shining on this spot. There was an old logging road leading in here from the railroad track. When it got to within two hundred feet from this place there was a bend in the road and one could not see beyond this bend. I happened to look up and I recognized the game warden coming hurriedly toward me. His face was red and he acted very upset. This first thing he said was, "How come (mentioning the section foreman's name) he told me that he didn't bring you down here. He told me a point blank lie." "You know Carl," I said, "I am not responsible for what he told you."Then he started walking in the shack. I must have had seventy traps hanging in there on the wall for I did not have time to find a suitable place to set them out. And there were the eighteen muskrats hanging still in the stretchers. "How come you got so many rats already? The season has only been open three days." "Oh", I said, "I found open water way down on that creek." By now my thought was on nothing except that beaver I had thrown out there by the brush pile. With this three inches of snow on the ground he could have traced my steps and found it in a few minutes. Then he started in on me saying a fellow saw me over there on that dam so he knew those were my traps. He said, "You just as well admitted you know those were your traps." "Oh," I said, "you know I am trying to make a little money trapping for groceries." "Oh," he said, "you tell so many lies - sit down here."There were a couple of boxes - he sat on one and I sat on the other. He took out a small book from his pocket and a pencil. Then he said, "Just when did you come to this country?" I said, if you are inquiring concerning my citizenship I was one the first day when I came over. Both of my parents were already naturalized citizens." He stuck his little book back in his shirt pocket. Then he said, "You better come on down to the lake with me and show me where you caught these rats." Still thinking about the beaver I was glad to get him away from here. We talked very little going down the railroad track to this lake. This was also the way he came in, yes two miles further, five miles the closest way in. My next thought was I only hoped now that he would not walk to the south end of that lake - it was quite a ways down, for there were my beaver sets. We walked out on the lake to some muskrat houses. One house had an open hole two feet wide and there were two rats swimming, repairing the house. We both watched them and neither of us said anything. Then he said, "I've got to go - so long, I'll see you again." He walked away swiftly. Neither one of us realized how thin that ice was. Both of us could have gone in. It was one of those soft mud bottom lakes - we would never have been able to get out. The day was spoiled for me by now. I headed back to skin the beaver. After all that had happened I was relieved when it was over and I knew that he would not be back for a while. We stayed two more weeks and as far as getting fur was concerned it wasn't what I had expected.

This time of the year the days are longer and we could get more things done. My friend the cook went back to stay in my shack and I went back to the farmer. I was always welcome there. By now this got to be routine. They had a big barn, hay on the top floor and the beaver hides were hidden underneath the hay. It seemed in those days I always had money. My thoughts for a long time were to buy the other two forty acres of land lying straight east of the one I owned now. This meant going to the courthouse and transacting for this. In those days two-thirds of the woodlands were delinquent tax forties. That is, if the original, owner had not paid the taxes for seven years then it became delinquent. Anyone paying this up would then own that land. To make it more legal if the original owners approved of giving you a quit claim deed this was good. This they did for $5.00 so now this day I bought two more forties - it made me feel good to think that now I owned 120 acres of land, of course, bought with trapping money. The lumberjack I had picked up over a month ago, the one who was cooking for me, now wanted to cut some tie-cuts. The forty across the main highway had the kind of trees that were tie-cut size. A tie-cut had to be not less than eight inches on the small end and cut to exact length eight foot allowance for tolerance was one inch each way. There was a ready market for them. Every sawmill produced railroad ties in those days. One got paid by the piece, the larger the better. From a 10'' they could get a No. 1 tie etc. It also happened that you could get two ties out of this 8 foot once in a while. This fellow was a real hermit. Now he wanted to build his own shack in a most unusual place. Two hundred feet back of this main road was a very large steep kettle hole, so called for they were shaped like a kettle. This was OK with me and he managed to do this by himself. He needed some material so I advanced nim some money. He went ahead and did get a warm place and this it should have been for he dug seven feet down on that steep hillside so the building was half buried in the ground. This also meant that it would be cool in the summer. After he got organized he took the phonograph and a pile of records over there so in this way he had music, the only entertainment he had. From a small nearby town the farmer had no trouble getting three men to finish clearing the land for the big rutabaga field I talked about before, clearing all around the edge where the plowing had started with that breaking plow. This way he could keep on plowing. Another man who understood the job took over the plowing from 5:00 p.m. to midnight. They rigged up two headlights from a car onto this tractor. As mechanics these fellows couldn't be beat. The farmer, who was getting up in age, did the sowing. Come to find out he was an expert in sowing rutabagas. Most people never understood how to sow them and would get them too thick and this would stunt the growth. The system he used was very simple. He took the axle and wheels from a wagon and installed a long large box and an end gate seeder. This was attached on the back and driving from a large sprocket from one side of the wagon wheel by a sprocket chain to a smaller wheel on the seeder. Then cloverseed mixed with the rutabaga seed of correct proportion was placed into a hopper. The reason for the clover seed is that it took one year to

47

get a stand for the clover. When the rutabagas are ready for harvest late in the fall, this clover is then three to four inches high. This causes no drawback to the growth of the rutabagas. Having had his measure so good when sowing the combination of seeds the rutabagas were 8-10-12 inches apart for perfect growth. This wagon sowing equipment had two poles, one on each side for a horse to fit in to pull it. One trip down the field would cover a twenty foot width. So this crop would not come up all at one time, he sowed it in three intervals a week apart. Harvesting would then be easier. They were harvested in the fall, shipped in carload lots and brought what was considered a good price. This was the largest rutabaga field I had ever heard of in this country. I received half of the income as I was promised. Just while we were in the process of pulling the rutabaga, we had eight people out there on the field to help, it rained slightly all night long and it was too wet to go on the field to work. So I drove over to my famous Finlander shack to burn some brush piles which were rather close to the log building. Being wet out I thought this would be a good time to do the job. never thinking of getting a burning permit. There was a law requiring this. Around ten in the morning a car full of people drove up. A man got out and walked around the side of the car where I could see him. It was the game warden, the same one I had had all my previous contacts with. Walking over where I was he said, "You got a permit?" "No," I said, "I thought it was wet and I wanted to get rid of this brush on account of fire danger." "That makes no difference," he said, "you're supposed to have a permit." "I know," I said, "but I thought it was all right to do this." "You come over Friday (that meant the County Seat) and see the judge." "Oh, why do that," I said, still trying to get out of it. "Now don't forget that I want to see you there at ten o'clock." I knew there was no use doing any more talking. The last time he came all the way down here to see me about those beaver sets on the dam and I know he was still mad. Being so busy with the rutabaga harvesting made me feel bad about the whole thing. One consolation was that I could borrow the farmer's truck and take a load of rutabagas in to town with me, see the judge and then go house to house peddling rutabagas. One could get $1.00 a bushel. Thinking this way I was anxious to get ready to go on Friday morning and to get there on time. At a time like that there always seems to be something going wrong. One thing I didn't like was I had long whiskers and a small beard. This meant I had to get a shave first so I went to the barbershop and got to the Court House one hour late. Walking into the courthouse you can see the stairway coming down from the second floor. I looked up and there was the warden coming down very hurriedly. He saw me and said, "Where have you been? You are an hour late?" I said I had a flat tire. "Come with me upstairs." To the right was a long narrow hallway that had a countertop on one side and a room behind this. Just as I approached a well dressed man came out. The warden talked to him and said,

"Here, I got this fellow." He was on one side of the counter and the warden joined him. He said, "You were burning out there without a permit?" "Yes, I said, "I guess I am guilty but it was raining that morning." The warden spoke up and said it was just drizzling. I said I was burning for the state's protection, too, because I thought when the sparks came out of the chimney they could catch the woods on fire with all those brush piles around. I told him I had built a house there. The warden said, "It is not a house, only a shack." This I didn't like so I said, "You know, some people have to live in shacks - everybody can't live in a mansion." He walked over to my side. I walked in front of him and I said, "What is the matter with you? You've been giving me a hard time all these years. What is the matter with you anyway?" "Oh, yes," he said, "I never forgot that letter you wrote me once." "Why," I said, "I apologized to you about that letter six years ago. Why don't you try to be a little bit diplomatic about this." "What did you say?"was his answer. "Diplomatic", I said. Acting kind of mad he walked away. Standing there looking into the office the man we had talked to was walking back and forth with his hands behind his back in a folded position. As he looked I motioned for him to come over. I said to him, "Who are you?" He said, "My name is Sheppard. I am the District Attorney." I told him my name and said that I had bought some tax forties and was just trying to make enough money to buy groceries. Then the warden came back and motioned to him to come into his room. I could barely hear them talking back in the corner of the room and could not see them. In a short time the warden came out and said to me, "Well, I guess you can go home for today." "Thanks," I said, and walked off. I thought then that the District Attorney understood my problems and was thankful they let me go. Of course, this time I would not have sat it out in jail. My time had become too valuable so I would have paid the fine. After all I had a truckload of rutabagas that I wanted to peddle that afternoon. Never seemed to be trouble selling that which has been grown on new soil. They are much sweeter than those grown on old soil.

Here it was late fall again and another deer season. The large level field the potato farmer had here was used by many fellows shining deer. Some would get caught as the wardens would watch these places very closely. A sad thing happened to the farmer I made my home with. Two of his horses were shot one night by men shining deer. Everybody figured the men must have been drunk. They never did catch them. This hunting season they had a $50.00 prize for the largest buck in weight. A brother of the farmer where I stayed was an expert shot. We knew of this big buck hanging around and when we saw his tracks they would almost scare one. So we hunted together tracking this big one up and down the river bottom. Following his tracks we found out how smart he was. He would travel against the wind so he could smell what was ahead of him. Then we saw where he laid down on a high knoll under a few small trees facing the way he had come. From such a position it would be impossible to sneak up on him. We got one shot at him one day. The bullet glazed a tree, and we found considerable hair but no blood. We never did get him. The truth about hunting season is every time a hunter goes out he can tell a different story. It seemed in those days I got one buck every year.

Gaining considerable experience logging I decided this winter I would start. I had met the manager of the sawmill in the town nearby and we had become good friends. He would advance me money when I needed it and also said I must get 4 or 5 fellows to help me. He was looking out for some of the oldtimers that would be good in the cutting of cedar. It was understood they would cut it where it would bring the most money. They would size up a tree after it had fallen and was limbed out for the best cuts like 7 foot cedar posts or say two ten foot or a telephone pole, etc. Now this meant I had to build an addition to the Finlander shack. This time we could afford to do it with boards and it went so much faster. The bunks were also made out of wood. We managed to get some old mattresses. One time coming back from Chicago in the Model T, I brought back two double mattresses rolled up so I could get them in the back seat. They were in good shape. When I was set for more help the place was ready. I got hold of five lumberjacks, none was married. I knew that I had to do the cooking so I would always be the first one up early in the morning and have breakfast ready shortly after the rest were up. About seven o'clock it was getting daylight and these fellows wanted to get a good start. Three of the men were cutting piece work and two were helping me by the day. We had to make all the logging roads, to skid the material out. We had two horses and they were worked single fashion. I had one bad job and that was I would have to come in a half hour earlier to get dinner ready. We did not have too far to walk for we were logging the forty the building was on. We were producing a lot of merchandise. I always believed in feeding the men good. They had to pay for their board. Using a lot of canned goods simplified the cooking. If I had told anyone in those days that our grocery bill that winter in that sawmill town was $600. no one would have believed me. The bill was paid in late spring after some money came in from the logging job. We produced 6,000 cedar posts and these would have to be peeled. The cost by the piece for peeling was $1\frac{1}{2}$¢, the standard length is 7 feet. I was very poor at this type of work not having the patience to stand in one place so long and this was required when peeling cedar posts. The ice was going out and this was beaver trapping time. One of the best camouflaged deals was having all those cedar posts to peel. They were piled in one long line by a regular well-traveled road. I had three men peeling the posts while I was trapping. I could make enough money to pay for having this work done. When one gets something so strongly on his mind it is hard to resist doing it. They say it gets in your blood. These beaver trappers have a strange way of getting acquainted. There were only a few fur buyers around dealing with illegal beaver skins so at a certain place on a certain night as many as six trappers would come with their furs to meet the buyer there. Several years back I met a man who used to be a state trapper - 1924 or 1925. The state, in those days, paid them by the month and furnished the traps, 4 dozen No. 48, new with steel drags. They trapped all predatory animals wolf, coyote, fox, bobcat, and porcupines. Private trappers got $20.00 bounty on wolves and coyotes, $5.00 on bobcats, and $2.00 on fox. There were about fifteen of these state trappers enough to reach across the northern part of the state. The best time to catch these animals was during the summer months. The average catch on wolves would be sixty, coyotes eighteen, and this in one month's time. Hides had to be turned over to the state. And so it was in those days, they were trying to keep the population down on these animals. Later, say in 1937, there were plenty wolves and beaver.

Sawmill Scene

My logging operation turned out so good that I bought a brand new Ford V8 pickup. Now I would think you don't have to work for anybody anymore. I thought that now I was in business, from now on I could be my own boss. How deceiving life can be when circumstances and environment can bring such thoughts of false illusion. They had me believing I was sitting on top of the world never knowing what was lying ahead for me. Most of the cedar posts and pulpwood was sold, also the skins from spring trapping. A friend came along. He was the guide at a large resort and he said he had found a good job for me. It seemed very strange to me taking a job like that. Besides my monthly salary I would make much in tips. Arguing back and forth I finally agreed to take the job. I was not in favor of logging the swamp through the summer months. We would have plenty time next winter to finish the logging on the remaining twenty acres. This resort work would be a new experience for me. I was told the job of running the launch would be mine. Now for the first and long time I would not have to do any cooking so it would be a big change. With all those things in mind this was sufficient consolation to look forward to what seemed just another adventure. It worked out all right. I found out that people liked to be waited on, helping them with their fishing poles, mixing the gasoline for their outboard motors, etc. One of the main jobs was cleaning the fish. Some had to be packed in ice for taking home or for shipping. All resorts had an ice house. People were in the business of filling up these ice houses all over the north country. They had the equipment and charged by the cake. When I was all alone in the launch, you could call it a speedboat; I could go 30 miles per hour. On one occasion I had eight people in the boat on a sightseeing tour. I was going along, not too fast and I was looking away over on the shoreline at something moving., I noticed the people looking around and getting restless. First I did not pay any attention then I happened to look straight ahead and here was a fishing boat 100 feet away right in line with the way I was going. I immediately turned the boat making a circle around so as to miss the fishing boat. I felt badly and apologized to the people. It took half a day to make this trip. When we got back I helped the people out of the boat and told them again I was sorry for what happened and that it would never happen again. I knew if they would talk about it too much it would turn out bad. And so things happened. One day a little girl about four years old, the only child of a doctor from St. Louis, fell in the water on the end of the boat landing dock. Her parents had gone to town. A number of people were swimming on the other side. She wandered away and got over to this dock and was walking backwards when it happened. I was about 200 feet away on the other side cleaning fish. A bachelor neighbor living nearby up the lake about the same distance away saw it happen. He hollered for me and kept on pointing toward the shore. All I could think was he saw a large fish. One seems to get a hunch when there is danger. I ran to the end of the dock as quickly as I could and I could see a dark spot about eight feet out and two feet under water. Making one jump I all but missed her, I raised her up and got her up on the dock. A young woman came running, I believe she was in charge of her. She slapped her on the back and she was coughing and coughing. Everything turned out OK, she was well. They called her Shirley Temple for she had curly hair. When her parents came back they looked me up and gave me $20.00. I didn't want to take it but they insisted saying I had ruined my good high top boots and I should buy another pair. That was the day when I was a hero to everybody - long since forgotten.

Time being our biggest enemy divides the spoils among us. What can our defense be? Who are our enemies? What power can we use to defend ourselves in this wilderness of life? As we get older strange thoughts of nature come upon us. All of us have to overcome many things - being as yet in a depression and a fellow like me riding around in a new Ford. However, if our riches increase and we do not set our hearts upon them that is no good. This never had any effect on me, glad to say.

It happened that the owner of this resort had a son up in northern Minnesota on the Canadian border. He owned two large resorts at the very end of a road, in fact, this was as far as anyone could go. From there on it was 80% water and 20% land, was very rugged, ravines running east and west often in a deep gully-like fashion for miles, making it impossible to build a road any farther. This was canoe country. When placing a canoe in the water you could go clear up to Hudson Bay hundreds of miles away. Very few people ever made that trip. Now I am getting ahead of my story. The son had been up in this neck of the woods for awhile and called it God's country. They were the first people to settle there. He had a good education, some in minerology.He was a good friend of the late James Fargo of the original American Express Company. At that time he owned thousands of acres up in that country all held for mineral rights. What happened to the late James Fargo? He died. The son here got to be administrator of this land. There were 1000 cords of spruce scattered here and there in the swamps.The son had come down to see his parents and that is when I met him. Finding out that I was a logger (people thought I was), he said he wanted me to come up there. He had 800 cords of spruce one and a half miles from this road, 45 miles up the road from the nearest town. He would contract this to me at a very reasonable price. I told him I wanted to finish my logging job next winter and then late spring I would be up to take a look. This is fine, he said. He was a very refined gentleman, never did much work, always working with his head, the most easy-going person I have ever met. I would see him standing near some rock cliff an hour at a time looking at a little stone in his hand with a magnifying glass. It was disturbing to me that I could not go up there any sooner to what he had called God's country. Lying in bed at night I would think about it and of all the things this man told me about the great trapping opportunities in that country and how beaver trappers, including some Indians, would go about this so as to stay away from the game warden. It seemed that it got so that I could not get along without that beaver and muskrat trapping money. The muskrats had been called the king pin of the fur industry for many years because they would multiply so fast. However, most of the money for me was in beaver. This then meant fall and spring trapping and most of this was illegal. When one has learned that we should obey the laws of the land one may look at this differently to be able to yield to temptation. Most violators think it is justifiable to kill deer and trap out of season for they think or say that these animals were put there for everybody to use. Years ago I used to think the same way. As time changes everything, so it changed me. It was right in the height of the bootleg beaver peddling years and I was gradually getting used to this racket, it being partly a result of the depression. In those days this was big money. A number of people, dating far back into our history, got a start from the money that came from beaver pelts and so it seemed with me. When the fur was prime it was impossible to miss it and I would go through all kinds of commotion in order to accomplish this. The late fall up to Christmas trapping would represent only one third of the catch. Every spring seemed to bring alive the call from the wilds of Mother Nature. It seemed as though everything was moving; the geese and ducks coming north sailing down on beaver pond whistling from the speed of their descent, curving to hit their target. There are always the red squirrels and they get very loud with their chatter. They seem to have a sense of alarming other animals when there is danger. The pecking of the woodpeckers comes very regularly in the morning and evening, breakfast and supper time. The loud squawks of the bluejays - they all have their own language, the hooting of the owl late at night could mean a warning to some creature. Often I would get mad at them when I saw then killing a rabbit. Here one had a romance of nature in which you could gather your own imaginative philosophy. We also had to finish our logging this winter here in Wisconsin. This was a big job for me but having learned more about it from experience helped. I remember this one winter. For the month of February it was 30 degrees below zero every day and the last two days it got to 40 below. One young fellow working for us froze his nose seven times one day. Not knowing in those days you should hold and warm the frozen part most people rubbed it with snow. It was wrong but it worked.

I never knew what a Sunday was, it was constantly work, work, work. It seemed it had to be this way - there couldn't be any loss of time. You can get stuck with this feeling and thousands of people have this problem. It took me twenty-five years to overcome it, constantly making up for lost time, afraid of going behind only all, of course, because of a frame of mind. How foolish to think this way as though you have nothing to eat the next day. When I finally learned I asked myself, who is going to take it away from me? Haven't I now lived forty years, had something to eat every day and a place to sleep? However, when we are young it seems we have to learn everything the hard way. This type of struggling that became a part of my life had made a rugged individual out of me. I could do many things that I would not even have thought were in existance six years ago. Even when it came to something like beaver trapping there was the urge to do better. That always in turn meant more hardships. The biggest problem was the game warden. That meant we had to go farther back in the woods and stay one or two weeks at a time. It never dawned on me that I could have gotten a pup tent and had more protection for sleeping. How long it takes for one to learn. I was a glutton for punishment, always sleeping under the open sky - there was a time it rained for two days. I did have a raincoat but in time one gets wet. Trying to keep the food dry gets to be a problem. Up a little creek I found a little tumbled-down shack, no more roof, just pieces of wood so I set the whole thing on fire. There were two doors made out of rough boards, I placed them near the fire so they dried out completely. As night was coming on it quit raining. I kept the fire going.Having an extra set of underwear I placed some poles and hung up most of my clothes to dry. The doors made a good floor near the fire and also the best place for sleeping as it was the only dry place. When one has rambled around all day you will sleep because you are dead tired. Every trip there were new experiences. I endeavored to find a balance to get some control of a new situation as it came along but this,of course,never happened.One would have to be an Indian to know how to work with nature instead of trying to fight nature.

We did get our logging done. There were some things we still had to sell but there was plenty of time as the spring trapping was not over yet. I knew a man who lived on the banks of the Pine River. He had a boy twenty years old. They did some logging. His wife had died and they were there all alone. They also had another log cabin, it was all in one large room, was clean and very nice. I told him I would pay him something if he would let me stay there. They did a little trapping up and down the river covering only a few miles. I would go light to ten miles. This was all new country to me. It was so late this day it would have been impossible for me to get back. The regular procedure was that I left their place early Monday morning and told them I would be back on Sunday. I would get up early often waiting for daybreak. In the spring of the year there are many birds singing and many pleasant sounds. They would start an hour before sun-up, increasing in numbers, adding on and on to what would become a melody of proportion ringing in your ears. This was one thing that would make you feel you were glad you were alive. Another thing, it served as an alarm clock. Their time was correct, one hour before sun-up. I would get up, start making breakfast and most of the time just as the sun was coming up I was ready to go. On the way back, looking over the sets I made the day before, I had two beaver. It takes time to skin a beaver and the day goes fast. At times there are a lot of things to take into account, the lay of the land, curves in the river swamps all making longer and slower walking at times.It was now late toward evening and the sun was about ready to go down. I was coming near a gravel road leading into a fellow's farm. I found out about this later on. He was a conservative modern bachelor, homesteading back there years ago from Ohio. He owned a lot of land, had a small sawmill and made a lot of maple syrup. Of course, we were scared of everybody. Sneaking around this place, we did not know who would squeal on us violators, I ran across this gravel road leading into heavy cedar swamp. There was a small stream leading into the Pine River here. Having a few traps left I decided to follow the stream to see if I could find possible upstream evidence of beaver like fresh cuttings of poplar, newly peeled sticks and limbs and houses and dams. I was wearing hip boots, for in the spring of the year with the ice going out almost everything was flooded. The swamp I had just walked in had water twenty inches deep. One thing was in my favor: it had a solid bottom of ice just as level as a floor. Do not forget, I am on new grounds. This meant I had never been there before in my life. Walking farther back into this swamp, hardly being able to identify the river from the rest, the thought came to me, why not find a place where I can stay all night. I was afraid that it might get too late and get dark. I liked to stay in swamps surrounded by a lot of water as this way I felt more safe. Wandering around I found a place where sometime ago someone had ploughed down a half dozen large cedar trees. No doubt it was a windstorm. This formed about an eight foot square of moss and ruts sticking out of the water a foot high like a little island. It just seemed so natural and I decided at once to camp there. Here I had the two beaver hides, some traps and some canned goods left for the next day. I would be going home anyway. I had other skins buried in the snowbanks back in the woods in a ravine where it was almost impossible for the sun to get in. Here you could find snow in the middle of May. This was the best place to keep hides before they are stretched ...just like having them in a refrigerator. I got my packsack off and piled everything on this island. There was very little dry wood to start a fire but some leaning cedars farther up had a lot of dead limbs. Climbing up a ways I lost my balance and as I started to fall one of my feet landed first. Here under the water were more dead cedar logs. From the force of falling a short stub of a limb two inches long and sharp, the size of a finger, went clear through the rubber boot into the center of my arch; went in very deep. For a moment it seemed I was paralyzed and thinking of getting lockjaw made it all the worse. Crawling, hanging on to a leaning tree I got up on this knoll and managed to get my boot off. Looking at it I could see a hole, triangle in shape, and my foot was bleeding. One thing I always carried was a small bottle of iodine. I tried to hold the wound open pouring the whole bottle on it. I tore a handkerchief into strips wrapped this around and placed my sock over this. Not having enough wood to keep the fire going I wrapped myself in a blanket the best way I could. I felt kind of numb lying there curled up like a dog. By now it was getting dark and I knew I would have to stay here all night. I shivered all night with the pain and you could say it was a miserable night. Early in the morning the first thing I looked for was something I could use for a walking cane. Limping on my toe with this one foot, it was painful but I knew I did not have any choice as I had to get out of here. I placed my things in the packsack, leaving everything right here on this knoll. There was no danger of anybody getting in here and finding my things. So I started out early. It would have been very easy for me to fall down in the water. I was glad when I got out to the gravel road. I had a distance of seven miles to go to where I was staying. It was a beautiful Sunday morning and I could feel the heat of the sun as I was hopping home. One time I thought I heard someone talking but I wasn't afraid as I wasn't carrying anything. Coming around a curve in the road I met three middle-aged fellows talking and laughing. When they saw me they were as astonished as I was. I had a heavy beard, they had never seen me before and I had never seen them. I walked to the side just nodding as I passed them never stopping and never looked back. I was glad that was over. What those fellows thought of me hopping along with that homemade walking cane, I don't know but I was a sight. It took me all day to get back to the cabin at the river. I cleaned up the best I could, got in my pick-up truck and drove thirty miles to see a doctor. Now I felt much better so I went back to my Finlander shack and stayed two days laying around there, having trouble with my walking. I was wondering what I should do with all the sets I had out and the eleven skins I had out there in the woods. Some way I had to get back out trapping. First I thought of using a boat but that was too big. Why not a second hand canoe? I managed to find one. For the first time I wondered why I had not done this before, doing all this walking when I could have been riding. I also found out there is much less chance of getting caught. Often walking from one small lake to another you expose yourself quite a bit. Here I could go up a stream to the end especially if it flowed to an out-of-the-way place. No one was living nearby for many miles around. Losing three days I was hopping fairly good and could get around. I made a rack for my pick-up for hauling the canoe. Now I had a job to get the packsack, traps and skins over on the Pine River. With the canoe I would go up from a certain bridge on a more suitable river. Knowing this part of the country well I got organized for this trip. I went back to my friends at the log cabin at the river and got myself all straightened out. At three o'clock in the morning the son who was making his home with his father, took me, canoe, traps and all I would need to stay a week starting rather far out in the woods where there was a bridge. After I got unloaded I got going upstream in what one would call a God-forsaken country. My friend took the pick-up back to his place so no one would know that I was out there. This week started out what I thought was really romantic, as part of a new adventure to me. I had two canoe paddles tied together end for end with rawhide string so it would be used like the paddling of a kayak. This way I had more control and could go faster. Often like here where the beavers had dam after dam the river would back up to form a lake-like pond. This at time got to be half a mile wide. When I found rocks the right weight and shape I would carry them with me as these

I used to make a drowning set. It is very important to drown the animals or they surely get away. These rocks are tied with a whirl or clothesline, using it double tied a certain way in the grooves around the rocks, getting rid of the sharp corners. This rock is tied on two lengths of chain from the trap. A six inch ring is made from the wire to fit over a large pole which is stuck hard into the river bottom. The ring slides down on this pole. (With a five pound rock going down also the chain sliding down it cannot come up and the beaver will drown.) However it takes about ten to twenty minutes for one to drown. Under natural conditions, swimming under water, they can go a long way but when something unusual happens to frighten them they lose an air bubble and it's like getting their second air. Now the water was high and it would often be two feet deep on the other side of a dam when going upstream like a waterfall. The current was strong so I would get out of the canoe and pull it over the dam. This can become quite a chore for it seemed that because of the pressure, one had to struggle to stand up. So, on the way up the best locations are found for making sets. Like most rivers eventually one comes to where there is high ground and often high banks. Toward evening I found such a place, heavily wooded and more so farther back. What I was looking for were large pine trees and these were mostly white pine. I saw some four hundred years old and one hundred fifty feet tall. Out of a tree that size you could get 2000 square board feet of lumber. There are still a small number of these old timers around. So up here I thought I was at least six miles from the bridge where I started, thinking that I should be safe here. Even when I thought that all this game belonged to everybody, yet back in my mind there still was a guilty feeling. I guess I wasn't as tough as I thought I was. I did find a half dozen good sized pine that I would use for stretching beaver. I brought nails and a hammer. When time is taken it is surprising what a fine job you can do of stretching, to know where to start for the correct size. Often you have to do some adjusting. When stretched right you could add a dollar to the value of a skin. Here is a good place - this is where I would camp. Also I figured this could be half of my destination. Tomorrow I would go farther up stream and make more sets. Now while I had the canoe it gave me something for a shelter. I carried it up to a nice level spot under a big hemlock. Four feet high on one end I drove several small post supports for laying on another pole to rest one end of the canoe so I could lay under there. I cut balsam boughs and laying them a foot thick made for more comfortable sleeping. The sun was almost down. Having had a good day I decided I would make supper a little early. I would have a big day ahead of me tomorrow. As night falls it is very still. The solitude can bring one unmeasurable consolation. Innermost it is a living testimony. Here one can meditate in understanding, watch the fire burning, the wood being consumed and swallowed by heat, one thing working against the other. One can get overwhelmed as one watches the night close in, hearing the water murmuring slightly as it is moving down the river. Here hope seems to kindle itself esteeming the whole of life's surroundings. There seems to be a time to be longing for an understanding between God, nature, and man so as to endure a vigilance while longing for another day. Even when one is wrong human nature will always make it right. Sleeping soundly one can dream at times of trapping. Here one can go far beyond oneself so the accomplishments and satisfaction become the heart of the matter. Now again in the morning with the sounds of the birds it was time to get going. So far out in the woods, yet so modern like frying eggs and bacon, toast made on an open fire, canned milk. Yes, I got a good start. Now up the river. It was a bright sunny day. I had to gather some rocks, they were important, and I took enough food for dinner. One can get so much enthusiasm eager for vigorous action with hopefulness that there is something new ahead. Not far up was a beaver dam. This was always located at the narrow part of the land on the highest point so as to get the water as deep as possible. One could really say this was engineering. Sometimes I could see far ahead and at times only a short distance. When one makes sets for beaver in the spring it is important to hide them from a warden who could come around in a canoe. Then scent is used. I made a dozen good sets on my way up. Here I came to the end in a big swamp on the river. Ducks were flying here and there. It was time for me to head back - it always goes better downstream than up. Way up here at this big swamp was a large old deserted beaver dam and here I had my dinner. This was an easy day and I made it back to where I camped the first night in good time for this was now my headquarters. Having three blankets instead of one this time I could keep much warmer than I did on some of my other trips, always sleeping with my clothes on. I took my shoes off and put on fresh socks for sleeping as socks were always damp from sweat in rubber boots. I should have been thankful for everything but I did not know how to pray. Another night, waiting for another day. The next day going down to look at the first sets I made I got three beaver and one otter. Now the work started. I got back late where I camped having skinned only two beaver. One I brought back not skinned and the otter. First I had to gather a pile of wood, this was always plentiful, lots of dead wood, some big chunks so the fire would last as I had to skin only one beaver by the light of the fire not being able to do all my chores in daytime. The otter was very hard to skin so I knew I would have to do that the next day. I realized that time would be pressing me to get back Sunday night to meet the young fellow who was going to pick me up. I got up early as the time had to count now. First thing was skinning the otter. In a dense part back of the woods I found enough snow to bury the skin and would take it home later to do a good job stretching. This time I had to go the other way up stream which represented one half of the trapline. I did not know how much time I would need to take care of matters so I kept constantly on the move. You can see where a set has been made in a bad location and this would have to be changed. On this trip I got two beaver and had time to skin them all out. This was good as I did not like skinning them at night. You could do a much better job in the daytime. Tomorrow would be Friday and then it would be time for me to go down the river toward the road where the bridge was. One can always make better time when going down and there is considerable current. This time I caught two beaver, skinned them out and the time just seemed to fly. Three or four miles can be a long way on a river with all the crooks and bends. On this day I had something else in mind and knew that I would have time to do this. And that was going further down the river just on the other side of the bridge to go part down aways. I wanted to see what I could find. The water was so high that I couldn't go under the bridge with the canoe so I had to carry it across. Approaching the bridge two hundred feet away was a very tall elder thicket with a lot of old marsh grass surrounding it. Here I parked the canoe. Very seldom would anyone travel this gravel road back here being thirty miles from any town. I went across the road with the packsack, first hiding the two beaver skins fifty feet back in this old marsh grass from where the canoe was. I had five traps, my knife, hatchet, whetstone and something to eat in the packsack. I was going over first to find a good place for walking leaving the packsack there to come back later to get the canoe. (The endurance one has when you are young is most marvelous.) I was tired and many things kept going through my mind. One thing for certain is that I do not want to hang around this road and bridge too long as the farther away from civilization the better. One good thing was the weather still was half way decent. Determination to do the things as circumstances called for would always be a matter of quick decision. I started out very early to go down stream first taking up all the traps on the way back. I don't think I ever worked this hard anytime since I had been trapping. When I got to the last trap up stream I was glad for now it meant the rest of the way I was going with the current. I was back at my camping place by noon. I caught three beaver up to this time, and would not skin them, just carry them with me. Somewhere up the river about a half mile from the bridge I would carry them back in the woods and skin them there as this would be safer. I wrapped the skins in the raincoat. Then I ran back to get the other skin. The rest did not take me long to get together. It was now Saturday. If all worked out, I would be able to meet the young fellow who was to pick me up on Sunday night. I was now ready for the last trip, partly melancholy, partly eager, a happy adventure. Taking out the sets, getting rid of the last trap I had two more beaver. One thing for certain was to stay away from the road. It was getting late. When I got all the beaver in one place, I carried the canoe back in the woods, the traps and everything I had. Most anyplace in those woods a trapper can get along. I had only this one night left. I had a bite to eat, some cheese and bread as I did not want to make a fire in case someone up on the road would be watching for me and they could then smell the smoke. It was at least two and a half miles down to the road. I had enough time to skin one beaver. I turned the canoe upside down placing everything under one end, then I got some balsam boughs under the other end and made a bed there, this end laying up on a chunk of wood so there was clearance for me to crawl under. I slept like a log as I was very tired. It must have been an hour before daylight when I got up. I was still afraid to make a fire. I had one can of pork and beans and some bread left and this filled me up. Here I had the two beaver to skin. I caught very few of what are called cub or small beaver. They were medium and large size. I had all day to skin them for my chauffeur would not come until late afternoon. He is living out in the sticks on the Pine River and will come in on the road from the east. The harder route is from the west. Around four in the afternoon I got done with the beaver, made three trips going northeast to hit the road half a mile from the bridge. I hid everything behind a large rock twenty feet from the road. The canoe I carried out last and this I left a hundred feet back in thick brush. It was getting dark I sat near the road in the woods waiting for the sound of the pickup and here he came. I stopped him just a minute and told him the warden had been around. "Nobody has been around," was his answer. We had to drive up the road about two miles, find a place to turn around, and watch if he could see anybody. In the meantime, I brought the canoe close to the road. He came back, got out and both of us loaded everything as fast as we could. I was excited but quieted down soon after we got started. The warden did not know where I was staying, also here I was in another county where a different warden had charge. However, any warden in the state of Wisconsin could arrest me. Each one had so much territory of their own it was impossible to even watch all their own. For that reason they did not go into the other county. It seems to be a never ending struggle. What a man won't do in order to make fast money. I had to stretch all the green fresh hides including the otter. A beaver trapper out of season never took time to trap otter but they would accidentally get into the beaver sets. One must find a natural location and often this would be where the animals can slide down some steep bank which they use mostly for playing and spend hours sliding down those slides. I nailed some boards together, making it 4x4 in size and placed a beaver skin in each side. They dry very fast. With this job out of the way I felt relieved.

It was getting late in the spring season and I decided to stop trapping as I was well satisfied with my total spring catch. Now the first part of May it was time to quit. Going back to the cabin on the Pine River I packed up all my things except the fur for I never, when going any distance, would have fur in the pickup when hauling the canoe. I hid the fur so that even the man living here and his son did not know about it, for in a few days I would come back to get them, then traveling by night. Now to think it soon would be over. All I had to do now was get rid of the fur. I headed back to my old homestead, the Finlander shack. The next day first thing I

The Old Finlander Shack

went to see the fellow who was shacking over by the kettlehole on my forty. He played the phonograph, we had some coffee and had a lot of things to talk about. He watched my place while I was gone cutting firewood stove length and split to keep himself going. There was a ready sale in those days for wood - no one was using fuel oil - all wood stoves. So he had a little income as I gave him the wood. There were some fence posts left. Farmers from down state would come up in the spring looking for these posts and buy them by the truck load. I wanted to get things cleaned up for shortly I would have to go to Minnesota and look over the logging job. I promised this man, who was now in charge of the James Fargo Estate, that I would do this. I had been thinking for some time about the deal he had made me logging 1000 cords of spruce. I managed to get the fur sold and got a good price. Like most people in those days the money you had was carried in your pocket or hidden in the house or someplace. So the day came when I had the pickup loaded down in case I would go back to log there. I would have this much less to move later on. It was not a heavy load. I had a fine hardwood rack made, all painted and it

Ready to Start

looked good. This I had to have and it also served as a good back support for the canoe. I would have to have the canoe to do some fishing. I had never been that far north and enjoyed the scenery up beyond Duluth following the north shore of Lake Superior. The shoreline was sometimes nearby and then again far off. There was a very high cliff. The stone was cut down to form a wall 200 feet in height to get this fine highway through here. At this point was a large stone historical marker saying from this point the Indians had crossed Lake Superior by canoe. Farther up was a small town - I got there by nightfall and stayed in a small hotel, the only one in town. They had a map of the northern part of this country. From here a gravel road led north wide enough so one could pass a car easily. However, some 25 miles north from there on this road was very narrow. It showed the place where I had to go, all the lakes and canoe routes. I bought this map and started out in the morning going around sharp curves, up steep short high hills and over solid pieces of rock some thirty feet long. Practically all the way I had to drive in second gear. There was so little traffic yet one could not take a chance on one of those sharp pitch uphill curves. Heavy trucks did come up this way hauling in supplies. There was a CCC camp up there. I finally arrived at my destination. I met the man again. I had not seen him since last summer at his parent's resort where I had worked. This was in Wisconsin. The layout he had here for a resort in those days would be considered up-to-date. It was on a very large lake and one could see several miles in one direction. The lakes up here had so many islands that this often would obstruct the view of seeing any further. The buildings were nice. The main lodge, a log building, was very fancy and of fine workmanship and construction. It was built practically on one formation of solid rock. Finlanders were hired to do the building of the clean looking, varnished, tightly sealed log cabins. I don't believe a cigarette paper could have been placed between where the logs joined one on top of the other. There was a six foot wide dock extending way out into the lake. They had a large number of canoes. One could quickly gather that this was a different country. We walked around slowly, talking, and he was showing me this and that explaining some things like outfitting canoe travelers as this was one mainstay of the business. Most people in those days rented their canoes. If you had one week or two weeks you could go out there in that wilderness making a large circle, without looking at the same lake twice. Now it was dinner time. The family consisted of this man, his wife, a little girl about six years old and a middle-aged woman, a hired person. This time of the year they were getting their cottages ready for the tourist trade. We had a fine meal - certainly different from my trapping food. In the afternoon we were going to look at the spruce, pulp, timber. There were a lot of spruce trees, not what are considered large. All had to be cut into 4' lengths. He made me a very liberal deal and I thought I could handle this operation. This meant that I would have to build a logging camp, a cook shanty, get beds, dishes and tools. When one is young it seems we don't think of these things until something happens and we have a need for it. I had to pay $150.00 down on the job. Then I came back to Wisconsin for I know where I could pick up some men. There was an old garage-like building four miles down the road from where the logging camp would be built. I found I could fix it up for sleeping quarters. An old wood stove was there and this we set outside to cook on. Then, there was a sawmill in operation twenty-five miles farther down on this same road. I made arrangements and bought all the lumber that we needed for two buildings, one 16 x 30 for cooking and eating and the other 16 x 32 for sleeping. I paid that fellow $150.00 down and they said they would deliver the lumber. The total bill was $230.00 and I was trying to hold some money back so I would not run out so fast. Having these arrangements made I headed south to get some men. I fixed up the pickup by placing a seat on each side. This could seat eight men. I went to a neighboring town where I was logging in Wisconsin. I picked up eight men. All had had some experience in the woods. Two were very young. They took along most of their working clothes, some bedding; two fellows sat in front with me and five in the back. I stopped in Ashland at a wholesale house to buy tools, nails, hammers, more drinking cups, some blankets and other things. I had considerable cooking utensils from my first logging operation. We had sufficient to get started. We had to stay in Duluth overnight. The next day we got up the road to the place we had planned for the temporary sleeping quarters. It was about three o'clock in the afternoon so we had plenty of time to get settled. Two fellows slept in the back of the pickup so that helped out. We had picked up twenty loaves of bread, eggs, bacon, enough to get along about five days. The resort owner, the one I bought the timber from (we can call him Harold) stopped to see us. He was going to town so I asked him to bring thirty loaves of bread as those fellows could eat. So far the worst part were the "black flies." They are very small and can be very annoying. Some people will swell up from the bites and that can become very troublesome. Every man had his own bottle of insect repellent as without it one could not stand it. This was the time of the year when they were very bad. We started to build and everyone worked hard, long hours to get our own place. We were getting ready to place the rafters one noon. This was in June and it was hot. There were so many horse flies and they keep buzzing around your head. Occasionally one would light and can they bite. Where they came from no one could tell. Surprising what one can get used to. They did sound like a swarm of attacking bees. The noise alone could keep you alarmed. After a few days they disappeared. I never could figure that one out. A mile back in the woods, south, was a slow flowing river. This area was mostly swamp land. Up to this point we could cut the spruce. I thought I might get a deer the next day, while carrying the canoe through this spruce swamp. Early in the morning there were two of us, one paddling the canoe very slowly and silently down the river. We had not gone far when there stood a deer partly in the water feeding on something. I was in a crouched position in front. The deer never heard nor saw us when I shot - down it went - it was a good sized doe. We dressed it out in good shape. Each one of us had a packsack so we could carry it easily. I don't know why we were so afraid as the game warden in the nearest town was forty-five miles distant. Of course, being new in this country made a lot of difference. We stayed a considerable distance back in the woods with the meat. We got a round point shovel and dug a hole in which to place a small wooden barrel to keep the meat cool. I went to one resort two miles down the road to see if they had ice. When I got there an old man came out first and then a woman, also dressed like a man. Both looked more like trappers than resort people. I told them I was looking for ice. "Yes," he said "we've got plenty of that." They had their own ice house and would cut the ice during the winter when they had a lot of time. They were real friendly and when I told him I was building this logging camp, he kind of laughed. I don't know what he was thinking, for he also had done considerable logging in his day he said, and no doubt knew that I was taking a bigger job than I bargained for. However, I didn't know it and was going ahead on this job just like an old timer. I got that ice back in the woods and also a wooden barrel I bought from the resort people. It seemed in those days people never asked a lot of questions when it wasn't their business. All I told them was that I could use a barrel. I placed a layer of meat then a layer of ice in the barrel and this was placed in the ground. I thought it would last for a few days. I covered it up in good shape. I thought it would be cooled off by night so I could get a hindquarter to make some steaks. I did the cooking then and tried to feed the fellows good. This I knew I had to do to keep them satisfied as they were not too happy with the whole set-up mostly on account of the black flies. They did some fishing on Sundays and got some good catches. I went back in the woods to get some meat for supper. As soon as I got near the place I noticed the brush was all torn up, the barrel was empty, nothing left. I felt badly when I thought how hard we worked to get this meat. It could be nothing else except a bear, the indications showed this. This was my first experience with a bear - the country was full of them - they can become your biggest enemy. So I had to hustle up to get something else ready for supper. I never did try to get another deer in the summertime.

The logging camp got built going through this period of considerable hardship. This was too much for most of the boys I brought up from Wisconsin and they wanted to go back now. Two would stay. There was nothing I could do about it and I couldn't talk them out of it. So the two fellows who stayed decided they wanted to try to dig a well, not for drinking water, but for the horses I would have to

Building a Logging Camp

get later on. The water coming out between the rocks looked bluish and had a very odd smell. How dumb can a person get - we should have known the horses would never drink that water so all this work was done for nothing. We would haul our drinking water from the resort. There was a lake across the road a quarter of a mile down dropping 300 feet at that distance, therefore we could not attempt to carry the water from there.

It was early Friday morning and we were going down to Wisconsin again. With an early start we could make it in one day, 365 miles, stopping in Duluth for dinner. Talking to an old time lumberjack there I found out that the bigger loggers had what they called man catchers. When men had so much pay coming the ones that liked to drink would manage to get to town even if they had to walk all the way. Those fellows had regular hangouts in Duluth and Superior. This man catcher would go around from one saloon to another where some were sobering up and had spent all their money and were then willing to come back as they called it, to make another grub stake. This gave me an idea. Realizing how hard it was to keep young fellows up there I would get these older fellows some that had worked all their life in the woods in order to keep them. Got back again often thinking of good old Wisconsin and took these guys right to their homes. I realized by now I had to get enough beds for at least ten men and the tools. In those days the logger furnished all the saws and axes for them. Then I knew I had to hire a truck to get those things up north. There were considerable odds and ends I had from my logging job we could use up there. That was it - we needed a 1½ ton truck. I had a friend here who had one and we made a deal - so much for the trip. This was all taken care of in one day. This time I brought John back here with me, the fellow who had made his home with me on that lake several years back. He didn't mind it, in fact, he liked it. On this side of Ashland we picked up another lumberjack. One could see he had been drinking. Started talking to him and found out he was a cook. The truck I hired

66

followed us. I had to buy more hardware so this gave him time to catch up. We would wait for him before crossing the bridge at Superior. All of us had something to eat at Duluth again. Needing more men I went shopping for them. We told the other truck to keep going and to wait for us where this gravel road leads north to our logging camp. It took us two hours to find five men. We would have taken three more but could not get them. I thought it was good that we got that many. Then you get thinking about lice - some fellows had them and others kept clean. We had double steel cots. The older fellows didn't like the idea of crawling up so high; cutting two of them in half gave us four more lower cots. The younger fellows didn't mind bunking up there. One good thing was we had enough room in the bunkhouse to do this. We finally got going cutting some pulp.This had to be in 4 ft. lengths and peeled, all piece work. It was cut by the cord and it was hard to say how many sticks it would take to make a cord. Being rather new to me this was the best way to do it. It was left laying and later when we finished peeling all of it, it was carried out by hand and piled 4 ft. high, 8 ft. long or 16 ft. to make two cords. In this way it would be measured. As soon as we had some piled up I would draw money on it as by now I was running short of money. Remember, I went to town to see the pulp buyers drawing $275.00 in advance. Shortly after that several forest fires broke out nearby. It was a dry season and they said the fire had started from lightning. They had the CCC boys fighting the fires. They had caterpillar tractors plowing around where they could. In the meantime fires broke out in four other locations. We would not see the sun for weeks. The whole country was under a smoke screen. We also heard of fourteen different places in Ontario, Canada where there were forest fires burning. We would hear planes flying - they were seaplanes taking in men and equipment to fight these fires. By now they were using and picking up lumberjacks from logging camps to fight these fires. In the evening the old timer's conversation would mostly concern these fires and they said they would not go if they came after them. And there were some who said they had to go if they swore them in. Some of the men, being set in their ways, just quit and left hiking. When they heard something coming they walked in the woods so as to miss it. One fellow told me, ''I walk at night as this is the safest. They allowed me two dollars for some grub to take with them for there was nothing for 45 miles where we could stop for something to eat.'' They all had a packsack. Some were not much for they were homemade but they served the purpose.

Now this was an entirely new experience for me - four fellows stayed. In two weeks the two fellows from Wisconsin left. They wrote to some of their friends and they came up and got them. Now there were three of us left counting myself. Here I had made this investment - enough equipment for eleven men, bedding, tools, and buildings. The result was we had 65 cords cut, now the peeling season stopped. The

COOK   LARRY   **Cook Shanty**   GUSS   SCHELS

cook was the first to go, one man that stayed with us all the way, he was the best man we had, had to go, this left John from Wisconsin and myself. We had to make a sleigh road from this main road, the one going to town, 1½ miles south to where the pulp had been cut, peeled and corded up. Sad to say but it took this old man and myself a month and a half to grub a gradual incline in one of these ravines so a team of horses could pull a sleigh load up there. This was done with pick, grubbing hoe and shovel. It took two months to finish the whole job. With a bulldozer that incline could have been done in 30 minutes. By now it was the early part of September. My money was practically all gone as I drew all the advance I could get on the pulpwood. Now things started to get rough. I advised a friend of mine in Wisconsin what had happened, this same man who helped me out on my first logging job. He said he would come and pick up John. He was the one who had been making his home with me some years before. He went back to stay with his brother. By now it was evident that my planning was to trap beaver. From the conversations I had with Harold, the resort man, the one I was dealing with here on the timber, I found out that back here on this road are a number of beaver trappers. Most of them I had met. My nearest neighbor was the champion of all the boys. There were about half dozen in all, each one having a certain territory they traveled. Well, my neighbor had built up a fine resort from the results of beaver trapping money. This consisted of a main lodge and seven fancy log cabins. He was the man who helped lay and brush out the road coming north here. There was this man and his wife and they lived in a tent. First he built one cabin and so on. He had been there for ten years - I would say he was sixty years old now. The main lodge, cabins and furniture were made out of diamond willow. This can be very attractive. Both of these people were experts at this work. Tanned deer hides were used for the seats of the chairs. They were removable so they could be washed. His wife trapped and hunted like a man. He had a reputation of being the most rugged individual in that neck of the woods. One of the wardens was a very good friend of his. When they were young he saved the warden's life by pulling him out of some rapids. For this reason when he went out trapping they did not bother him. This I learned later. Since I had been here I met him a few times. He seemed like a reasonable man. Now I wanted to go and see him and have a talk with him about trapping. By now I was in bad shape with money, you could say I was bankrupt as I had $3.00 left in my pocket. I stayed in the logging camp all alone and did not realize how cold it can become. I had not drained the water out of my pickup and in the morning I noticed the radiator cap was pushed up. It froze so hard it pushed the cap up so the motor was frozen. This made things worse than ever. Here I was with $3 in my picket and no transportation. The pickup had only 5000 miles on the motor - all I could do was just let it sit there. This also meant I had to walk to the neighbor which was two miles. I had planned to see him before this. When one is used to riding, walking two miles can be a long distance. So I got myself ready to go and in a short time was on my way. When I got into trouble I had a way of talking to people, fabricating my words to make my feeling known when looking for sympathy. "Oh," he said, "we can fix that up." He was what you would call a smart old fox. Then he explained to me that he had to get his winter wood up first usually cutting 60 cords which is a lot of wood. He had a motor driven wood cutting unit. We got going working on that wood pile immediately. They furnished me with meals. I had to get up early to walk over there and get there in time for breakfast. The mornings were rather chilly so we would work fast. It is surprising how the body warms up from movement, I had an alarm clock, this was a must, as then I could sleep soundly. Somehow I couldn't get myself to worry about the circumstances I found myself in. All my years I found it to be that way believing that whatever happens has some reason. This was part of my nature. People who have known about me said they just couldn't understand that things didn't bother me. Of course some people thought I was crazy as my answer would always be that everything will be all right. This kind of a disposition has been a great help to me and hope has never failed me. We sawed, split and piled wood for a week. Nearly all the wood was close by and was now worked up. He had an old truck so we went up the road to get some dead dry trees. There were plenty of them. What could I say as I was now at the mercy of this man and he was the kind that would take advantage of something like this. His wife was different - she never liked the way he did things and she was not afraid to tell him so. He would tell her that she didn't know what it was all about and tried to make her believe that she was dumb. Some people can get highly wood conscious, that is a fact, for I have seen it. They would fill the whole woodshed with wood and not use any of it. They gather more and more for their present use until the wood in the shed starts to rot. Like a beaver he didn't know when it was enough and many of the trees they cut are wasted. If a white man could be like an Indian this would be different. This I have seen often. They cut wood as it is needed. It can be ten degrees below zero and you can see an Indian, no cap on, cutting enough wood to make his breakfast. One time a white man asked an Indian if there was going to be a hard winter. "Yes," the Indian said, "bad winter coming." "How do you know," asked the white man. "Oh," said the Indian, "white got them great big woodpile." Yes, I believed in getting in wood, too, so you don't have to dig it out of the snow. Like everything else one can overdo it like this man here. Now, while he had free labor, why not take advantage of it? Another good excuse was that it would be two weeks before we could go trapping as it would have to freeze up some. Where we were going occasionally we would have to cross certain points on water and wanted to wait until the ice was thick enough to hold us up. We were in the cabin, the one they used to live in. After dinner he would talk about some of his experiences while beaver trapping. There is a great danger of going through the ice and up here more than one had disappeared. On the very lake he was on, just a few years back they found the snowshoes of a trapper on top of the ice. These are called air pockets where they can go in and sometimes the ice appears a little darker on that spot. The hard thing is with snowshoes on it is hard to get out. You have to get them off first. Most of the time these fellows wear heavy woolen clothing and when it get soaked it becomes awfully heavy and holds one down. He did like to talk about it and you would wonder if it was true or not. This one spring he was seventy feet from land on this lake where he went through the ice. The lake wasn't too deep, eight to ten feet, and he started walking and crawling on the bottom of the lake. One time he said he made a hard jump, the ice was very thin near the shore as it always melts there first, to see if he was going in the right direction. His head came through the thin ice - yes he was going the right way. He went quickly down to the bottom, kept going and said he made it. He could not swim. Here on this lake, which was only fifty feet from the main lodge, they would cut a hole in the ice ten feet deep and let their moose and deer meat down to the bottom in wire baskets. One winter they went to Duluth for two weeks. Keeping the meat in this way it would not freeze and no one could find it and steal it. This was all illegal. This territory was in the Superior National Forest, no trapping or hunting was allowed. One year they opened the season on deer after twenty-eight years of no season. This large protected area, Superior National Forest, joining the Quetico Provincial Park, was located on the International line about a hundred miles west of Fort Williams. The area has 2,140 square miles of virgin forest. Considerable game can be found here, there are lots of lakes, rivers and streams, a paradise for outlaw beaver trappers in those days, but not anymore. This wildlife is now more carefully protected. Here in this wilderness I would have a chance to travel. The old time beaver trapper said that it would take us five days to get in by going cross country, as he called it, by compass. It was our understanding that he would grubstake me all the way through if I helped him cut his wood. This meant he would take me to Port Arthur, loan me enough money to buy some woolen clothes and rubber boots that had leather tops; the food I would need for thirty days, like 30 lbs. of flour, using this every day for making bannocks on an open fire. This takes the place of bread. The flour is always mixed in right proportion, a little salt, even a little sugar, and baking powder. We needed rice, barley, peas, navy beans, oatmeal, prunes, all dried food, no canned goods as that would be too heavy to carry. Weight was very important. One thing he also told me was that when we got in there from that point on after we made camp he would show me in which direction to go. I would pay him back in fur, green hides, not stretched or dried, $8 for beaver and $15 for otter. This was all fine with me. This time of the year while the weather was cold the skins could not be dried so one had to transport them while green. The green skins weighed more that the dried skins. I did not know what a struggle trapping might be in this wilderness. We were about fifty-five miles away from any human beings, not even an Indian. He said it would take us at least five days to get in there. I said I heard he was a good friend of the warden. "Don't worry about that," he said, "he never follows me when I go out there." Then he said if he ever saw a man take a beaver out of one of his traps he would shoot him right there. I had heard before that he was that kind of person. One great consolation was that I was safe with him as far as the warden was concerned and I figured I would now be able to get on my feet again and get a new motor for my Ford pickup. The setback I had on account of the logging job did not break down my spirit. One will always sacrifice willingly for the contentment of freedom. It just seems now that I was yoked together with these happy hunting grounds surrounding us in every direction, many waterways, lakes, rivers and streams to the southwest the way we had to go. This inland route had to be followed. At certain points it was the connecting link to get on the other side to a beaver dam. he told me that most of the traveling was done by landmarks. One remembers them instinctively.These were some of the things I learned about the country when I heard people talking about it.

I had a week to get ready in my logging camp for my trip. One thing I thought I should have is a sleeping bag. I had some twelve gauge canvas, the kind used for covering a canoe made of wood.I also had a very thin small mattress pad.I made a square sack out of the canvas large enough so I could crawl inside and place the mattress inside. My partner would take six traps, his food and sleeping bag (one of the best on the market stuffed with duck feathers). I believe you could sleep in this if it was twenty below zero. His load weighed about 65 lbs. He also had a 16 x 18 foot square of bedsheets sewed together. This is used for shelter and then waterproofed. It is formed with poles in a ⅔ round circle in teepee form. The sheeting is stretched around in a secure fashion. Each one of us had one set of this covering, weighing about two pounds. Thinking that I had to catch a lot of beaver I took eighteen traps. When I got all my things together enough so I could stay a month, my load weighed 80 lbs. I was overdoing it some, like taking 18 traps and such a heavy clumsy sleeping bag. No one told me any differently and I didn't know any better. I found out later, to my sorrow, just what can happen.

The night before this, being the last night I could sleep under a roof, I went over to the neighbor just so I could talk to someone and also to tell them I was all packed for the next day.Early he would come my way and we would start out from here. We could leave from right behind my logging camp, walking about four miles into the woods from here which, in a general direction, would be southwest. For an old fellow he still could walk fast.   One thing was certain I could not tell him what to do. From the time I knew him I could sense what type of person he was. There was now six inches of snow on the ground,not bad walking except in some places where the hazelnut brush got kind of thick. This brush was the worst for tearing clothing. Most of the time I was walking some distance behind as I had this 80 lb. load. He carried a good watch - I had a dollar watch.We stopped for lunch, made tea and had sandwiches. We both had plenty. Around three o'clock in the afternoon we came to our first beaver dam. Here the water was open out twenty feet. On the other side you could walk around the edge of the flowage on the ice only walking near shore for a half mile where it ended. We knew that the ice was not safe. Here he started through a long swamp. I placed all my confidence in him, thinking that he knew where he was going. He had always gone out in the fall with another man. Taking me along this time did not change his plans. These fellows had a certain way of doing things and they always stuck together. However, I did not know anything about this until nightfall and we were making camp. Then he told me we were going to meet another fellow out here at a certain place - he had come in from a different direction. There was nothing I could say - he was the boss. There was no trouble sleeping after a trip like this. In the morning it was always best to get an early start. One doesn't have much on his mind except the thought of getting there.

Now the second day we were making good time. Occasionally, when there was a rock handy of the right height, I would rest the packsack relieving the weight. I also had a headgear rigged up where part of the weight is carried from your forehead - this is a big help. I was always looking for noon and night to come. Rest was welcome even if it was only five minutes. The scenery started to change now and quite often we had small hills to climb. We did get down to the river bottom and we saw some large tracks. My partner said they were from timber wolves. The creek must have been eight feed wide and they could jump this in one leap. Looking over the tracks more closely, he said there must have been about four of them. The day seemed to go very fast. Walking slowly now on highland we approached a creek. It was a good place to camp for the night. We were tired, made a hearty meal and hit our bunks. Our sleeping bags were put on top of a one foot thickness of balsam boughs. We always slept with our clothes on and extra socks to keep warm. Now the third day was coming up. One seems to be refreshed and hopes are high thinking that we are getting closer. There were a few beaver scattered around throughout this country we had traveled; further in they were more plentiful. It was estimated there were 70,000 beaver in northern Minnesota at that time. After we had been going for several hours I noticed that the cords up the back of my legs started to ache. Walking more slowly I now got farther and farther behind my partner and at times I could not see him. He stopped and waited and said, ''What's the matter with you?'' I told him about my legs hurting. ''Oh,'' he said, ''you've got too heavy a load and you have to start double packing now.'' I knew he was right. Then he added, ''you just follow me and you can camp in the same place where I camp.'' ''Good,'' I said, ''then I should be able to find you fellows.'' Then he said,''Just keep on going in our tracks and you can't miss us.'' It all sounded good. After all I was supposed to be a woodsman. Right then and there I took out my traps and other things to get about half the weight. This was a relief and we could walk much faster. We made camp together here on this third day - it is evening now. It seemed he talked less and less every day. We always made a good sized fire for there was plenty of wood. One thing this time of the year we did not have to worry about forest fires and bears, for it was the beginning of winter. When morning came, now the fourth day, he left me and I started back to get the other half of my pack. It was nearly noon when I got back with this load where we camped and I thought it would be a good time to have lunch. The back of my legs hurt more and more. By now I was limping. I had new shoes, they seemed to fit and I just couldn't figure out why I should get this lame. Taking this same load I had, I forced myself to walk as fast as I possibly could. Well, by nightfall I didn't reach any place where he had stopped so I looked for a place by a large rock formation shielded from the wind to make camp. Now, I thought, this is my first night in Northern Minnesota where I am out like this all alone. I got a fire made and started to boil some rice, I had some cooked deer meat and put that in. This made more than I could eat so I would have some left for breakfast. I had a tin plate to eat out of. While I was looking around for more dry wood, wolves started to howl. It sounded like two or three. I took the tin plate and hit it with a large spoon. This made a lot of noise, however the wolves kept right on howling and did so for several hours. I had a lot of wood and had a good fire going throwing an old pine stump on top that would burn all night. I was rather uneasy as this was my first experience with wolves. My legs did ache and I rubbed them. It was partly swollen up the calves of my legs. This troubled me considerably but being tired I went to sleep. I counted the days as one would under such circumstances. Now, this morning is the fifth day. There were some coals left and with some birchbark I would have heat in only minutes. I warmed up the rice food and it tasted good. The fresh air and all that walking gives one a good appetite. Now I had to go back for my other half of the pack. It was very discouraging having to go back. This morning my legs were more stiff and sore than before. I knew I had no choice but had to keep going. The starting was the most difficult - I had considerable pain the first mile and after that I limbered up some. When I got back it was three o'clock in the afternoon. It could not be far to where he camped the day before as by now I must be a day behind. So, with the pack I had now I thought I would keep going until dark and by then or before I should come across where he stayed. Yes, I did find it before dark. Having some extra time on my hands I decided to do some cooking. I had some canned deer meat left so I cooked a little rice, barley and peas and when this was done I added the meat. This would be good for two or three meals. It was getting much colder and I was wishing I had the other half of my pack here. There was constant pain in the cords and muscles in the back of my legs. I knew that I had to make it to catch up with them for the other man would meet him there. There are so many things about when you are way out here and things start to happen. I managed to keep fairly warm through the night and stayed rather close to the fire. I placed several of these black charred pine stumps on and they hold the fire for some time. There were plenty of them lying around for they were the remains from forest fires no doubt many years ago. They contained a lot of pitch and this preserves them for many years and they do not rot fast.

Now this morning, the sixth day, I wondered just how far it would be before I caught up with them. I worried about my legs for this morning they were worse. I know that I must make it and also if I got going they would limber up some. It was a slow process yet remarkable how far one can go. I knew I had to keep on moving so I managed to get going slowly. There was a six inch depth of snow and this trail had been traveled over two times, first by my partner, then I came along and now I am going back. Now when I came back again it would be more packed and this made better walking. Both of us also brought our snowshoes. These we would need later on. I made the trip and got back but it took me much longer to walk for now I was limping every step. Another night - it was getting much colder and the wind was blowing making it all the more miserable. I took the large waterproof bed sheeting, folded it up to make a large blanket and used it as a cover. I managed to get by for the night. I thought the rest would help my legs not realizing how badly they were inflamed. Having gone this far now I was glad to think that today I would catch up with them. For I understood the other fellow was around this territory. It took all the courage I had to make it for now it was very painful to slip shoes on. There was no way of finding out how far ahead they were. I had to have patience and the capacity for endurance. There was no one around I could complain to. When one finds oneself wandering around in a God-forsaken place like this and in the condition I was, I could not stop or hesitate any length of time. Time can become very valuable. I did not know then what was ahead of me, to find out how little my partner, the man who helped to bring me in here, cared about what would happen to me. I struggled on and by noon a big snowstorm came up. The scenery changed and it looked more like new land for it was a flat large river bottom, very few hills. I carried only half of my things; one always takes all the grub and traps on the first load when double packing. Now the snow started to cover the tracks that I was to follow more and more. This was open country, like a small valley, and the wind was whirling around in all directions. It was snowing very hard. Just ahead of me I saw a beaver dam, not very high, going clear across this small valley. It must have been 1000 feet in length. here I noted the tracks, only seeing part of them, and then I knew he did cross here. It was very difficult to walk on this narrow slippery dam. Considerable water was running over. I was afraid I might fall in so I had to take my time. This was one thing I could not afford to have happen. There was a rather steep bank where the dam joined the land. All I could do in my condition was crawl up there. Up on the higher elevation the wind swept harder that ever. There were places where the tracks had completely disappeared. The snow was blowing against my face and with my head in a downward position I could not see far ahead. At times I was guessing for direction. Yes, I noticed I had lost the tracks. Up ahead a distance I could see a heavily wooded area. When I got there it was a very dense forest. Looking around, walking up and down in different directions I thought I would find the tracks. Here they were and I felt a great relief for the wind could not hit here and the heavy balsam trees kept the snow here from coming down. For this reason the tracks could be seen here. By now it was also getting dark. All day I had been limping badly. I wondered how I got this far and was almost sympathetic with myself. One has to behave so as to banish all fears. Walking around a sharp turn heading north I saw the large teepee tent. First I thought I was dreaming. One man walked out hurriedly to get some balsam boughs - it was my partner and he didn't even see me coming. When I got there the other fellow middle aged, was cutting up some meat. We said hello to each other and shook hands. My partner came back with a big armful of boughs. "You got here," he said. "Yes," I said, "I made it but I'm in bad shape." I told him my legs were all swollen up in back. The one fellow was still working cutting off large steaks from the hindquarter of a deer, getting ready to fry them. He spoke up and said, "You had your shoes laced too tight." "Oh, my gosh," I said, "here I'm trying to figure out what caused it." The tent made from this waterproofed bedsheeting was large in size and there was plenty of room for three of us to sleep in it. I got in one corner and sat down. It did not take long and they had a good meal ready. All of us seemed to enjoy it. Then I told them how it was almost impossible for me to find their tracks. "Oh," the new man (they called him Jet), "You were lucky for I have just come back from there. I killed a deer on the way in and went back to get the hind quarters. Did you come across that beaver dam?" I said, "Yes, that's the way I came. I thought those were Jeff's tracks." (Let's call my partner, the resort man, Jeff.) He said, "You could never have found his tracks for I couldn't even see them," I knew about Jeff's disposition - he had hardly said a word since I came back. I thought to myself, he wasn't worried about me. I realized that I could never have found them if Jeff hadn't gone back after that deer meat and the thought alone frightened me. Then Jeff spoke up and said, "I got two big beaver - I caught them in a trap on the way in. One of them was alive yet when I pulled them out." When it came to human feelings I found that he was very cold. All he thought about was beaver. I was trying to clear my mind, thinking of how I could have got lost, and the condition I am in, what a terrible time I had walking, and to think that Jeff would do this to me when he had promised to show me directions when we came out here. I was more dependent upon these fellows now. They were going to hit the hay and so was I. They slept together in Jeff's eiderdown sleeping bag and I had my homemade one. I was trying to sleep, thinking of my misfortune, enduring the pain in my legs and thinking of how I struggled to get here. I didn't mention anything about half my pack being back where I camped last night and nobody said anything. All this was completely new to me and I had to learn that a man was fighting his own battle out here. I was overtired and did not know when I went to sleep. The first one to stir was Jeff. He was a very restless character. No doubt he had trapped more that anyone up in this country - everybody was afraid of him. I got up in a sitting position and noticed that my legs were sensitive and hurt, so I just sat there for a while. Jet got up. He had also been in this area before. These fellows knew this whole country. They started to make breakfast frying more deer meat. Jeff had started to make bannock thirty minutes before. The secret is to get a good fire going to get hot coals, placing them under a log so the heat is reflected out. You use a frying pan having handles that can be tilted partly in an upright position. The flour, already a prepared mixture, is then mixed with water to make a dough. Browning nicely on one side and then turning it over, this makes a delicious substitute for bread. I am still sitting there watching. I finally said to Jeff, "I think I am in bad shape." Trying to get up I turned on my side and as soon as I got weight on my feet I knew they were highly inflamed from constant abuse ever since I started this trip. The heavy load, the new tightly laced shoes had caused it. The fact was I couldn't walk on them. What is going to happen? Not trusting myself to talk to Jeff, this by now got to be a natural reaction since I thought how he would have left me back there when he knew that the snowstorm would cover his tracks, I said to Jet, "Why don't you help me out this time and go back there and get my stuff?" Not giving him time to answer I said, "I'll give you two traps." A trap so far out there was worth $50.00 a piece. I also knew that he could find it as he had traveled that river bottom the same direction I came in. All I had to do was give him an idea. Those fellows were real woodsmen. Jeff never said a word and I don't think he would have gotten my other pack for me. This now was a relief. Jeff started out immediately on his trapline and said, "I'll see you tonight." Jet went after my half pack. So, here I was rubbing my legs. Both of the men said I would be able to walk in a couple of days - all I needed was some rest. This was encouraging inasmuch as I was also sad. It seemed there was nothing around to burn except those old pine stumps. They were sitting around like stones in a graveyard. Most of them could be pushed over. It was now getting very cold, they thought that through the night it got down to ten below zero. Jeff and Jet had gathered a pile of these stumps and I was hugging the fire very close trying to keep warm. The wind was blowing strong, we had considerable protection from rather thick woods, but still the smoke was blowing in all directions. You can feel the pine smoke in your eyes for it is strong, no doubt from the pitch. Never before had I had trouble with my eyes and did not think anything of it. My eyes watered and occasionally I would rub them. Jet came back with my stuff late in the afternoon. He took two of my traps and said, "Over there on the side hill I skinned out a beaver and I noticed a fox is eating on it." He wanted to catch the fox. In this part of the country were some silver foxes and a number that were crossed. "That's good " I said. Jeff, the hardhearted wicked beaver trapper, came in a little after dark. I sensed that Jeff just had to get wherever we were going first. He caught two beaver. he now had four to start with. Jet had two. Jeff had six traps. Jet now had eight traps and I have sixteen. I told Jet about my eyes being sore. I don't know if he knew what he was talking about but he said you can get snow blind. Now I was using my own food. Whatever they had brought out between them for food they shared. While they were around they kept the fire going. About one hundred feet down a slope was a little creek and that is where we got our water.

Most all of this water flowing in different directions came out of a beaver flowage. I never trusted the water so I would boil it all the time. One never drinks much water - I got started on tea as that could be made in a hurry. Three days had gone by and I could not tell any improvement in my legs. My eyes were very sore and fire red. I crawled around like a person with a broken leg. The two men left early every day on their trapline. I don't know where they split up as they said they were going southwest. Jeff said that morning when he left that he never saw a man get such a tough break in all his life. On the fourth day I noticed immediately that my eyes were highly sensitive when looking at the snow. Never having had this experience before I didn't realize that by keeping close to the fire all day the pine smoke had inflamed my eyes and it hurt to open them. Yes, the next day they were worse. Crawling down to the little creek I managed to get some water. I heated it in an aluminum pan I brought along for washing, put a towel in it and got it as hot as I could stand it, wrung out the towel and placed it over my eyes. I would do this over and over laying flat on my back for ten minutes at a time. I placed other rags over the hot towel so it would stay warm for a little while. One can do lots of things in a desperate situation being out here fifty-five miles in this wilderness, knowing that you must get well. In those days there were no helicopters, the canoe routes were frozen so if something serious should happen they would have to carry you out all the way on a stretcher. This would take several weeks considering the distance and the terrain surrounding the swamps. So, for the next two days I kept soaking my eyes with the hot towel. Inasmuch as I just barely could hop on my legs this became a second hand matter. Now, if there is one thing a person will worry about it is your eyes, In time of trouble we call on the Lord. With conviction a believer can overcome one's fear not knowing then that the fear of the Lord is the beginning of wisdom. It took me many years to learn that. In those days I was very proud and thought I had the whole world at my feet. As I said before, I did not know how to pray and it never entered my mind. Now it is seven days since I came here. My

78

legs pained but I would walk favoring the one leg that was worse than the other. My eyes were better so I told Jeff and Jet that I would try and go out and see what I could find. They had a good start and did not tell me how many beaver they had. One day Jet had very good luck and he just had to tell me. He caught three otter in one night. He had a set on a beaver dam where there were a lot of minnows swimming around, so many that they covered his trap on this certain spot. When a family of otters come along or two families, there could be six or eight. They are great for traveling. That is what happened. If one gets in a trap the others won't leave. He had three traps around there intended for beaver. Then another got in a trap and another. Otters sometimes will stay a week still looking for their mates, as they do mate for life. Man being the biggest enemy to all animals often will destroy even when it is not necessary.

Jeff and Jet left early in the morning. About two hours later I started out limping, very slowly at first and after about an hour it went a little better. I don't know why Jeff told me to go north but I did for I believed what he told me that I would find some beaver there. I wandered around first going up a gradual long hill and then to the northeast sloping down; I followed that heading down into a creek bottom. Here there was a thick growth of elderberry. The snow was around ten inches deep. However the wind blew the snow in those places and was so heavy that I had to crawl along to get through. I was dressed warm and with all that exertion I was now sweating. I followed the creek afraid to walk on the thin ice for it is treacherous when water is moving below. Where the current is here the ice can be very thin. One is always tempted as the walking is so much easier. I could see a beaver dam ahead and noticed it was frozen solid which is a sign that there are no beaver. Yes, I found the house, walking on the top of it and it was dead. Where the heat of the beaver in the house escapes, the front is snow white in a frozen form. Here it started to dawn on me that these fellows were sending me into a territory they had trapped before. Farther up there had been another colony at one time and this was dead. By now, about three in the afternoon, I headed back for my legs still gave me pain. I did have my boots laced very loose now so there was freedom for more blood circulation. This was part of my trouble before. I got back just before dark and no one was there. I stirred up the fire with those pine stumps; it never went out. I started to make a stew. They had brought in the hind quarters of a young beaver. These are parboiled at least ten minutes and then the water is throw out and fresh water is added, with barley, rice, navy beans and some bouillon cubes thrown in before it was done. Cooking this stew with beaver meat is good and nourishing. This is one of the main diets of a beaver trapper. A trapper will eat about two pounds of beaver meat in a day. I tried to save food and eat more wild meat to make it last for when one starts getting low on food, it is time to move out. All cooking is done in a gallon pail, yellow coated inside. These are sanitary - they have a wire handle. A long pole is placed at about a ninety-five degree position and the pail is hung on the end above a moderate fire. This works out very well. While the days are short the stews are then cooked at night. If the fire is right when the stew is half done,it will keep on cooking. Should the fire be a little too much,it often boils over just enough to put out some fire, which slows it down. This can become automatic if arranged just right. The boys got home late as usual. First they said, "How did you get along today. Did you find any beaver?" "No," I said, "I got way over there on that creek and everything was dead." I thought I would bring home a point and said somebody had trapped there last year. Jeff said right away, "Oh, you went the wrong way. I told you to go north to that lake." Now the lake he mentioned (later on) I had been to several times, not this year, but I knew there were only a few beaver there and they would be hard to catch at this time of the year. The reputation this very large lake had was that near the outlet, west, was the largest now deserted beaver house in this whole country. I judged it to be eighty feet in length and some said it was larger. The beaver just kept adding on and on. Also here on this lake was an outlet going down to another scenic lake. It was a half mile from one lake to the other and it would drop three hundred feet. The rock formations here are very high and rugged. Using the canoe route you would have to portage from one lake to the other,   which involved considerable climbing. Sometimes one or two parties might venture through here in a season for it is a remote area. By now I had lost confidence in what Jeff was telling me about where to find beaver. I started out on my second day, my legs were better and my eyes started to clear up, I felt better all around. They started out before I did. I took something along to set six traps,thinking if I found any at all this would be enough to start. One thing a person must have is an ax or hatchet and matches. The kind we used was a small double bit using one side for chopping beaver dams, the other to keep sharp. Matches are always kept so they can't get wet if one should fall in somewhere. The large lakes and channels are very deep from 200 to 1400 feet in depth. One reason why the fur keeps prime longer in the spring is in places the water stays cold to the 15th of June.   Walking about two miles I came to a long narrow body of water.   Somehow I felt that I must get on the other side in order to find some beaver. It was about 200 feet across and in some places in the middle it was not frozen over. Being very desperate I thought I would try to walk around the open parts to get across. On shore there was a log going out about six feet. I started to go in a foot of slush and stepping quickly got my feet on solid ice. Looking up and down this chain of water something told me not to go. Glancing down I saw a deer track and noticed it had made a circle and came back. That was it.

I hurried back on land, made some tea got out my lunch and enjoyed it. This was the first nice day we had and the sun was out. I kept on going further north and the only way I could go following this body of water. About three in the afternoon I was going up a steep hill. On top was what I thought a high elevation, here I climbed a large jackpine, the limbs came way down to the ground so it was easy to climb - just like a ladder. Going up as far as I dared looking in all directions, all I could see in the far distance were what looked like chains of mountains. It seemed at the time I got some satisfaction out of this, not that it helped me any. Now I knew that for this day I would not find any beaver so it would be best if I started back as it got dark early. Lying seven days in the tent, two days out here scouting, nine days in all and no beaver. The boys, I thought, must have twenty each by now. It should be no problem to average two a day with six to eight traps. Most of my traps were still in the tent. Man is guided in many ways in this life but he will never admit it unless he has some close escape from death. Our assurance of self reliance sometimes fails.

I pursued this unknown valley in a region that is not known to many individuals living out and around my logging camp. Certainly very few people would come out here looking for comfort. There are many thoughts that wander around in a man's mind while tramping here in the heart of this wilderness. It seemed that somehow, after all that had happened, I couldn't worry just because I had not been able to catch any beaver. It was a good thing that I had patience. A force within you tells you to take naturally whatever comes along.   So, I silently headed for camp - no one was there yet.   It wasn't long before Jet came - he was the fellow one could talk to. I knew that neither one was on the level with me. I said, ''Which way do you fellows go anyway.'' ''Oh,'' he said, ''we go way down southwest.'' We were just talking and here came Jeff. ''Did you go up there by that lake?'' he said. ''No,'' I said, ''I tried although I never found it.'' ''You have to go further south.'' ''I'll see what I can do tomorrow.'' I knew right along that they did not want me to go down there in that direction and wanted to steer me away from there as these fellows highly regarded their privacy when it came to trapping beaver. Certainly I was able to figure that out. However, I was in no position to argue or talk about it to them. I had one thought and that was the hope for another day.

Like a dream an extraordinary enduring force persistently surrounds oneself. The uncertainties of new tomorrows haunted me. Where the challenge is not blind there is hope which in turn can bring understanding. One can become adapted to the tests that lie before you. Why, one at times will struggle within to find the same combination here as in the wilds of nature, forces against forces where energy lodges in position to overcome physical weakness. The last nine days of my turmoil have impressed confidence within me that I will make it. My two companions have, to a degree, worked against me in a way that made me think that I was isolated to a certain area to trap in. I also realized that they had found the place before I did. One thing that I am very proud of is that I never did interfere with their trapline, meaning, not one time did I ever follow their tracks.

I had not found any beaver location as yet and the main factor was I was a complete stranger in this neck of the woods. Jeff had not kept his word to show me around as he had stated before we left on this trip. Now I was very eager to get started the next day. My mind was made up that I would cross the body of water that stretched like a large river from north to southwest, sometimes wide, sometimes very narrow with high rock walls going up ten to fifty feet. This I found out the next day. Taking ten traps I traveled two miles down thinking that anytime I must run into one of them. No tracks, but down here was a place where I could cut a large white birch that would reach the other side for there was a bottleneck in the river. After the tree fell it made a fine crossing. Exploring this primeval forest of rivers, creeks, and lakes it is interesting to see how much nature has to offer. Most of the country has not been spoiled by the hands of man. I got up about two miles now on the west side of this chain of water and I noticed a very small creek coming down a long sloping hill. I could not see any water running. There were some elders growing there and in order to grow they must have water. Coming close, standing still, I could hear water running underneath. I followed this as one could easily see the way it was going up and up. I did not walk far here - a good sized beaver dam was in sight. As I got right on the top of it here were men's tracks going across. I could not believe my eyes. Trying to study the tracks I wondered who could be out here, not a game warden. Oh, no, it must be Jeff. But why didn't I cross his tracks before? Where does he cross this chain of water where I had to cut a tree? In the meantime, still thinking about these things, I walked on the other side of the dam. Here on the upper part of the dam you could see the form of a large beaver flowage. Where the dam hit the land it was an eight foot high rock formation. Right alongside of this he had walked straight up the beaver flowage. Now here I thought I cannot follow his tracks as two men cannot trap in the same place. How quickly I made a decision is hard for me to forget but I said to myself, you are going right straight ahead into the woods here. I had never been here in my life. Without hesitation I started walking. The growth of timber was not too thick so one could see several hundred feed ahead at all times. It seemed I could not have walked more than a half mile when here in front of me was a river. Looking down there was a long large dam. One, at the moment, does not know how large this river is for this dam formed a considerable large body of water. Next, looking up the other direction, there was a very high large perfectly round house. I am sure beavers do not know what their houses look like nor their dams. However, at times when you see such perfect work it makes you wonder. This was the most welcome sight I had seen since I was out here. I made three sets some distance apart on the dam. Then I went upstream toward the house not going near it as I wanted to be certain not to distrub them. They do sleep in the daytime. You never trap beaver in the winter at the house; the easiest place to catch them is on the dam. Here I had some sad experiences. While digging your hands are used for making a foundation. Most of the time here is a mud bottom. In placing the trap, to do a good job, you have to get your hands in the water. The hands then start freezing, soon cracks appear on your fingers and then when mud gets in there the cracks get larger and larger. Once it gets started you try to wash them with warm soapy water but they never heal not until you get off the trapline. I did tramp farther up and found another colony within a half mile. There are always the house and more dams and I made more sets. Never have I found as many beaver as there were right here in this area. I went further, the river made a bend, there were more beaver and I set out eight traps that day, all I had time for. It was much further now to walk back to camp and I would have to get started. I was happy now with the prospect of having sets out and to think that I did find some beaver. I made it back late and Jeff and Jet were already cooking supper. "How did you get along today?", Jet said. "Not bad," I said, "I found one place and it looks pretty good." On the way back I was thinking, Why should I walk so far back here, why can't I move over where I found the beaver and set up camp for myself. With this in mind I told the boys that it was a long way over there and I thought that I should move over there. Jeff said, "Yes, that will save you a lot of walking." I believe they were glad to get rid of me. They never said how many beaver and otter they had and I could not get myself to ask them as I thought that would be asking too much about their business. So the subject never came up. They did say that when they go home they would come and let me know. "You can find your way in on the canoe route," Jeff said. Now the lakes were frozen and were in good shape. At that time I was never thinking about going in for I thought I was just now getting started. I had been saving my food all along, eating beaver meat every day. One did not think of any dessert; drinking tea was on the menu. How quickly one forgets the troubles we sometimes have, nothing pleasant, so perhaps that is the reason, like the way I suffered in this shelter. Now this was my last night here. How fast things had changed in those few days. I must have been thankful only in a silent way, an emotion of a feeling that you cannot explain, with much expectation and the state of excitement about my new project, setting up this new camp, to pick out or to find a good location. This time of the day in the forest or just before you go to sleep, positive thinking conveys clearly the duties for the next day. With this state of mind I should got have any trouble going to sleep. I got up earlier than usual for this was a special day for me and there was much to do getting my stuff packed. One good thing was I had brought my own tent material. We all left the same time and after walking some distance we shook hands and I said, "I'll see you guys later." I was very ambitious now walking faster than ever being anxious to get there, first to find a good place for camp. Having had some experience I was now looking for two rock walls close together. I walked around covering the area rather well and I did find a good place not realizing then that I would be camping here three years later in this ravine forming two rock walls twenty feet high spaced some thirty feet apart. One would have thought it was man-made and was built for a railroad track. Here on the south wall was a recess two feet back forming a square like a chimney. What a perfect place to set a teepee style tent up here arranging it so when finished this square part of the wall is left open for the smoke to go out. On one side two feet is left open for an entrance. The other space a two-thirds circle, forms up to the wall making that part completely enclosed. Having an extra very torn old blanket I wrapped this around the outside and then banked this with two feet of snow. Inside I put some balsam boughs one foot deep. When placing them they are placed stem down slightly leaning. This way it gives it a cushion effect. I left a space of rockwall like a fireplace. Reflecting the heat certainly means comfort on a cold night that money could not buy. After tramping around all day on a trapline coming home to a place like this is welcome and becomes a part of life. A wood supply is ready in case you should get back late. You always stay out longer on moonlit nights for the trail can be seen in the snow. After getting the camp in good shape I could devote more time to go and look at the traps for now I was not so far away from the locations where I had traps set out. I had the hind leg of a beaver that had been cooked, I put this into a frying pan with some lard, browning on both sides, and ate this with bannock. Good lunch - surprising how much it means to a person to have food in the stomach and how far one can go on this energy. I hurried to get over to that river. A gypsy-like adventure seems to surround me from all directions, like a stranger wandering with imaginative vision around nature. On the dam to the first trap, no beaver. Out of the eight sets I got three beaver. I reset these three as well as I could and left the others the way they were as I would not have time to make any new sets. Skinning two beaver will take a good hour. The dollar watch I had was set in front of me so I would be constantly aware of the time so as not to start day dreaming. The knife has to be sharpened several times for one beaver. I brought two round carborundum stones with me. One I left in camp in case I should lose one. Also there was a one pint mason jar tightly sealed for reserve matches. The third beaver I carried home as is. This one would have to be skinned by the light of the fire. I had to hustle to get back before dark for it was a cloudy day, there was no moon, and it made a difference. My first three beaver was a good start. I certainly did go through a lot of unforeseen unexpected misfortune, spending all this time and only three beaver. However I was glad that I had a start. As in every other walk of life things do happen beyond our control. Fifty-five miles out here - at some uncertain moment one could break a leg and this, I thought, would be much worse than what had happened to me in the last two weeks. Now I was happy that I was alive. Here I was in my new establishment, well protected from the wind. Getting a good fire going inside the tent after a good bed of coals was a necessity as one had to make bannock and also enough for the next day. If there was no stew, some would have to be made. The opening I left open for the entrance in the tent was handy as eight to ten foot poles of wood could be placed in here reaching the fire inside the tent by the rock wall. This came in very handy; as the poles burned off you pulled them up again in the fire. This saved wood cutting. The opening on the tent, a square hole of rock wall, worked just perfectly. This created a draft like a chimney and for that reason I had no smoke inside. I did have to keep the fire within reason, otherwise I couldn't stand it from the reflection of the heat of the rock. It was, in fact, a cozy place as I sat here ten o'clock at night skinning the beaver I brought home. It really was nice and warm. What a difference from the other place. One thing man appreciates out in the woods in cold weather is a fire. Here I confined the fire so that very little heat could escape. There was enough material left that was on the tent so the entrance could also be closed at night. Man will never understand the full value of wood where today, in the manufacturing process, they have products where the waste materials can also be used. The heat of wood has saved the lives of thousands of people. There is also a feeling of comfort watching a fire burn. When the darkness of night surrounds one and you hear the sound of the wind, the trees are cracking loud like a shotgun when the temperature gets down below zero, what such a small shelter against this rock wall means on nights like this cannot be counted in dollars and cents. Here one in solitude can find moments of thought seeking to find your soul. The very essence of your heart comes to harmonize with these surroundings of nature, things one does experience, thoughts of life come here in this deserted lonely place that I had not thought of before in my everyday life, a magnitude of observations unfolding at times like a dream. I am trying here to explain my feelings as they came to me under the circumstances. Environment often thus originates our conduct of action and thought.

This was my first night here. The accomplishments of my new trapline, my shelter, all gave me a secure feeling. I went to sleep in a hurry. I was very anxious to get an early start in the morning. With eight traps now out and eight more to set is sometimes more than a full day's work depending upon what the occurrences of this day on the river will be. There is always something new, like exploring miles up the river for the first time. Often smaller creeks come in and it never fails but there are beaver there. Sets where the traps had been snapped had to be adjusted for better position. Here you almost trade your thinking with the beaver. You know, in your imagination, his reaction as he approaches that trap and of course, you think you are right and the beaver is wrong. Often you are so certain that when you come back something of the unusual must have happened if the trap was snapped again. Often to corral a beaver one would take dead dry sticks made in a horseshoe circle, placing the sticks close together. They freeze in where the hole is cut in the ice. In the back corner, place small fresh sticks of poplar fastened down. Here at the entrance of this the trap is placed. One does not make a set like this in the wintertime, only when you find a place where the depth of the water, etc. is in your favor for this can become a time consuming job. I started early in the morning and the experience I had had gave me a lot of confidence. A trapper is full of anticipation and gets to be a rugged individual.One reason the cooking is done at night is you could not afford to take time out during the day to cook. Actually, you are fighting time every minute. From now on the weather will get colder each day, the food will get shorter so there is a constant battle existing from known elements and unknown elements that spring up at times unforeseen. Such is the destiny divided in degrees and out here in this wilderness this can become discouraging at times. While out here often thoughts of mixed emotion can arouse your imagination. These are things existing here in the confines of nature that one is fully aware of at all times. This I have learned the hard way. Here I am approaching the beaver dam. Looking over the eight traps set, I had four beaver so the three best sets were left and five I took out. This meant that I had to find thirteen good places for sets. Having time and a lot of new territory ahead of me that was the thing to do. There are the two old beaver in every house with their young now almost a year old. The trapper after catching the two large ones,which is the case most of the time,will pull the traps and go to a new location for the price you get for the small ones was discouraging. However, when the one year-olds become two year–olds they have their own family and house.These, when caught, would be medium pelts. Most of the beavers, the older ones, weigh 65 to 85 pounds, the medium 50 to 65 and the small so-called cubs 25 to 45. So, like today, catching four beaver, two medium and two large, you do not carry them very far skinning them near some rock wall for this whole area is full of them. I made a fire first then got my dollar watch to lay in a position so I could see the time at a glance. After cutting the legs off first and then around the tail - these are like leather, I started skinning always satisfied if I could make it in a half hour. Today I had three to skin out, one I would carry home, this would be the smallest one out of the four caught today. In cold weather they freeze stiff in a hurry so it is best to skin them at once. The one I took home will be thawed out in the tent. There is a special place for things like that. They are skinned laying down, as this simplifies the job. It seemed the further I went west the more beaver I found. Also, the country became more rugged, deep ravines running southwest for miles and at times one solid rock formation one quarter mile long. Tributaries of small streams braced the framework of the larger river in a fashion creating a paradise for beaver. All of this was very new to me and increased my love more every day for this unparalleled high plateau 16,000 feet above sea level where the watershed dividing line is established. A small distance south of my camp the streams run into Lake Superior. Here, where I am trapping five miles north, all water runs north to Hudson Bay. This was a busy day for me and I did make some fine sets.

I knew that I couldn't lose any time when I got my last trap set to get back by dark. When I got back I saw where someone had walked around on the side. This seemed strange to me. The first thing I thought about was the beaver skins thinking that they might steal them. However, they were buried in the snow and would be hard to find. After getting inside the tent house, up on the rock wall in a crack was stuck a piece of birchbark. Looking it over carefully I noticed some writing scribbled with a pencil. It was very hard to read but I could make out they were going in. Yes, it was Jeff going in tomorrow. Well, I couldn't go along for I did not have enough beaver. In fact I was just getting a good start and besides I was saving my food by eating a lot of beaver meat so I decided that I would stay a while. I did not know how many days, as those things are uncertain and you do not want to think about that. A thought came to me. I hoped I would not have any trouble finding my way back out as I had never been here before and we did come in cross country by compass following one might say a guide who had no doubt been southwest of here a dozen times. Now I had no map but I had looked at a canoe route map before we came in. Jeff had one for the route out of here starting considerably southeast from my location. After eight miles a well established canoe route starts. I had such a perfect picture of this in my mind, building up so much confidence, I thought there was no way I could miss. Since I learned to know these fellows I knew they would never wait for me. Here I had all my traps out for the first time. They must have had twenty-five or more skins and at an average of three pounds each seventy-five pounds would be a heavy load for Jeff as he was past sixty years of age. Now after tomorrow I would be out here by myself. Being busy it would be impossible to get to sleep before 11 o'clock tonight. There was always one beaver to skin. The cooking of meat takes time. Awareness of the condition for self preservation seens to take on more meaningful action. There are many things a person does not have to eat on a trapline such as cake, fruit, potatoes, pie, milk, vegetables etc. One does not think about it and never seems to miss it. There was little rest, seven hours sleep, sound sleep and thirteen hours on the go, doing something. The endurance one has when you are young is amazing. Every day now it meant to start at daylight. I had another surprise this morning - it had snowed at least six inches. Now the snow was getting rather deep and I started to use snowshoes. One does not like to use them until the going gets tough. When the weather conditions were such that the

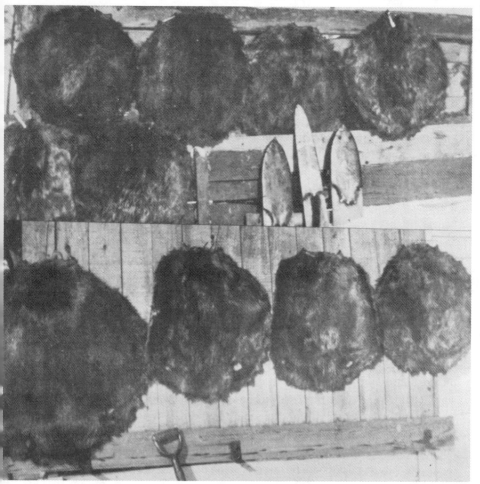

Beaver, Muskrat, and Mink Skins

snowshoe trail had frozen hard enough to walk on, then I would carry the snowshoes as I could make better time. Scouting further ahead to break a new trail I would again use the snowshoes. I got out on my trapline which was now five miles in length, had sixteen good sets out and this is more than I ever had in my life. Also, when I had looked at the last trap I had seven beaver. This was the most I ever caught in one night. What a job to skin them! The time one loses here and there it would take at least four hours to skin them so I decided to carry two of the smaller ones home. I did the best I could to make a few new sets. One likes to change the traps, take them out where two large beaver had been caught out of one colony and move ahead to a new location this way increasing the chance of catching more big ones. Every day the same routine. I don't think I had ever been more busy in all my life and then having to skin out two beaver at night after all that hiking in one day. I had no thermometer to tell the degrees but when trees crack at night that is when it is cold. This is caused from frost. Sap in the trees freezes and expands the wood often cracking the tree open on the outside making a very loud noise. While skinning the beaver here at night under the shelter I also had stew cooking. I never got tired of beaver meat. Food was getting low. A week would be the longest I could stay. The last day before leaving I would cook extra chunks of beaver meat to have to eat on the trip back. On the canoe route I would take four days to get in because it was more of a straight direction. Then the day came when I knew I had to go back. My total catch was thirty-six beaver and one otter; I decided to take half of the hides. This would give me around sixty pounds with a few other things. The balance of the fur I would hide. I had a burlap sack and I placed the hides in it. Walking along the trail not far off was a good sized rock. Standing on snowshoes heading south I threw the sack six feet over the rock west and down behind it went. I would come back later and pick it up. The tent and everything was left there, the traps all in one pile behind a stump as I would be back in early spring before the ice went out and before the bear came out as they would surely tear up the tent as they love to do that.The morning I was ready to go it had, started to snow. It was about eight to ten miles to the canoe route. This meant that I had to walk back exactly the way we came in this distance. I took a last glance at my camp tent below as I was going up the hill that led me out of this ravine. One tries to think of so many things at one time, and of all the comfort I got out of such a little place against that rock wall. It seemed just like leaving home. We have moments in life like that here but of course, my circumstances were different; an understanding of the forces of nature that can give strength and take away strength, creating a challenge that at times must be measured in spirit by such means where it becomes the center of your very life. There is no doubt that starting back from this point the journey was different in comparison with other trips I had made on a trapline. I had a good start and I thought I was making good time. On this lake, about one mile across, going south there was an outlet forming a small stream and this was the way I had to go. By now the wind was blowing and it was snowing so hard that when looking back twenty feet I couldn't see my tracks. Here at this outlet we had walked on the ice when we first came in. The snow had blown off in some places and you could see the ice. This, of course, is more safe walking. As it happened this particular day the sun had come out and thawed some and a little slush was forming. I was walking without snowshoes so my tracks were left in this slush. Then overnight these tracks froze. As the weather gets colder these tracks stay there until spring when the ice goes out. A day later at that time Jeff and Jet came through there and saw these frozen tracks. Even then they still would not walk on that ice for fear they would break through. They said, "You know, in some places in there it is twelve feet deep. Boy, you think you can walk on water, don't you." You know how it is, you can make much better time that way than walking around on shore. You find out some days what can happen. In those days, when I had a lot of nerve, at times I tried to do the impossible. This was the day it happened. Approaching the outlet it immediately narrowed down to twelve feet. When I was eight feet from shore I went in; lucky it was only four feet deep. I broke a circle three feet across to get out of there fast and to get some relief. I managed to get the packsack up on the ice and then pushing hard with both feet, snowshoes on, got up to the rim of the ice of the hole. This, of course, didn't do me any good, sitting in that position propped up there. It would have been impossible for me to get out that way so all I could do was go back down again. It was a good thing I had snowshoes on as they kept me from sinking down onto the mud bottom. The water was up under my arms. I did get the packsack off for that was resting on the ice, got the ax out which is carried so the handle stuck out in back, wrapped rags around the double bit blade and then shoved the pack ahead on the ice which was getting thicker toward shore, three to four inches. I was chopping and breaking to get out to the bank. It was very cold and stormy and the wind whipped across the big lake. It was what you could call a blinding snowstorm. I must have been in the water about ten minutes so now things were in bad shape. First I must make a fire. While walking through these thick elders I broke off every dead branch I could find to use to get a fire going. By the time I had gone two hundred feet my clothing, especially my shoelaces, were frozen stiff. There was a high knoll ahead. There were two large white pine trees - yes, this was a good place to make a fire. Leaving the pack there I looked for birch bark and more wood as I had to have some heat, barely being able to walk and shivering by now. I had a knife and matches so did get a fire going. You would stand so close at times you wouldn't care if your shoes burned up. The laces had to be thawed so I could take my shoes off. I had two suits of long underwear. When they get dirty they usually get rather black; the dirty one was in the packsack. Being able to hold it up on the ice when I fell in it did not get wet. I got the underwear and a pair of my dirty woolen socks out of the pack and standing on the packsack I changed my underwear. What I did not notice was the fire was burning two feet high now and the heat going up. Six feet above a heavy pine limb had a foot of snow on it. I thought nothing about this as I was anxious to get my underwear on. The heat of the fire released that snow and it fell right on top of me. At a time like that one thinks the world is coming to an end. I got out of it the best I could, wringing out my pants the best I could, and being heavy wool this was hard to do. I was trying to dry the pants and was still in my underwear. I had my pants hanging on an elder that I bent over near the fire and kept turning them front then back, front then back to get the heat from the fire long enough so they would dry out. The pants were just steaming and this means that they dry fast but you have to watch them so they don't burn. You always scorch clothes. especially socks when trying to get something dry in a hurry and you are cold. I did not have a pair of socks left out of four pair where the toes were not scorched so by now they did not have a toe in them. So now when I put them on I had some rags, splitting a piece five inches wide I would first turn part of a sock over my toes, then place a rag over so while placing my foot in a shoe this would hold the sock in place and the toes were covered. The insoles of leather-top rubber-bottom shoes are important to help keep you warm. One always has several pair of these. This time they were more than welcome - they were in the packsack. The worst thing to dry out in a hurry is the inside of those shoes. I struggled there half an hour before I could get all my clothes on again. It would have been something if somebody had taken a movie of this. I had an old grey long-sleeved sweater in the packsack, another thing I changed. I stood by the fire a little while when I was ready to go - it felt so good. I lingered on, not wanting to leave. However, time is always important. I did not have too much food left and I was thinking that by night I might be able to make it where Jeff had killed the deer on his way in. There would be something left for he only took the hindquarters. I did have a bite to eat just before I left hugging the fire very close not knowing that the sleeve of this old sweater got hot enough so it was smoldering. I probably was in so much distress that I never noticed it. I must have gone two miles, swinging my arms; happened to have my head turned to the right and somehow glanced at my arm and noticed that my sleeve was gone. I could not believe my eyes - just couldn't figure out how this happened. Getting alarmed I was wondering what is happened to me? You must be going out of your head - you'd better watch yourself. My mind started wondering why I did not smell or see this before warning me to watch my step. My clothes were never completely dry. However, if one keeps on moving walking fast you can keep warm. It did quit snowing at three in the afternoon and the wind started dying down. All I could think about was that deer meat up there on a heavily wooded hillside; also the moon would be out if it cleared up as it had been cloudy all day. Still following this river bottom soon I would have to go over the ridge and start in the direction going northwest. It was getting dusk and it was clearing up. I slowly climbed up a long fairly steep hillside and I knew I would find the deer meat up there. Yes, when I finally got there I could see the moon coming up through the trees. As I got near this rock wall where the deer meat was I noticed a lot of coyote or wolf tracks. Getting within eight feet I could see hair from the back of deer sticking out. They were feeding on it. I knew then they were not coyotes or wolves, just foxes. There was considerable meat left. Jeff had taken the hind quarters only. Now the front legs were mostly gone. The wolves or coyotes would have taken everything by now. I dug out the back and rib side and cut the best part of it in one chunk. One seems never to learn, it seemed this was the way with me. I started to do some foolish things. One reason I believe this happened was that by now I was used to having a shelter and something came in my mind that I had read years ago in a book called "The Wilderness Trapper." It said for a temporary shelter lean poles up some rock wall and cover it with balsam boughs. Oh, yes, I must have one of those shelters. Thinking nothing of it I set the packsack down near the meat, took the ax and walked through the woods east, looking for a good size rock wall. There was enough light from the moon so I could see fairly well. I went a quarter of a mile first straight in and then turned north and found a good sized wall. First I started to make a fire by this wall. How foolish one is when your mind at times like this is not working right for on this rock wall there was so much snow and ice the larger the fire got it melted the ice and snow and this kept putting the fire out. I just kept throwing on more wood in the meantime cutting poles and getting balsam boughs until I had it finished. What a job. I was tired from my trip, then the blade of the ax was dull so I had hard chopping. It must have taken me an hour and a half. Instead of following my tracks back the way I came I had to short cut. The moon was much higher by now and almost full so I could see good. I started to walk straight through the woods to get to where the packsack was. Yes I came out right where all the stuff was, was somewhat surprised and happy. Taking everything along, including the meat, I started out straight for that shelter. I placed a lot of wood on the fire as it took a while to get going. Now to make something to eat. To save the little meat I had along I would eat the deer meat. I had no water so I melted snow in the gallon tin pail to drink - had no more tea. Taking half the side rib part of the deer I put a stick on each end to hold this securely on the fire to brown until the juice ran out, then turned it over and did the same on the other side. No salt. Here I was chewing all the meat off the ribs like a caveman - I ate until I couldn't eat any more. That was my supper. Now the next thing was to cut more wood and put more on the fire. The wood was not plentiful here and I had to chop some green wood. This also burns if it once gets started. Now to get back to this shelter. It was terribly cold and I had trouble keeping warm. I placed more wood on the fire, took everything out of the packsack except the hides and used this to stand on because I wanted to take my shoes off as they were somewhat frozen. I turned these upside down on the poles where the balsam boughs made the roof. I was turning to pull in a stick of wood as I wanted to dry out the boots. The flames were whipping up rather high and all of a sudden the balsam boughs caught on fire. They have a lot of pitch in them and burn like gasoline. In just seconds the roof was gone - I quickly grabbed my shoes and threw them out. So here I was, clear sky, moon shining and cold. This night it got to 32 degrees below zero, this I found out later. I was chopping wood all night to keep from freezing to death. A few times I lay curled up like a dog stretched out on a few beaver skins by the packsack. You soon lose strength when sleep is lost and this food was not like having warm liquids in your stomach. I had some more deer meat and started out early as I knew that I had lost a half day in time and had lost distance. Walking only a few miles my legs felt very numb. One gets worried because you are afraid of freezing your feet. I had heard of trappers up here in these places freezing their feet so badly they could not leave their camp. It had happened to Jeff. So I walked up to a tree pounded my toes against it very hard but felt nothing. I had been gathering white birch bark along the way so I sat on a log, made a small fire and it is surprising how quickly your feet get warm. The only way to warm them is to take your shoes off and I had some trouble using the rag after what was left of the socks, folding them back first, then the rag to be sure that the toes would be covered. I started out again. In another mile I would come to the canoe route. One finds the portage the hard way as they are hidden away in bays, and at times you walk a considerable distance to find it. There is no other way to go and this was the first time in my life that I had been in this part of the country. Yes, I found the first lake. This was a long narrow lake almost like a river three miles long. I noticed in the afternoon, looking west, that the sun could barely be seen through the very dark cloudy sky and looking back I noticed that my tracks seemed to be very close together. Yes, they were. Then for the first time I got to thinking that I must be getting weaker. At no time does one want to confess or think of the results of such a condition. I was glad when nightfall came. It was very cold and the main thing was to find a good location that had good shelter and lots of dry wood around. Before getting dark would be the best time to find a place to stay on this portage for the night. It is never hard to find a suitable place. Tonight I would make two fires about six feet apart, get them going good so green wood and larger birch would also burn. This would then hold the fire. Perhaps then I could get a little sleep. I carried enough wood to last all night, found a couple of pine stumps and they were a big help. When something like this is accomplished you derive a lot of satisfaction. Now I was tired and hungry. For dinner I ate one piece of meat while walking and melted some snow. I had six chunks of beaver meat left. I had the frying pan with me and some lard and I knew that I had to take it easy on the meat. I took two of the smaller pieces and browned them on both sides. What a sight I must have been sitting there between these two fires eating. The crackling of wood broke the silence and sparks of many colors were flying in many directions adding life, whisking themselves in mid-air. I ate slowly. It is difficult to imagine the consequences in true nature, a union of mood uniting man with nature through the passing night. A strong feeling existing within causes you to ponder your surroundings. Being aware of my thoughts I was always thankful for what I had. Also there was much contentment and after having had something to eat I was now able to get some rest. I stretched out four beaver skins, fur side up, on top of snow that I had tramped down; on the outer edge I covered them with snow to make certain they would not catch on fire as I had to keep it going. Morning came and I knew I had to get started. This was the third day, I was not making good time and I was slowing down. Certainly it would take longer now to get to my logging camp where I would be staying for some time-later going back to Wisconsin. I had four pieces of meat left and realized that I could eat one for breakfast. One thing that tastes odd is water melted from snow. I was wishing I had some salt and thought this will never happen to me again, running out of salt. One cannot make mistakes like I did on many occasions out here far from nowhere. Depending too much on self-reliance is no help when forces of nature are working against you. I was eating this meat very slowly trying to make it last as I also wanted to soak up all the heat I could before leaving the place. The sixty pound load was getting heavier and heavier - I started from a kneeling position to get upright after the packsack had been placed on my back. I was on my way and it seems that the spirit of adventure never leaves one. Following the canoe route out here for the first time one is concerned and eager to see what lies ahead. The grim fact remained that the odds were against me this third day on my trip. I felt myself getting weaker and weaker causing me distress and I was looking for a windfall or rock where I could perch the bottom of my packsack for a rest at every chance I got. By doing this often I lost time, it got colder, mostly my feet. Then when it got so bad that I was afraid of freezing them, I had to stop and make a fire and get warmed up. The other thing was I was hungry. It was now ten in the morning and I knew that I couldn't eat as yet. I had three pieces of meat left. I was making very poor time so it could take me five days instead of four. It was frightening to think this but the fact remained it was so. Pressure from cold and hunger can get a firm grasp on a person in a hurry.

Then there are harsh sounds from one's imagination, often an irrational notion or belief, the thought of not being able to make it. Things of uncertainty by now often appeared from out of nowhere, things I never thought would be in existence. Feeble of mind and strength I found myself in this condition so that toward evening walking up a steep hill I used my arms grabbing my pants above the knee to help lift my leg. Yes, it happened way before dark. I walked by a place where there were a lot of pine stumps. What a blessing, for many of these can be pushed over, having been there seventy years or longer. When the forest fires destroyed these trees, the second growth that is standing here now, mostly poplar, white birch, balsam and pine (some now up to ten to twelve inches in size) would have to grow about seventy years to get to that size. I had trouble getting the fire going and after it was started I just sat there and rested for a half hour. Not having to use up any energy cutting wood was a life saver, at least, that was the way I felt. This was the first time a feeling of isolation came over me and I was thinking about the outside world. I had restrained myself from eating all day as I felt that I should save the three pieces of beaver meat I had left. Being so cold also helped discourage me from opening the packsack. Now that I got warm and had a little rest I felt better. I took one piece of meat and warmed it up in the frying pan. Again I melted snow water. I would eat very slowly poking around the fire with a stick. One's thoughts wander in all directions always trying to offset the good from the bad. A good sized pine stump that was lying in position near the fire made a backrest. Again I removed all things from the packsack except the skins, using them to sit on. There was nothing I would change for I would doze here through the night partly in a leaning position against this pine stump. Now my third night, tomorrow will be the fourth day. I had two pieces of meat left and couldn't understand why I did not bring more meat along. I was thinking back over the past year, learning all the time the hard way. It was a cold moonlit night and the trees never failed to crack. You do not care to hear this sound as this is an indication of zero weather. Thoughts of human nature will reverse and sanction emotions of hardships to justify the cause, once capability to reason becomes sluggish and unjust. Within inexhaustible energy not to give way or surrender, a motion of mixed feelings gets to be a natural process. So the night did go and the morning came. The thought of food was uppermost on my mind. I was restless to get going after I had another piece of meat, always the same procedure in warming it up, and the snow water to drink. How much this meant to me, to think that upon a quarter pound of meat one can go all day carrying sixty pounds of weight. Enduring the cold weather, is, however much worse and can take the life right out of you. Never would I have dreamed the morning I left my camp that this would happen to me. One cannot find time to feel sorry for oneself. In the struggle for survival this I fully understood. As the circumstances were, I knew when I started out this morning, the fourth day, that I could not stop anymore if I was going to make it. I had about a quarter of a pound of meat left in this small chunk. The meat had been cooked back at camp in salt water so that I all had been doing is warming it up in a frying pan to get it nice and brown on both sides. With all the determination that I possessed I started out on this canoe route leading into civilization, not knowing how many miles I had to go-I thought I might have seven to ten miles left. I could only guess as Jeff and Jet thought it would be four days regular walking. Knowing of all the time I had lost now it was different. One has so much more hope when surrounded by such environments. How one will sacrifice and not surrender and one, in such times, has a lot to give. I found when nightfall came I had rested at least fifty times never taking the packsack off--only resting it on something to relieve the weight, and this had become a slow process. Stopping to make a fire takes time and not knowing how far I had to go made it confusing. I stopped just long enough to get this last piece of meat out of my packsack - I had to keep moving as it was cold. I ate this as I was walking catching some snow off the lower limbs with my mouth holding it in my mouth until it dissolved. Each mouthful made a little water. When eating now one wants to get the cleanest. On all this trip there was about fourteen inches of snow. Having to pack a new trail with my snowshoes was very tiring. There will be another moonlight night. I stopped every three hundred feet or so resting the weight of my load. Realizing by now that the only way I would make it was by keeping going I trudged along in a slow wearisome fashion physically refusing to stop. It seems at this point a supernatural power takes over also finding out that it was not the food anymore that would help me. By now I had become weary and the grim fact remained that I had to keep going. Leaving behind me this snowshoe trail I did not have a natural step for I barely raised my feet high enough to clear the other snowshoe. I must say that on this journey toward one o'oclock at night I was stopping every 150 feet. Here, after midnight I did get out to the gravel road. I could make no attempt to describe the feeling I had when I saw this gravel road here in the moonlight. By now I was shaking all over from cold. This road had been traveled considerably all year round so I managed to get my snowshoes off and threw them in the woods. For I could find them later. What a relief this was, going straight down to my logging camp which was two miles from where I came out of the woods. My fatigue was now influenced by hope, rejoicing that I was alive. It was a slow process getting there but I made it. The door here at the remote logging camp was not locked, it had a barrel heater and a pile of wood as there was a lot of room. I got the fire going and that was all I could remember as I went to bed with all my clothes on, except my shoes. Having dozens of army blankets I took six of these and covered up. My body was shaking for some time and after that I went to sleep and slept until late in the morning. Not once did I think of eating. To get to sleep under a roof, after all this time, seemed strange. One realizes the meaning of comfort. All this environment here becomes like a millionaire's mansion and it took me until ten o'clock in the morning to get going. The first thing I did was hide the skins. Then I went down to Jeff, the resort owner who had grub staked me, to get some groceries. I never caught a cold but was somewhat stiff from hiking. I was surprised as I thought while coming in on that trip that I would get sick. Also with all that hardship I thought I would think twice before going out there again. How soon one forgets all the hardships as soon as one gets straightened out and recuperates!

Going down to Jeff half way down around the curve I heard someone whistling. Meeting almost head on right at the point of the curve, here was Jet the partner who was out with Jeff trapping beaver. "Oh," he said, "what a surprise. We thought you were dead when you didn't come in before this. We thought you went through the ice and we would come out tomorrow and look for you." "My," I said, "I never thought you fellows would do that." We both walked back to Jeff's house. He was glad to see me and we all had dinner together. We had so much to talk about and the homecooked food, including potatoes, really was a treat. Jeff said it was 32 degrees below zero, this was on my first night coming in. The last few days it was 20 to 30 below. "No wonder," I said, "I had such a tough time trying to keep warm." Jeff said I had some experience and I was lucky I made it. "And you walking on that thin ice out there. I told my wife," he said, "that you can walk on water." We had made this deal on price at the time we went out. Immediately I said that I would bring the skins down in the morning and then he would pay me for them. Thinking about my snowshoes I said I would go and get them early in the morning. Jeff said he had to go to town the next day and I offered him a good price if he would help me tow my pickup down. He said he would - money often talks. First he would run up and get the fur for Jeff, then he would take out what I owed him, that was only $32.00, and the rest I got. He also knew of the other hides I had and I said I would go and get them later. Jeff and Jet were very close friends and this winter he was staying in one of his cabins. It was 45 miles to town and one had to be very careful towing a car on this road. I was very happy to get it in the Ford garage. They would get a new motor for it and at that time the cost was a little over $100.00. Jeff and I both got a supply of groceries. It would take three weeks to get the pickup fixed and this was OK with me. When we got back and got these groceries in the logging camp and got settled I felt that all had been worthwhile, thinking now that I would get on my feet again. I had sufficient blankets and by hanging them up I could fix it like a wall. This made a smaller room corralling the stove in the middle - easier to keep warm. It was now three weeks until Christmas. I made up my mind that Christmas Eve would be a good time to go back and get the balance of the hides hoping we would not get too much snow by then so I would be able to see the old snowshoe tracks. This would help a lot for better walking. I went down to Jeff's place several times. He had gone over to the Canadian side to get diamond willow to make furniture. They were working on a frame, making a double bed. It looked very good - pieces were placed in the most suitable places. It made a good pasttime for the winter. One fault of mine was I did not have enough patience to do this. I never told them when I planned to go back for the rest of the fur. Apparently all was well concerning the wardens. When It came to this I was somewhat leary as I could not afford to have anything happen. The time went fast. I did some reading and I got out around the camp finding enough wood to get by. This I carried out in long lengths and then cut short stove lengths with what was called a Swede saw. They are very handy, fast cutting and light. I was preparing for this eight day trip, four days in and four out. I borrowed Jeff's sleeping bag that was stuffed with feathers from the breast of wild ducks. I took plenty of food, frying pan, tin can of tea and this would be light weight on the way in. On the way back I would have about 65 pounds. The sleeping bag will be the main comfort for one never knows what the weather conditions will be. The time went fast and two days before Christmas, early in the morning I started out. A mile and a half back of the logging camp was the river I spoke of before and this I followed. It was well frozen so the only thing to look out for would be spring holes. One can make good time and further down will hit the portage route. Walking along at a good pace in the distance I could see an object ahead in the river. Coming closer I could see this was a moose of considerable size, one third of the body above ice and frozen in. Knowing this river has a mud bottom he got stuck in there probably as it was freezing up. I had seen sick moose out here in the woods before and I then thought that this is what must have happened. Had foxes started to eat on it? This one can tell from the print of the tracks in the snow. One often likes to think in terms of coyotes and wolves. These are around but are found further out in the woods.

I made good time getting in there and could say it was an enjoyable trip instead of one of hardship such as I had experienced a short time ago on my way out. Comparing conditions I could honestly say I was thankful. I made it in here in three and a half days instead of four. The camp against the rock wall was a welcome sight. I got up some wood and now, two o'clock in the afternoon I had plenty time to rest as I wanted to stay for one night in this "old place," as I called it, where memories still lingered from the times I had here before. I don't think I could have found a better place for shelter especially in the middle of winter. While I am now old this is one place, God willing, that I want to see once more. Of course, it would be in the summer time going in by canoe with my two sons as I want them to see the evidence from heat and smoke burned into the rock nine feet high on the rock wall like a lasting monument dedicated to the end of time from a beaver trapper, as that dark black formation in that rock was there to stay.

Notice home made broom

Trapping Shack

One at times in life gets involved in many things, alluring attractions. Money can become the principal object of the matter. I had never learned a trade only knew how to make a living from the woods, either trees or fur. In those days trapping beaver was fast money. I will say you had to learn it from hard experience. This was in the CCC days and jobs were few. Trapping became the backbone of my life no matter how complicated it got. Having had a lot of food and time to rest I saw no reason why I could not get started back early in the morning. I found the fur - it was in good shape, frozen solid like a rock. I made a cushion out of the sleeping bag inside the packsack as those frozen skins would have been like rocks when pressing on my back and this would have been torture. At daybreak I started out thinking that now it was after Christmas. My feeling was this was the safest time for going. One good thing was they did not have any snowmobiles in those days as this would have made easy traveling for the wardens. I don't think they were much for hardships. I do know they had a good cabin on one of the lakes on an island rather far out. I knew that this would be my last trip in this year and I had so many things to look forward to keeping me in the best of courage. My walk displayed energy interweaving strands of a poetic mood, also reflecting the present thoughts of life. The weather has a terrific influence on a trip like this. I can say up to now the weather has been very moderate, like 10 below and when dressed warm for packing this is ideal. The security of knowing that I had a sleeping bag was half of the battle.

Late at night on the fourth day I got back to the logging camp. It did not take me long to make something to eat and after a day's hike like that I hurriedly went to bed. My thoughts were that I had many important things to do and uppermost in my mind was to get the fur down to Jeff. He always seemed to have money and paid me cash on the spot. I was afraid to walk down the road in the daytime with the fur so in a roundabout way, going through the woods, I went to Jeff's place. I was a happy fellow when I got rid of that responsibility and had the money. The first time Jet would go to town I would go with him and get my pickup and he assured me that within a week's time he would go. I told him I would give him $2 to help pay for the gas. One thing I could never get myself to do is mooch on people that often want to help you. We did go to town and my pickup was ready. He told me to take it easy to break in that new motor. I had the money to pay the bill. This pickup has been just like a partner as everywhere I went, it went. Now again to hear and feel the wheels rolling under me gave me the satisfaction that now I could go again. So the next morning I packed, and took all I could load on as the weight would not hurt the pickup, only the bulk. I knew then that I was not going to log anymore here. Thinking back at what I had experienced last year while here, all the forest fires, etc. I had enough of logging in this country. I owed the man $750 on stumpage and thought then that he might allow me this if I gave him the camp buildings as with lumber and labor the buildings cost me $500. I did not want to go fourteen miles up the road to tell Herman, the one who sold me the timber, as I knew it was a poor time to do this. I thought he would find out soon enough by next year in the late spring. I was loaded and very anxious to get started on my trip back to Wisconsin. At ten in the morning I stopped in at Jeff, his wife and Jet and thanked them for everything and told them good-by. I couldn't help the thoughts in my mind the last day when I was double packing when the snowstorm came up, how easy it could have been to get lost if it would not have been for other circumstances at that time. Those are things hard to forget even if you try.

Every day was a new day. Somehow being able to come back to Wisconsin again made this a special day for me. I looked forward to seeing old friends in Wisconsin. I would see the manager of the lumbermill first as he would give me a job working in his sawmill for the winter. I got as far as Ashland and stayed there overnight. Coming down on U.S. 2 the next day freedom was present all around me, a feeling of being released from this bold and stern northern country where there is so much wilderness, rich in minerals, and forest and the home of many fur bearing animals. Such a great change takes place when one leaves that north shore area. The scenery changed; here were farms, and villages and towns, long strips of tilled ground and this all seemed different. By three in the afternoon I arrived at the little sawmill town. My old friend was glad to see me again. I had supper at his house and I had a lot of stories and tell him. It was late at night when I walked up the steep hill to the boarding house. There were always some empty bunks and it was always warm in there. He gave me a job and early in the spring I would leave again for Minnesota to trap beaver. He paid $2 a day and board and that was good wages for so called common labor. The board was figured at $1. For pastime there was a poker game every night and once you get started at this it is hard to quit. Yes, I had to play poker. One night I played a hunch, that is where from the beginning most everyone had fair cards. This was draw poker, eight fellows playing. My hole card was an ace and a king showing; several of the men already had one pair; everyone drew the third card betting was fairly high right along and so far the pot had $12 in it. The fourth time around I got a king so this gave me two kings and this ace in the hole. I bet $1 and two fellows dropped out and five stayed; the man next to the last one around to me raised another dollar for he had two pair, one pair showing and to make the other pair was the one card in the hole or blind that he had. One more man dropped out. The last card around two fellows had two small pair now showing up; my last card was an ace making me aces and kings and it was the highest hand around and $32 in the pot. That was the most money I ever won in a poker game. Then, of course, I bought everybody a treat. According to the law of averages you usually break even. Most of the time if you played all winter you would be lucky if you broke even. Some men sat around the bunk house telling stories, some watched the poker game and some were reading while others went to sleep early. In this mill they sawed an average of 28,000 square board feet. The reason I am bringing this up is the fact that two men piled all this at 50 cents per thousand except the railroad ties. He did cut some railroad ties; I used to peel them. They never would handle over 26,000 board feet a day. I used to think of all the money this fellow made; 26,000 feet gave each one $13 a day. We used to slide the lumber on tough strong leather aprons using the whole body as one unit like action only lifting part with the arms. Then there were rollers mounted on lumber piles and also a thing called a lumberjack for balance and placing in position. If a plank 2 x 10 x 16 feet long a 1'' board once dropped in position in the right place it never had to be moved again. Yes, these men were experts and strong and their faces looked more like leather. Today it would cost $4 a thousand to pile this lumber compared with 50 cents in those days. You could not find men in Wisconsin that could pile 26,000 feet in one day. These men piled this every day all winter long - that is what one calls old-timers. Soon that generation will be gone forever. These are also the men who would play jokes on the new men brought into camp and the young fellows working in the woods for the first time. The foreman would go right along with it, like sending one of these fellows over to the blacksmith shop to get the sky hook which has a two foot round hook on it. After a while the man would come back and say he couldn't find it. They had the same joke about the lumber stretcher.One thing they did not do or allow in those days was to sharpen an ax with a file;this had to be done with a grindstone.

Often one heard of the old time trappers. Also here and there you could find them shacking in some remote place. I have seen them staying in what you could describe as a root cellar located on top or level with the ground. This I know, that every trapper has his own way of doing things in catching or shooting the animals. South of this little sawmill town is a thirty mile stretch and east forty miles of solid woods, some creeks, a few lakes and a lot of swamps. One can imagine how much more wild this was a generation back. Here a trapper from this small town would track a pack of wolves until he would catch up with them.This would happen on the third or fourth day as by then he could get in shooting distance from them. No doubt he waited for the best weather conditions, full moon and probably about six inches of snow. The wolves had no chance to eat. He was using a high powered rifle. Wolves brought $20 bounty. One night in our sleeping quarters (bunk house) this same old fellow told us that while he was mink trapping ever so often someone would steal the mink out of his trap.So,one day there was a nice mink in one of his traps. Then he said he waited there to see if he could catch the one who was stealing his mink. After three hours of standing waiting behind a tree he saw someone coming through the woods. He had his rifle as he was never without it at any time. "Well," he said, "you know it was an Indian taking my mink." Then he quit talking. There were about eight fellows sitting around there listening, everybody was quiet. Finally one fellow spoke up and said, "What happened to the Indian?" "Oh," he said, "I guess he is still there." A friend of mine used to be a state trapper here in Northern Wisconsin in 1924 and 1925. They could catch them all year around, however, in the summertime was the best time to catch them. The territory for one trapper was a twenty mile square or a line twenty miles east and west on the north edge of the state. One time he found where a family of coyotes were located. He went and bought a sheep for $1. Then he killed it in the locality where the coyotes were howling every night. He put the hide in a hollow stump and covered it so the ravens would not get it and the entrails he cut up and buried in many places. The meat was cut up into walnut size chunks and this was used as bait at the traps. Then he set out seven traps one hundred to two hundred feet apart. He left the traps unattended for three days. When he looked at the traps he had caught one coyote and it was all eaten up except for the one leg in the trap and all the bait near the other traps was gone, also the decoy baits; one trap was uncovered by a coyote. So, he put another trap beside it and baited all sets. Again he left them for another three days. When he visited the sets the first trap had a timber wolf. The next set was the place where he had the two traps. When he came in sight of it there stood two big timber wolves side by side. Well, he believed that one was in the trap and the other one just standing there waiting. He had an automatic 22 so he could shoot quick. Bang, bang, he hit both. They hollered like hounds, kicked in the ribs and don't you know, he said they were both in the traps, one in each. He said he had a load to get out to his car. At that time he was trapping for bounty. I don't believe that this could happen again in a thousand years for both of these wolves had to put their foot on the trap pedal the same second at one time for as soon as they get in the trap they jump violently. Too bad he couldn't take a picture as very few people would believe him.

The winter months seemed to go by fast. The ice was going out in Minnesota one month later than in Wisconsin and this gave me time to get some legal trapping done in Wisconsin. Beaver season was open in early spring and one could always catch a few. I would stay right here at the boarding house paying $1 for board and I would sleep here. The manager of the sawmill did not care and was glad to see me make more money. I was anxious for the time to come when I could start out. Ahead of time I got things together - I needed traps and wire to fix my snowshoes as often one does use them. I got acquainted with a young farm lad from a town fifty miles away from here. He had worked here several winters. Saturday nights he would go home to his folks and stay over Sunday. He was a single fellow, very sincere and honest, someone I could trust for when it came time to go to Minnesota I thought I would have to play it very safe to go in there where I was trapping. Somehow I thought no one would know about it except this farm lad and I could trust him. He would take me up so we would get to my logging camp about three o'clock in the morning. He would not stop at all but go back to Wisconsin and I would go further up in the woods and start trapping. When I came out of the woods I would call him, he would come and get me and in this way nobody knew that I was out there. He liked the idea and it was something new to him to drive a practically new pickup. After the season opened here in Wisconsin, about two weeks ago, I had five beaver and the limit was twelve. In back of the boarding house was an old woodshed and this made a good place for skinning and throwing the carcass out on some wood pile. At night they would freeze and dogs running around at night would drag them around. There was a Finlander cook who always got a big bang out of a joke. He took a couple of these carcasses and cleaned them all up, par boiled them and made a fine stew. Not saying anything he served this for dinner. About thirty men ate it and said nothing as it tasted good. However, when the whole story got around a few fellows got mad and told him never to pull a trick like that again.

When the legal open season was over I had a total of eight beaver. This was considered good. Legal skins would average $15.00 a piece. Working at $2.00 a day didn't count up fast. Besides I was doing what I liked to do, was my own boss, and I liked to roam around in the woods.

The time went fast and I had to get ready to go back to Minnesota within a week. My traps were out there at the tent shelter. I would try to rough it as far as the weather was concerned. The ice would be going out and it would be getting warmer each day. This meant that I would not have to take a sleeping bag. The main thing was to take a lot of food as I was going to make a long trip out of this. I thought of all the experiences I had on my first trip in and out last fall so this time I would do it better. You have so much confidence at times that it actually stops your thinking. When buying groceries I thought I would add a few luxuries like a couple of pounds of butter, raisins, sugar, prunes, powdered milk, oatmeal, bacon, navy beans, lard, and most important 35 pounds of flour for making bannock. Yes, this time I would start out right. If I had only known what was ahead of me, no doubt I would have laughed if anyone had told me. I had the packsack, packed everything in waterproof bags, sharp ax, whetstones, matches, two woolen blankets and a good sized piece of water-proofed bed sheeting.

Early on a Monday morning we got going taking out time as we did not want to get there before midnight or later as I felt this would be the safest time to leave the road up there and to start walking into the woods. Everything went exactly as planned. It was much cooler up here than it was in Wisconsin. Forty-five miles up this road was where I had to start out. We got there at two o'clock in the morning. The snow was frozen so I put on my snowshoes as in this way no tracks would show on this hard crust. I told my friend good-bye, he would go up the road three or four miles to find a place to turn around, and then go straight back to Wisconsin. He had all the information that in a month and a half or later I would let him know and he would come back and pick me up. My pack here on this second trip weighed 65 pounds. You can walk along at a good gait with this weight. Why a trapper has such high hopes is at times hard to understand. There are, of course, many other things in life hard to understand and even though you get to be eighty years old you still do not understand them. When you deliberately challenge the elements of nature you might know that things can happen. The sun was shining brightly and by noon I had come to a familiar spot at a creek. I stopped and had a well prepared lunch that the cook at the boarding house had made for me. He was so big-hearted you might know he would die poor. At one time he had also trapped beaver. I started out again and you could tell by the sun that it was high noon. I came to a bay recessing near shore like a small lake by itself. From here, around a sharp bend, I would follow the larger body of water going in a southwesterly direction. Looking all along the shore line I could see where the water in some places had opened up, thawed out, two feet out. However, at the point where I was there the ice came solid up to shore. Now I should have known not to trust that ice. All I had to do was cut a ten foot pole so when one goes in, most of the time just breaking a two foot round hole, this pole, two or three inches round, is sufficient to help you as you hold it in the middle. When breaking through instinctively one will act fast, very seldom getting wet further up than your hips. Was I so brave or was it because I didn't know any better or too much in a hurry to take time to think. This time of the year there is always water on top of the ice, three to six inches and sometimes more. Here there was about three inches. I walked out on the ice and everything seemed fine and fifteen feet out, in I went. I was lucky to this day that this was a very unusual lake as it was only about four feet deep. Lakes around here are usually very deep often twelve to thirty feet straight down from shore and fifty feet deep. This lake had a gravel bottom, I immediately set the packsack up on the ice and jumping I managed to get out. I slid the pack on the ice toward shore and back on land I was. Woolen clothes really soak up a lot of water. I had only one more pair of pants that I thought to use for sleeping and, of course, only one pair of shoes. As long as I would have to make a fire to dry out some of my things I thought this was a good place to make it. The sun was shining. It did not take me long to get those wet clothes off. I had an extra suit of underwear and some extra socks. Ringing out my woolen pants the best I could and all the other clothes, I hung them up in the sun and had a fire going on the side to help dry them out. Looking in the packsack I noticed things got a little wet but the waterproofed bags saved the food. After two hours nothing was really dry. One thing that helped was an extra pair of insoles and with those and dry socks one never feels that. So I was ready to go. Here to the west was a large spruce swamp and I don't know to this day how large this low land area was. Well, I got in this swamp thinking of going around to get down further on the other end of this lake and then get a pole and walk the ice. The snow was very deep and there were a lot of windfalls so it was hard going. I kept on walking and walking and never came out to high land. The sun had gone down and I was still walking but very slow for in this jungle of woods I had gotten very tired. Now ahead I saw some tracks, no this could not be my tracks (I considered myself to be a good woodsman) but yes, there were my tracks, and then I knew I was walking in circles. This bothered me for this proved that I had not gone anywhere. I wandered around until dark and then I knew I had to give up. I cut large spruce limbs, making a teepee, and a pile of boughs to lay on. I made a good fire and hung up my clothes that were not dry. It was time to make something to eat and I felt better after eating. I had a considerable variety of things to eat more than I had any other time out in the brush. I moved around the fire slowly doing this and taking care of that. A process of establishment seems to be in order if one does not get annoyed or desperate under such conditions. I did not stay here in this swamp because I wanted to get out of that swamp. It was a misfortune that forced this upon me and I had no choice. There are many thoughts that suddenly come upon you with overpowering impulse pleading to give counsel. How free I was just a few days ago and tonight I felt that I was partly lost in this swamp. One thing a person never likes or wants to admit is that he is lost. I was also very tired and when I thought I had everything under control I dozed off to sleep occasionally waking up now and then. Having had no sleep the night before that sleep was a necessity effecting me in the form of a nightmare. As soon as the darkness started to disappear I got the fire going and cooked some oatmeal after the snow water was melted, for there was no water around. Then I fried four slices of bacon and when the oatmeal was done I dumped the bacon, grease and all, in the oatmeal and mixed it all up to give it a flavor. It was warm and it tasted good out here. I packed all my things and started out in what I thought was the right direction. I kept going for two hours and to my great disappointment came back on my tracks again. By now I was getting somewhat confused and frightened as by now I had considerable tracks in this swamp. Then I knew for certain that I had been walking in a circle all this time. Sad as it was, it didn't help conditions any to have a cloudy day. This swamp, the deep snow and all the obstruction confronting one was a battle in itself, not to think that I was lost and forty-five miles to go and the ice going out fast. It would be impossible to walk cross country as in the first place I did not even know how to go. I wanted to get out on the lake and find the canoe route. By now I realized that I had started one week too late for when I fell in the lake showed that the ice was getting thin. One thing I could not do was follow the track I had just run into as then I would be back where I came from. In desperation a person will do strange things at times. It was more like crawling around in this swamp than walking. All I can do, I thought, is go in the opposite direction. Looking ahead as far as I could I picked out a tree and went over there; from there looking in the same direction ahead I picked another tree and in this way I thought that I would at least be going straight forward. How foolish that I did not bring a compass along. Yes, I would know the way, just follow the canoe route. I came out on a lake and I recognized it to be the one I came in on last fall. I should have known that I could not be too far out of the way as I did start out right. I was so happy I could have cried. I realized that in order to be able to walk on the lake I must at all times carry a ten to twelve foot pole. There are places on lakes and rivers where there are weak spots in the ice and air pockets. The water and slush three inches deep made it harder walking. This swamp kept coming back in my mind - how could I possibly have gotten mixed up like that. Ordinarily I have had no trouble walking cross country five or six miles to come out at a beaver dam on a river the only spot one could get across for quite a stretch. This I had done several times and I surprised myself how close I did come out on the point. After I ate I cut a good light pole, the kind that I knew would not break, and started out. I got out on the ice and nothing happened. A bay located on the south side was the last ice to break open. Here the sun never got to this area. this is the place I was looking for, reaching that part of the lake going southwest. Walking in this slushy water my feet were soaking wet. One likes to wear the best ten inch leather high top boots money can buy, somewhat on the large size, so felt insoles with heavy woolen socks can be used. Surprising but no matter how wet you are if you keep moving you stay warm. The swamp was still haunting me like a nightmare although I was able to walk here where it was more level. I had lost considerable time and was not making good headway and this worried me. I was glad when I came to a portage. These are well made, a good trail that at one time had been cleared out. These, at times, are two miles long and some are only one hundred feet.

Now the second day out, yes, I did have to keep track of the days. This was the only thing that concerned civilization, all the rest was wild out here. Everytime I came to another lake I noticed there was more open water showing on shore. This was becoming of great concern knowing that I have to walk the ice to get in to where my traps were. The creeks and rivers will go out first and this is no country to get in or out of for someone like me on the ice or by canoe. To travel on land cross country one has to know the landmarks, use a compass, and it takes two days longer like when I came in with Jeff, the tough guy, on my first trip in. He was the one who showed me this place first.

Here another day is coming to close and I traveled right up to the time it started to get dark. Desperation can rush one on and on. I stopped where I could get water, made some tea and did some cooking. Wood was plentiful so that was no problem. All in all, from what had happened I felt relieved and more settled here at this place. One cannot help but enjoy it for every night the place where I sleep is home for the night. There is that feeling that surrounds you that everywhere you look and everything you do has a touch of nature. This also seems to grow on you and becomes part of your life. As a structure must include the right kind of frame work to hold up; so it seems to effect a trapper trying to find something to hold on to in time of trouble. I got a fire going in good shape for I would need coals tonight to bake some bannock mostly for lunch on tomorrow's trip. The nights out here often become very still but there was nothing to think about yet and I did not have to worry about bears. Should we get a real warm spell then they can come out any time now. Trying to get as comfortable as I could for sleeping meant piling up boughs one foot thick. My socks were hung up and I had to dry my shoes the best I could. Dry insoles in the morning is a big help. So, another night, I was glad to be alive and hoped for another day. The weather was good, not too cold. To get out of the wet socks felt good. I had four pair of socks in all and two dry pair I needed for sleeping. I had cut off rubbers for slippers and these I used often. I had all my clothes on, a big old coat. two blankets on top of those boughs, quite a combination but it made for good sleeping. In the morning I knew it was the best rest I had since I left Wisconsin.

This was the third day and I got up very early for a good start. Ahead of me was one of the largest lakes for miles around. It had many islands. I had my pole for safety as I was walking in five inches of water. At noon I stopped on one of the small islands and had a bite to eat. My pack seemed heavier, it was hard walking in the water, and the situation was getting worse. It was a cloudy day and it appeared as though rain was on the way. Going around a number of these islands I got off my course. This lake was some six miles across. I noticed, on the lake, a long dark line going ahead as far as I could see. Yes, I recognized what it was, snowshoe tracks. The width and all corresponded. The very heavy slush which was snow on the ice was gradually melting. You could see very plainly where the snow had been packed by snowshoes as this was darker in color than all the rest. How foolish I was to think that this must go down into the country where I was going. There was no mistake in my mind but that I was going southwest. It was late afternoon and I was walking more slowly now following the dark outline going straight for a good sized wooded island. Never in all my life would I have believed that I was going to run into a small cabin here. It was no more than twelve feet long and eight feet wide, had two small windows and by pushing in hard on the frame it moved. So I tried harder and got it open. I crawled inside and all that was holding the windows were nails driven in side ways. There was a bed made from wood and a single style double bunk, a good combination cook and woodstove. On a beam in the middle partly supporting the cabin were cloth bags of food hanging on wires. This was done so mice could not get at the food. They had small pieces of soap laying there. I had heard that the wardens had a cabin somewhere in this area and I thought perhaps this was the one. I wasn't there very long before it started raining. I did not know then that it would continue to rain for two days. I took a water pail, crawled back out and ran down to the lake to get water. I wanted to wash my hands and face and when warming water this would be a treat. The door had been locked and I never touched the door. I took what I needed out of my packsack and left the rest outside covering it with waterproof sheeting. I could never have gotten this in through the window. I had everything in there I needed so now I would do a little cooking. There was pancake flour there so in the morning I would make pancakes. I felt good to think I had the good fortune to stumble on to this cabin especially on a rainy night. I could hear on the roof that it was coming down hard and heavy. No one would ever have to worry about a warden or anybody else coming in now. The ice was going out faster than ever with this rain. I did not know then that this night would be the best night of my whole trapping experience. Rain or no rain I knew that time was getting shorter and that I had to get out to my traps and shelter and the only way I could get there was on the ice. When you are young you have a lot of courage and it seemed natural that things happened the way they did. You always have a lot of confidence, never fully realizing how disastrous things like this can be. It was not late when I went to sleep but I forgot about everything and slept. When I woke up it was daylight and it was raining but not too hard. I made some pancakes as fast as I could and some extra ones to take along. I was soon on my way closing the window as best I could. I kept the waterproof sheeting out and this served as part raincoat over my head and over the packsack. I folded it so that it could be used this way. This is how I started out. After walking a few hours I had to take the waterproof sheeting off of my head as it got too hot and I strapped it on top of the pack. Now there was more water and slush on top of the ice. Approaching the shore line of this large lake I did come out on the portage. It felt good to walk on land, however, it was sad as none of these places between lakes were very long. I kept my pole with me at all times. When I came to the end of the trail I saw the smaller lake and it had ten feet of open water all along the shore line as far as I could see. I knew that my life depended upon it that I would have to walk on the ice. The idea came to me that I must cut a tree, one that is long enough to reach so I could get out. There are many trees lining the shore and to walk around some of these lakes would take days. There were ravines of solid rock running east and west, very rugged, many rock walls of considerable height - no that was out of the question. The first tree which was very handy was a good sized white birch. What made everything so bad was that it was raining. I was keeping track of my time - this was the fourth day. I had my pole, got out on the ice and nothing happened. The dark line shadow from the snowshoe tracks was barely visible at times. There were black lines two inches apart running the full length of the lake mostly in a north-south direction where the ice had parted. I looked very closely now to see how thick the ice was - it was 6 to 8 inches thick. Immediately it came to me how this had happened. In the winter if it is cold enough to freeze ice, if the force becomes too great it expands. I have heard this often - it makes a very loud continuous noise as it starts from one end of the lake going clear across. This works on the same principal as the cracking of the trees. I was glad to know what it was. One thing good to know was the thickness of the ice. I was fortunate enough to find a bay on the south side on the other end of the lake so I could get off. It was still raining and by noon I was getting soaked. Being on land now I started to look around for a suitable place for a shelter. Beside a hill side here was a completely broken down old log cabin. It was partly rotten. Having become very desperate by now I said to myself - make a fire here and burn the whole thing up. This cabin had been made of small logs. When I got the fire going I took several of the logs and laid them in a position so I could stretch my waterproof sheeting over them. While I was doing this there was a cloudburst - the way it came down! I covered myself with the waterproof material I had. The rain lasted for a half hour and as soon as it let up some I stretched the covering over the logs I had fixed just a short time before. I was wet all over and was starting to feel it. I knew I could not go any farther today. Just about the time I had this shelter fixed so it would stay in place another heavy shower came. There was so little room under this small tent-like affair that after I crawled under I had to pull in my legs to get them inside. The weight of the water on the top formed a small valley and it ran off like a spout barely missing my feet. I was getting practically no heat from the fire and it had practically gone out from this heavy rain. Soon it slacked up and I crawled out and threw the remaining logs on the fire. I knew that if I moved around I had a better chance of keeping warm. My packsack was getting heavy for me. This always happens as the journey gets longer. Thinking about this I got a foolish idea in my mind-that was to make a sleigh and in this way I could distribute the weight and I would not have to carry all of it. I was very restless and had to do something to keep warm. I started to walk along a steep bank up from the shore line of the lake trying to find suitable white birch about four inches around. First I would hew out two skis for the runners. On a hillside one can often find a tree with a perfect curve. Scouting at least twenty minutes or so I found two. I took these back with me and threw a lot of wood on the fire and got it going in good shape. Then I thawed these out. They had to come from the center to maintain the width. When I got done they looked good. Then I wanted to dry them. In the fire they went, I pulled them back and forth and when they started to burn I took them out. They were coal black but very light. I had nails along as these I needed to nail the beaver skins for drying. In spring all skins are dried as in this way one can pack many skins. I hewed a cross piece and had to build it up for clearance. It got dark early and I did not finish the job. It never quit drizzling and I had to rearrange my shelter. I was glad it did not rain more heavily. There was a large spruce nearby where the limbs had grown

110

way down to the bottom. I cut some limbs to make an X frame to support a ridge pole about six feet high. The limbs had a long slight curve and could be placed in position one over the other two thirds of the way around. This alone can shed water for a half a day. I laid some on the ground and made a fire in front of the entrance. You are constantly guarding your packsack as you do not want to get your food, blankets and extra clothing wet. Extending a roof-like affair in front gave me room to hang up my pants and socks to dry. I did this after I had something to eat, the food that I had prepared in the cabin where I had slept all night. I was thankful it happened that way. How little I knew in those days about divine power, that which is outside the range of the accepted and known course of nature. The rain made everything very miserable, yet when I got dry underclothes and pants, two pair of socks, one for sleeping, I felt like a new person. It never stopped raining. I got so much comfort out of this little shelter and an experience such as this is hard to describe. I was unhappy in the morning for it was still raining. Changed clothes again and made breakfast, at all times using everything sparingly as the longer the food lasted the longer I could stay, at least until the black flies started to get bad in the middle of May. Now to finish the sleigh. It was done and it looked more like a toboggan - I only had to fix a rope for pulling. I knew I had to get going so I got all of my things together. Across the portage over to the next lake was the way I would have to go.

It was now the fifth day and I should have been there had all gone well. I was not even half way but this I did not know and I also did not know that I was lost. When I arrived at the next lake the scenery was strange. One recognizes new territory at once but what could I do? It would be impossible to turn back or try to find out where I took the wrong portage route. This was a long narrow lake and from what I could see it had already opened up fifteen feet out. This meant I had to cut another tree to get out. Like it had been today, I can see a long tall spruce hitting that ice and then the water flying. The water was deep here. First I pushed out the sleigh, empty, with a pole up to where the ice started and also the limbs on the tree. This was no time for me to be scared to walk out on this tree eight inches in size and I had to carry the packsack. Only a few feet out my pole did not reach any more. From here on I would have to take it slow and balance. I made it for when I reached the place where the limbs started it gave me more footing. I stopped here throwing the pole ahead and working the sleigh out with me to the very top, that was out a good fifteen feet on the ice. Knowing that this would be a poor place to load the sleigh I pushed it ahead once more with my pole which was a good ten feet long. Here the water on the ice was not less than six inches deep. I started out with my packsack on to get over to the sleigh. I hadn't gone eight feet when in I went. I made a perfect two foot wide round hole and I was hanging on the pole arms straight down in a stooped position. It all went fast, barely getting in I got on the pole with my knees, hands ahead on the ice and partly crawled out. I believe it all happened in a minute, I was so conscious of this so reaction came fast. I got to where the sleigh was loaded on the packsack and started to pull it. I went ten feet and I couldn't understand why this should pull so hard. Then in a hundred feet the snow packing underneath made it impossible to pull. I couldn't understand it and who would have believed such a thing as this. All the hard work, the skis were almost perfect but it was no use to try anymore. For the sake of consultation I would save the runners and some day get them when I was up here in a canoe - I would save them for a souvenir. I knocked the sleigh apart to get the runners and thirty feet from shore I threw them out one at a time as I could always get them. I found later these were only thoughts. I had mentioned before that this was a long narrow lake and so it was two-thirds of the way. The dark faint line could still be noticed going straight down the middle of this lake. The dark open streaks appeared in many places and it looked now as though the ice was about six inches thick. Farther down the lake widened out on both sides running into bays. My biggest worry was to be able to find a place to get off of the ice down here on this end. I went up to the very end of the southwest corner and there I could get off. Here the ice was better than I had seen as it was in a place hidden from the sun. The sun does not rise so high as yet. I knew that from here I would have to go left, or south, to find the portage. It must be noon for I was hungry and it was also time for a little rest. The pack was getting heavy and I thought several times of double packing. What was most encouraging was that about ten o'clock it quit raining. I was still partly wet - woolen cloth can take a lot of water but when I fell in I got soaked good on the lower part of my body. Walking so long in the water got to be a natural thing. Under these circumstances everything you do can become doubtful like knowing, when I set the knife blade on my finger throwing a shadow in opposition to where the sun was, what the direction would be. From time to time I would do this while there was no sun today. Yes, according to the sun I was going southwest the way I had to go to get back in to where I was last fall and to my traps. It was not far through the woods to the portage. I made lunch and tried to get my thoughts together. One thing certain was the ice was going out fast and I was fighting against time. The fact was, I started out too late. One in Wisconsin never knows the exact conditions and just when the ice goes out in northern Minnesota. It does depend upon weather conditions and they vary at times. This year it was one week earlier as one could see. Getting lost, at least I did not know where I was, I believed that I was only partly lost. You sense a restless condition, part imagination and part true like a shifting wind - gladness mixed with sorrow. One thing I knew was that I could have drowned out there and also knew that walking on the ice was the only way that I could get out. I walked on the portage to the next lake and this was all new country and elements of nature were the most complex part of the whole surroundings. I was certain that when I got to the next lake I would have to cut another tree to get out on the ice. When first approaching the lake the first thing was to look to see how much open water was there. Every time it was more and here it was not less than twenty feet. Unfortunately, the breaking up of the ice starts from the shore all around the lake. The only hope one could have would be to find a bay in the southwest corner to be able to get up on land. So far I made it. I was half soaked but could overcome this as long as I could keep warm. Carrying a load like I have often made me sweat. Here was a lake that I could see across, also saw the two islands very heavily wooded. Those I wanted to stay away from as by now they would be surrounded by water. It was four in the afternoon and I knew that I had several hours yet to hike in hopes that I could get off the lake. I realized by now that not getting off the lake could be called a game of exploitation. I could see here against the skyline heavily wooded timberland to the west. The two islands, only covering about five or six acres of land, were round in shape, there were a large number of white pine standing here and there and it was a scene like two monuments standing there in the middle of the lake. I was very near the extreme south end for that was the only place where I could get off, and every time that happened uniting myself with land was a step of new hope. I knew I had to go south to reach the portage. One reason I knew how to find the portage was out on the lake snowshoe tracks would leave the dark line and they would go straight to the portage. When I came nearer to shore I could not follow the tracks. At first I wanted to walk on the lake to the farthest point down. There was no choice, it had to be in a bay and they are mostly hidden from the sun. On a long lake, winter or summer, in a canoe, portages are often hard to find. Arriving on the portage was refreshing, here where the connecting link for another lake begins. My pack was getting the better of me, the straps had cut into my shoulder blades and they were sore. Tomorrow would be my sixth day and I decided that I would start double packing as all day I had been walking rather slowly. In the meantime with these thoughts going through my mind, I kept on walking never knowing how long this portage would be. It was about a half mile long. Here now was a new lake and I walked up to the edge to see how the water was. It was thirty feet out from the shore to the ice and there was no tree in sight that I could cut that would reach. Having some time before it would get dark I set my pack down and walking up along the north side of the lake about a thousand feet. Here the ice was closest to the shore and there was a large old poplar (aspen) that could be fallen in that direction. I had my ax along, one carries that like a hunter

113

carries his gun, I chopped it down as this would save me time in the morning. The weather felt much warmer today but the nights do get chilly. I tried to find a good place to stay here for the night. After getting back to the pack I walked around on the south side and I saw fairly good sized rocks in the distance. Fifty feet back from the lack was what one could call a cubby hole - two rocks in triangle shape. I cut poles the same old style one gets used to and I knew how far the waterproof cover would reach for protection on two sides. I lugged some boughs as my first thought was to get a place to lie down. What a relief, I thought, to get these partly wet clothes off. The water was gushing in my shoes all day. I hurriedly made a fire out of birch bark - what a blessing the bark was for a fast fire to keep you warm and for cooking. I got water from the lake and made tea and this was all free. With all my sorrows still there were dramatic moments.It was a relief to change my wet clothes for dry. I made a pole rack near the fire to dry the wet clothes. I had to watch this closely while cooking so I would not scorch the clothes. The socks usually do get burned a bit. I took time and cooked some navy beans and threw in a little bacon. There would be enough to take with me for dinner as I cooked enough for that. A trapper gets used to living in the wild woods and it gets appealing, the free life is more satisfying but it is also a solitary and dangerous life. Alone here in the trackless forest demands endurance of no ordinary kind. Silently one pursues the way, no whistling, no talking or singing. I said before that I had not learned how to pray so such though s did not enter my mind.Now I know that it would have been a lot of consolation. I sat here looking into the fire, admiring the color of the flames. This was the only thing moving. It was nine o'clock, I stirred up the fire, bundled up the best I could and lay down. Often one does go over the happenings of the day before in your mind before falling asleep. The only time you wake up is when you get cold. This time of the year the birds start singing an hour before sun-up. As soon as I hear them I get up and check the weather. Wearing my old rubber bottom slippers I could walk around and then in no time I would have a fire going. Kindling was always readyfrom the night before and that included birch bark and small dry sticks. All wood finds its place in our life and so does the birch bark. It's been used millions of times for making fire, the Indians used it to make their birch bark canoes, and it is truly a treasure for the woodsman.

This was the sixth day and the first time the sun came out in three days. What a welcome feeling this brought, knowing that it will help melt the ice but not as fast as the two days of rain. The sun would now guide me in my direction of travel as I knew the sun came up in the east. I would have to walk in water but it was much easier to keep warm when the sun was out, and it also stimulated my feelings. Ihad had a good rest, had oatmeal for breakfast with sugar on it, and some tea. My dinner was ready to take along, the navy beans I had cooked last night. I divided the weight of my packsack about even for today, for the first time, I was going to try double packing. I distributed it so that all the things I needed for making camp I would take, like the two old blankets, I must have my clothes, and my homemade covering for a tent. This was a must in case I didn't or couldn't get back. At times like this I felt that I was all set. I got a fairly good start as it was six o'clock in the morning. What a difference half of the weight made as now I was only carrying about thirty pounds. I had more freedom of movement and how much easier it would be for me to get out should I fall in the lake again. The danger of doing this was greater than ever as the lakes showed evidence of this. In no time I got down to where I had cut the tree and where it had fallen on the ice. This was sixty feet in length and I needed that now, the longer the better for safety. Nothing went wrong and I started out at a faster pace than before using my pole. I could not see the end of the lake, it was not wide, more narrow slightly winding and a half mile wide in most places. It never did get any wider and it took me until noon to get where I could see the end, about four miles. The water was never less than six inches deep on top of the ice and this slowed me down considerably. A very faint dark line could be identified going very straight from the snowshoe tracks made by somebody last winter and the ones I followed now for some time. I had no idea who it could have been at that time of the year and where this person could have gone. This was a mystery to me, and never will this man know that someone had followed his tracks. Arriving at the very south west tip of the lake I met with a sad surprise - there was open water all along the shore and this left me stranded on this body of ice. What could I do - it was four miles back to where I had cut the tree to get on to the lake. I started to walk back, I always had the pole with me, on the south side of the shore line. One hundred feet out away from shore was all swamp land bordering the lake. A ways down a tree of fair size was leaning out - I got there and it was a large cedar that had grown in a long curve leaning fifteen feet out. Where the heavy limbs started growing straight up the ice was about five feet under the tree and it was at that point four feet up from the ice. When I approached it and saw the condition of how this had grown, I knew that this was the only place where I could get off and I would have to take a run for it and grab the tree. I threw my pole over on shore and then I ran as fast as I could to get hold of that tree - the ice broke. I had to use the last ounce of strength I had. This is what happened. With the weight of my packsack hanging, part of my legs dangling in the water, I worked myself up on the trunk of the tree as best I could. From here on in, as in all the rest of the places, the ice had gone out. The farther I got in, the farther my body was hanging in the water. It was now up to my packsack. The lake was very deep here but there was nothing I could do except hang on for it would have been impossible to try and get up and around. I did manage, on one side, to touch my foot on a cranberry bog

115

sticking out here in the lake. Pushing myself up, after I had one foot on the bog, I started to stand up and the bog went down quickly and I went down to my waist. I scrambled to get more footing on the bog and to find more solid bottom as ten feet out the water was gradually getting more shallow and I finally got out in the solid swamp. It is most surprising how far a person can go and what one can do when it gets to be a matter of survival. There was no stopping, I thought, to change clothes. The snow in the swamp drifted in here two feet deep and it was slush, soft from the rain we had had. In fact, it was like walking in water. I did not have to lift my feet, I could push through the slush. I worked my way over to the portage as I knew where I could find it. By now the wet clothes became so unbearable I had to change. I put on the old pants I used for sleeping, changed socks and insoles, wiped out the shoes on the inside with an old rag the best I could and felt better, I should have known that the shoes would be soaking wet again as soon as I got to the next lake. Trying to wring out the heavy pants is like wringing out a wet beaver hide. I was concerned about getting my clothes dry but this would have to be done late in the evening. I came to the portage and it was now past dinner time so I made a little fire and warmed the beans in the gallon pail that was the chief cooking utensil. Felt better now after changing clothes. One has two sets of long underwear and these never get washed on a trip like this and do get mighty black by the time one leaves the trap line. Had my beans and was ready to go. This was a short portage and the lakes often lay close together. Same problem - open water thirty feet out getting so now that this was nothing new. I had to walk around on the shore again looking for a tall tree to cut to get out on this lake. There was a large white birch on the very edge of the shore leaning out on the lake. It did not take long to fall the tree as my ax was sharp. A heavy leaning tree will break off about one third up from the unbalanced weight. This is a big help. One side of the ax was kept very sharp. When camping and cutting wood at night one becomes conscious not to get cut on the foot or leg as out here this could become a fatal thing. I took my pole and balanced out on the trunk of this tree. There is never a complete feeling of security when doing this. One mistake here can lose you a half day of travel or perhaps a day. If you should lose your food with the circumstances being as they were here, my being lost and not knowing if I ever would be able to find my trapline, this in time would be disastrous. Gradually thoughts of disturbance flashed through my mind, constantly ignoring the fact that this was all strange country. All went well to make the ice. It was a challenge to get on as well as to get out of here. Further down on the lake was a large formation of rock walls going up twenty to fifty feet in height. You get the impression that this whole area is more rugged than it is farther north. I was splashing through six inches of water step by step, the sun was very bright, and the sky blue, and I had not seen the moon for three days. It should be out

116

tonight. My spirits were down - these moments seem to come. The scenery was getting very wild, high cliffs such as I had never seen before. I got to a narrow channel, it got to about twenty feet wide with solid reddish rock walls now up to sixty to seventy feet straight up. The faint snowshoe trail went right through this channel. It was all very strange, I stopped and thought this must be wrong, this cannot be the right direction that I am following here. This can never be - I must change my course. Instinctively my behavior turned me saying to myself that I must go straight south. On this side the shore line was very steep also, two hundred feet up as far as I could look and sloping back. Very little sun could shine in here and for that reason the ice went solid up to the shore. Jagged rocks of smaller walls were sticking out all over. By hanging on to small trees I would just make it up here sliding back here and there. Now here while I was climbing I saw my first bear tracks. At first I did not want to believe it and actually bent down for a closer look - yes, it was a bear track. I knew from the jumps he was taking up this very steep rugged incline that he had heard me coming and left in a hurry. When I got on top The walking was not bad as there was about five inches of snow left on the ground. There were larger trees here and, in general, this seemed rather heavily wooded. I thought I had walked about a mile going up a large wide ridge. It was getting toward evening. By now many things kept going through my mind - where will I camp tonight. Seeing that bear worried me - he may find my other food that I left back where I stayed last night. Thinking nothing of it I took off my packsack and set it down. I climbed a very old large jack pine high up here on the ridge. The limbs were way down to the ground so it was easy to climb. I went up to almost the very top looking in all directions as far as I could. Well, there was a chain of timber lines way around. Looking partly north I saw two small lakes. I said to myself, you've never been here before - you never saw this before. While up there I was almost certain I heard noises. Listening very intently a light wind coming from the southwest carried the noise of rushing water - yes, I could make it out. It was water and here on this watershed it was running partly north to the Hudson Bay. Then I knew for certain that I was really lost. I climbed down from the tree not knowing just what my thoughts were. My condition must have been very desperate. A weakness of intellect takes over, it is fear. The foolish things one does when this happens. Never thinking about my packsack or anything else I start running straight down the long slope. It was north, the way I started out, and not paying any attention I just kept on running very fast. I had read once that if you ever get lost, don't run - it's the worst thing you can do. This was going through my mind and I tried to tell myself to stop. I became like a ghost running through the woods, faster and faster. A thousand things seemed to be going through my mind and I just kept on running. Going down a steep gully I saw a lake. When I got to within fifty feet of it I recognized this as the first lake I had walked this morning. Only a few times did I think about God out here. This was a time that completely revealed the emotion of my needs and my troubles. Holding my arms around a tree I started praying a sad very unusual prayer saying, ''God, I thank you if you only let me have a few beaver,'' showing that I had beaver on my mind. There was no more fear and everything of suspicion was gone. First I had to go back and get my packsack. Coming back here I had to cut a tree to get out on the lake and a new walking pole for walking on the ice. It was getting dusk but there was no rest for me until I got back to my other pack. This meant that I had to walk this lake down to the portage where I had camped last night. Also, I knew that on this lake I could get off of the ice on the southwest corner. It was rather dark now, I cut that tree, found a ten foot pole and made it out. Now out on the lake it was much easier to see. I had a mile to go to hit the portage and I was happy when I got there. It was like coming home and to know that I had all my pack with the food and other things. All the entanglements I got into that day and all the struggle I had, and here I am back at the same place I started from this morning, and time was so precious and the ice was going out faster every day. I had lost a whole day. It was essential that I change direction. I made a fire big enough so I could see some distance around and gathered a good supply of wood. I had to do some cooking. My good woolen pants were wet and my socks - this happened when I was hanging on that cedar tree. Surprising how much time all of this really takes. I was glad to get my shoes off. I had some pancake flour and these I made now to take the place of bannock and besides, flour was one thing I was saving. If I could only get out to my trapline. There I could get beaver meat in a short time.

Tomorrow would be my seventh day and there was no denying that I did sense a feeling of being completely encircled out here in this wilderness. There was no way that I could have turned back. Soon the ice will be such that no one can walk on it. This, of course, was no opinion or impression, it was a fact. Life takes on a fixed meaning when convictions become a driving force. Steadily the evidence of my conduct like running through the woods today unexpectedly came upon me. No doubt I was restless and looking at my watch it was now eleven o'clock at night. I had to keep a fire going to get my pants dry. I had them hanging high above the fire so the flames could not reach them - this was the only way to get them dry fast as the heat goes directly up. Not satisfied with today I hurriedly made up my mind to follow a body of water that I noticed coming into this lake from the south and for a second thought I constructed the idea that straight south was the way I had to go. The moon was shining brightly so why not go now, just take the ax along, to see which way this is going. (To state here, if there had been another man with me and we were lost under these conditions we would never have gotten out as two men could not agree on anything one would call rational.) This is what happened. Walking down a steep embankment one hundred feet down on one side I saw open water. Then I heard a loud splash - it was a beaver and he either heard or smelled me. This was the first sign of beaver on this trip. I wondered what I would accomplish if I would keep on going down. Even here in the moonlight the country was rugged and very impressive. Here the land dropped gradually and I could see the ice. I came out right on a point of water showing ten feet from shore. While standing here looking it over, a bunch of coyotes were howling very loud. I hated this for I knew they were running deer. Here I did a very foolish thing and it could have cost me my life. Someone was watching over me and it was not my time to go. I am a strong believer in this, as we are born to answer a purpose and not until the purpose is answered are we called. To proceed, here within fifty feet from where I was standing was a chanel thirty feet wide and a twenty foot high rock wall on either side. A long tall spruce stood at the very edge. Chopping it down, out on the ice it went. I must have been very excited or at least I was not thinking for here I walked out without my pole and this is the only thing that can save you if you break through the ice and fall in. Walking out on the end of the tree up between the channel no more than a hundred feet I stopped; the moon shining as it was showed every shadow like reflections on the surface of the ice. I noticed a dark spot thirty feet ahead of me and immediately recognized it to be an air pocket. It came to me that I did not have a pole. This was very frightening. I turned around and very slowly, step by step got back to that tree. When I got to the tree I ran on it to shore. Here was a relief partly isolated yet calm and thankful and feeling land under my feet never felt so good. If I had broken through the ice no one would ever have found me.

It was now after midnight and I went back to the little camp I had fixed the same as I had last night. I was a happy person and went to sleep. Rest and provisions can do much for a person giving you new strength and new life. Our mind can confuse any mental state, activity, feelings, mood or desire. Here, under the circumstances, lost the way I was, I was beginning to pay strict attention to signs of uncertainty. All day long, in this kind of environment, a person thinks out loud. It is a creative imagination forming a picture of the acts that are taking place and at times become a fantasy. There is a reaction of harmony corresponding in many ways in rhythm with nature. I was changing my direction of travel tomorrow and all would be entirely new. All went well even though I had had only five hours of rest - it would have been hard to do without this. The fact that the weather was nice was half the battle.

This was a new day, the eighth day. The danger of ice going out fast became bewildering. Ever since I started I had been trying to save food, not thinking of it in those terms, but the fact was I was getting weak. Today I would be double packing again, often thinking, if I would only get to where my traps were. Since you know the bear are out you respect them. When a bear is in the vicinity, can be a half mile or more away, if the wind is in his direction he can smell food. More than one trapper lost all or part of his grub. A friend of mine walked in thirty miles to get thirty pounds of flour and other things as the bear got what he had. I packed one half of what I had to take along and the rest I wrapped carefully in the waterproof sheeting in such a way that it was the shape of a paper bag when blown up. I wrapped wire around to hold it shut, I had a role of cable like wire such as is used for a clothes line, this was fifty feet in length. Then to find a high rock. Here it was hung down in the center about eight feet down. This has to be a rock high enough so the bag is at least ten feet up from any solid footing so the bear cannot reach it from below. Above, back some distance the small cable is fastened to a tree. This a trapper calls a cache; where animals hide their food is also called a cache. One thing was, and that is very important, I did not have to worry about the bear getting this part of my grub. So I started out the way I went last night down that long steep slope. Came down to the place where I had cut the tall spruce and took one more look at where I had walked out there last night without a pole. Here in the day time I was able to see better and visualize the danger I had taken. The way the high ground embraced the shoreline here provided fairly good walking. As long as I could go in a southerly direction it was much better walking than walking on the ice. What a relief it was to get out of walking in the water where in no time my feet were soaked and were wet all day. It was very hard walking and tiresome but I had to admit that going through the woods, even though it was not level by any means, was better walking. Now I had completely gotten away from the body of water I had followed earlier. Here it looked like the beginning of an elevated woodland area. There was even much more self reliance in my walking and I knew I was making good time. I impressed upon my mind a want of mutual fitness and convinced myself that I was a trapper and that I could make it. I held on strong to my convictions and overcame all my fears and acquired unbroken uninterrupted steps in my walk. This is also an expression of freedom and one thinks that all is well. I thought I heard water running -- there was a light wind. Yes, standing very still I could hear it plainly south the way I was going. Walking very fast in a short time I came out on a portage. Looking east just two hundred feet was a big lake, I had seen this lake before and also knew the name of the lake. This was the same area where Jeff kept telling me to go north last fall where I could find some beaver. At that time I had approached this territory from the south and never came this far north where I am now. This is the lake with the old beaver house, one of the largest in the country. Here also is the place where in a distance of a quarter of a mile the water dropped three hundred feet down to a fine lake below here. The U.S. Forest Service had a large upright red metal box standing on the side of the portage trail. I noticed the door had been ripped off and all the fire fighting equipment, including considerable first aid material, was scattered all over. At first I did not want to believe that it was a bear. Here one finds a primeval wilderness, rocks had been blasted out in some places in order to get down on that three hundred foot drop to be able to portage a canoe, and the most astounding of all was a large cedar tree that had practically grown straight across where the water was rushing down, formation of rocks laying in there on the surface as large as a battleship.This time of the year with all the ice and snow going out there was so much water it came down dropping here on a 45 degree pitch. The water would splash twenty feet high in many places when coming in contact with those rocks. Heard trappers talking about this tree, that this was the only place they could cross between north and south at this time of the year and when on foot going cross country you immediately rocognize it as such. The trunk of the tree was two feet and at no time was it less than eight inches where one could get off. At this point there were large heavy limbs. In order to get down on the ground on the other side you had to hang on to the limbs and then partly fall four feet down in order to make it. From here it was two hundred feet up, very steep and I kept hanging on small trees so I could make it.By now it was noon so I sat up here on a rock and had a bite to eat watching and listening to the water below. On a clear day the sound would carry two miles. If I hurried and went back I should be able to make it back here by late tonight. I pondered this over in my mind knowing that it would be impossible to get back again by night. So I said to myself - be satisfied, now you know where you are; you can find your traps from here and be there in a day and a half. This I did for now it was more easy to calm myself since I knew where I was. I could never figure out how I changed direction back there taking this course and finding this place. Today, while I am writing this, I believe that I had guidance. Understanding of spiritual matters always came slow, to learn that it is in a spiritual realm where alone there is to be found forgiveness of sin, life and salvation. Twenty years later my thinking changed, discarding misery to find that the fear of the Lord is the beginning of wisdom.

I was bothered when thinking about double packing as it took twice the time. I had brought my snowshoes this far by hanging them on the back of my pack but I decided to leave them here and hung them on a tree. Also, I had already planned that in early fall I would come back here with two canoes and have someone along to help me build a log shack and make it bear proof and put supplies in it, food, etc., that would keep for early spring trapping. I thought I could pick up the snowshoes then. By twilight I got back once more to this familiar place for now it was my third night here. I knew that this would be my last night here and it was a happy thought. I discovered, when I got over where I had the balance of my pack hanging down on that rock, that the bear had been here as there was a path worn on the bottom going back and forth where he was trying to figure out how to reach it. I had to climb around on top pulling all I could to get it up. How glad I was that I had enough sense to protect this from the bear for he is the trapper's biggest enemy and the woods are full of them around here. Farther up in the wilds of northern Quebec, also a paradise for trappers and hunters alike, there the wolverine is the trapper's worst enemy. They are shy, shrewd and thieving, called the North American glutton. They follow the trappers' footsteps and destroy the animals as they are caught. They have great strength, short legs, very sharp curved claws. There is not a more cunning or crafty animal living than the wolverine. He hunts day and night during the winter months to find a trail of a man and when he finds it follows it unerringly until he finds a trap and then destroys the animal and the trap. When a wolverine has established himself on a trapline the hunter's only chance is to change ground. The Indians gave him the name "Evil One." I was glad there were no wolverines around this neck of the woods. The trouble I had with bear was enough to keep me on constant guard so as not to lose any food or fur. I decided to make a good sized fire to scare the bear away. Those were my thoughts then, but a bear does not concern himself too much with a campfire, a forest fire, yes. These bear in the wilds do not touch a human being, only the female in the spring when they have their young. They will not bother you unless you deliberately cross their path. For this I was thankful as many nights I was so tired that nothing in the world could keep me awake not even the bear. And then I found out that all along things were happening, contacts I had with them or they with me, and they did not touch me. Most of these bear had never seen a human being and were afraid. However, they were very hungry at this time of the year just coming out of hibernation and were looking for food day and night. They are very fond of beaver meat and occasionally catch one mostly in the fall while they are out cutting down trees. So what happens is they also follow a beaver trapper on his rounds to get the carcasses. Then they have a feast for what they find on the ground, by nature, they believe belongs to them and will eat it even though they are close by. If I hang a beaver carcass in a tree, which I have done a few time, then they carry it a long way before they eat it as they believe they are stealing it. First night, like tonight here, I was leary of the bear but as time went on I learned to live with them. The nights are peaceful and this was the first time since I started out that I did not get wet - I was dry. Wearing several pairs of woolen socks and all the clothes one can manage to get on, you keep warm. I was trying to piece together the last few days learnings and it was something like a miracle what happened to me. I was relieved to think that now I would be able to get out to my traps. I would eat a lot of beaver meat so I could save on the other food and stay longer. Later on the suckers would start running and there are creeks where they can be caught. They can be cooked and this would be something different for a change. So, I was looking forward for those days to come. I had more rest this night than any night I had spent out here. The pressure of urgency also had partly disappeared and I was more calm.

I gathered up my things and started out now, the ninth day. I knew my way through these woods so the portage was easy for me to find. Also, down here there was evidence that at one time a number of men had camped here for there were stakes driven in the ground and also a square frame also out of poles in the form of a single cot for sleeping. First they had car wire fastened going across every eight inches and had woven willow boughs into this in a neat fashion - a good place to sleep off the ground. The only thing I could figure out is that the CCC boys flew in here with seaplanes to fight fire in this remote place and they had made it, for it was last year they had a number of fires going the time I had to quit logging. They had considerable of this car wire that is a little thicker than one eighth of an inch and can come in mighty handy for a beaver trapper. It was rolled up about fifty feet in length. I had used some of this wire before to hang my grub down another rock wall on my first trip here. I made it down here by ten in the morning, very good time but I did start early. I could just as well fix a little something to eat and then get going again. I decided to take half across the rapids on the cedar tree, that was all I could possibly take and then up that mountain-like steep hill I described before. At that time I could easily see the layout as I had told it, climb down on those limbs and from there crawling on hands and knees hanging on anything you could reach in order to make it up. I was very glad when I reached the top but I had to go back once more to get the other half of my pack. My mind was made up that when I got them both here I would repack and make one pack out of it from here on. It would be slower walking but I didn't care. There is considerable excitement aroused, even though I was very good on balance, when walking on this cedar tree over this waterfall, something one should have a movie of. Here in about a half hour's time of struggle I had all the things on the top of this hill. Repacking everything that was there made one good load. I left the snowshoes over on the other side hanging on wire down a rock wall a way back in the woods. They could be hanging there for years as it would be a miracle if anyone could find them. The bear could not get them. They break up anything including a canoe. The safest way to leave it is right side up, if it is upside down they surely tear it up. The best way is to make a rack out of poles seven feet high with cross pieces so the canoe can be laid upside down so the bear can walk underneath and look and then he is satisfied.

It was eleven thirty on my dollar watch - I certainly was getting my money's worth out of that watch. I had to get down on my hands and knees to get up with my full pack now although, it didn't weigh much less than when I first started out. It was that I had gotten much weaker. The sun was out and the sweat was flowing freely. I kept going south resting now and then. By four o'clock, the sun was up a good distance in the west, I came out on a high rock cliff. Looking down I saw a large beaver pond between a long gully and recognized the place at once as I had been there before. Overcome with happiness I knelt down on the top here and this was the second time I prayed, no doubt thanking the Lord for letting me find this place and seeing this part of the country again. I felt then that I had really made it. In order to get on the other side I had to go west around this part and further up there was a small body of water clear up to the end. I cut a large spruce tree to get on the other side. It was a good sized job to do this and I would have been further ahead if I had gone up to the end and walked around. I realized my mistake but ever so often a man will do a foolish thing on a trap line. I knew exactly how to go from here to get to the tent I had against the rock wall last fall. I should have been there five days earlier. There were more bear out now and I only hoped that they had not found the place and torn it up. If all goes well I should make it there by tomorrow for dinner. To think now, that this would be my last night to make camp. I walked until almost dark and kept looking for a suitable place on some creek for the lakes here were further apart. Down here the whole layout of the country was different than further north. What had happened when I was lost a total of seven days was that I was walking southwest, the right direction, but five miles too far north. After I got here then it was easy for me to figure this out. I found a very friendly wild-looking place by a small stream where the water was going down rapidly over the rocks. Two feet above the water level was a solid base rock triangle corner and then a wall straight up twenty feet. I made a pole frame in no time to fit the purpose. This was good protection, the snow was all gone in open places, and all I had to watch out for was forest fires. I gathered wood to get a fire going for by now I was hungry. I thought I would cook up some rice and prunes, something different. I was never worried about food now for there would be mushrooms, beaver, suckers, and I would try and snare a deer with the car wire I had and I knew that if I placed it in the right place it would work. I know a trapper, one year, shot a small moose out this way. I did not want to carry the 25-20 with me for it was too much of a job I thought. Up to now I had not become a modern trapper and was learning every day the hard way. A constant harmony of freedom is in existence at all times, giving strength silently, defending and giving ability of power, stimulating a form so that at times everything that surrounds you becomes a small world all your own. There is understanding joining hand in hand with nature here, the fire burning so close to the small stream that the reflection in connection with this babbling water falling down on the rocks portrays a picture of sound and color. The rapid succession of this sound can become a personal matter talking freely, confusing the stillness of the night, thoughts of consultation, a state of rest stimulating the conscience. In moments like this one is aware of the facts existing in the form of activity corresponding in a realm of nature. I have now spent thirty years in the woods and get carried away when trying to explain my feelings as many of these incidents occurred. The murmuring rippling sounds of this stream did put me to sleep. When morning came I heard the same sounds now intermingled with songs from the birds. Certainly I could regard this day a special day. This was also the tenth day from the time my farm lad friend brought me up the road forty-five miles at midnight and let me off there to come out here. He would never dream that it would take me so long to get out here. The main thing was that I made it. For breakfast I had leftovers from last night. I packed up all my belongings and traveled the best way I thought for good walking. This is important when carrying a load even if the distance, at times, is further. I was encouraged knowing that I would get there soon recognizing most of this woods where I had traveled before. About eleven o'clock I

A BEAVER SKIN

125

approached the ravine and from here it was a quarter mile to where the tent was located. Hidden some from the heavy timber stand one had to get within two hundred feet before it could be seen. When I came around this point I was anxiously looking ahead - yes, I could see the tent. I was a happy person to know that the bear had not torn it up. Now my pack came off as I would not have to lug it for a while. I ate some dried fruit and made some tea as I did not want to take time to cook as I was anxious to set out a few traps. I took eight traps and went up the river. This time of the year beaver are on the move. On some dams where the ice is out is the most easy place to make a set. Some of the smaller ponds had open water but only in spots. It is entirely different trapping in the spring in open water as one can catch more beaver in two weeks in open water than in comparison with trapping all fall and winter. The water opens up around the beaver houses first due to the activity of their constantly swimming around under the ice before the lake opens up. Many of the houses are out in the middle of the pond, but one does not set traps on a house, first because there is too much disturbance and secondly there are many other good locations. On the first upper main dam were some of the smartest beaver I ever dealt with. There was the cutest little creek coming down a small valley going by in all styles of winding one hundred feet from my camp. A beaver can make a good sized lake out of a little stream where very little water is flowing. This I found out. I had cut a narrow trench in the dam to entice the beaver to fix it up again having a trap set there all hidden in the mud. They don't want to lose any water and are alway watching out for the dam. Here is what happened. When the trench was open it was easy for me to dip water out a half mile down from where I camped. However, as soon as the beaver closed this trench, which he did every night, it was hard for me to get water for cooking. I had to dig a hole in the creek bottom for more depth in order to have water. All water was boiled, I was very careful in that respect, also the same with any kind of wild meat. Early in the morning, going down for water, I could tell that the trench was closed again. Every time with expectation I would look at the trap to see if I had a beaver. It never worked that way and I don't know what that beaver knew about a trap but, he would shove sticks ahead snapping the trap or he would bury it. This went on for two weeks and I knew then that it was the large female beaver that was doing this. Also, from observation, I could see that the year old was not allowed near the dam - the mother was guarding them away from the trap. Being stubborn I made up my mind that I was going to catch them. I set the trap again and I thought I was fixing it better every time but I was thinking right along that I was wasting this trap and should set it somewhere else. So, this is what happened. I did set one further up near the swamp and caught a small one there. I took the trap off this main dam, here was a nice looking structure ten feet high and eighty feet long reaching across from one bank of the gully to the other. Two hundred feet down was another dam holding about five feet of water and another dam farther down, each dam supporting the other. They have to have considerable depth in their living quarters so they can survive the winter. They describe the beaver as a famed architect and builder. They lay up a large food supply for the winter dragging felled logs to their burrows then gnawing away the bark. It didn't take me long to get a trapline established going out ten miles in different directions from my camp. I made another small camp on the north end of the line underneath a very large spruce where the limbs on the bottom had partly grown into the ground. In all my days I had never seen such a tree with so many limbs. I had to fight my way in to the trunk cutting two feet off of the limbs going in there so as to get to where I could cut them off at the trunk. One thing I have to say is under this tree without any covering it could rain hard a full day shedding water sufficiently so one would not get wet. However, having this extra waterproofed sheeting stretched over this on top was extra protection. When night comes a trapper looks forward to this shelter as he knows it is his home. I did not know then that I could not call myself a good trapper, but I thought I was. I often went through so much unusual commotion with an impulse of urging action and there was no need for it. The bear alone was a problem and he alone would keep me on my guard all along the beaten trails that he now helped establish for as soon as I started to skin a beaver they came from all directions and followed me around day and night. One truly gets to understand them as I had to in order to live with them. They were not shy and often very bold. One large brown cinnamon bear came up behind me while skinning a beaver, I never heard him coming and he was whining in a very low tone. When I first heard him I couldn't figure out what it was making this kind of noise. I looked around and here he stood straight up, the largest cinnamon bear I had ever seen. He never moved and was not afraid. Thinking he was a little too close to me for comfort I opened my packsack, took out a tin plate that I used to eat out of and rattled it against the blade of an ax. It took a lot of noise making before he started running but he only ran seventy feet behind a large rock. All I could see of him was his head and he was looking straight at me. He was waiting for the beaver carcass for this would make a feast for him. I cut off the choice hind quarter and on a young beaver this was the only part the bear did not get. I would say that my consumption of beaver meat averaged a pound and a half a day; also, the average catch ran close to three beaver a day. I developed enough chores to keep me on my toes and often it became a struggle especially when the weather got bad. One thing important was to watch out for rain as the hides, at this time of the year, were dried on large white pine trees stretched partly oval shaped. It pays to keep on rearranging the skin in order to get the right shape and size. They stay that way after they dry and it takes two to three days depending upon the weather when drying them out in the woods.

Then the time came when the bear was not satisfied with the beaver meat I fed them or rather what he took and I discovered one day that they had pulled two hides off from a tree. I used eight penny nails, two inches apart, sufficient to hold as the skin dries and has a tendency to pull. Well, this bear came along and ripped this off without any effort. The small skin I found ripped straight through the middle. This alarmed me and I wondered what I could do. They don't eat the skins, only carry them a short distance and them let them lay. So I got an idea. I would nail a beaver

READY FOR THE TRAPLINES

carcass straight above the skin. I had a beaver to skin so I thought I would watch and see what would happen. Yes, in a short time a good sized bear, more black in color, came walking very slowly up to where the skins were nailed. Only one of the larger skins had the carcass hanging above it. When he got near he stood straight up, took the carcass, placed it under his right front foot and walking in an upright position sneaked along very slowly constantly looking in my direction. He kept on going that way until he disappeared in the woods. I knew then that if they find something not laying on the ground they feel they are stealing it and will often go

128

for miles before eating it or storing it away. Otherwise, if they are hungry and find it on the ground, they will eat it right there. I realized that the skins were valuable and often conditions were such that I could not hang a carcass at the right time to protect the skins. On my rounds across country I found a lake, not large, about forty acres, in size. I could not help but admire the scenery here and every time I came by I would stop and look for just a few minutes. Half way around, bordering a spruce swamp, there was a solid formation of spruce trees where the limbs would hang over and in the water. On a still bright day the reflection of these trees in the water, mixed with a blue skyline would have been a picture for an artist to capture. Around the northwest side on a hill were two large white pine trees. Many of these stand a hundred years and are still sound. From these I can hew planks and when nailed side by side this would make a 3 x 6 square like a door. This I did for nailing on beaver skins for drying. It was large enough to place four skins on each side. I had brought along a clothesline and a pulley. I found one of these large pine trees standing out in an open area, it had limbs twenty feet long. It was easy to climb. On one of the most suitable limbs I hung the pulley way out with wire. Any interference from the limbs below was cut off. Hanging this homemade works of wood in the center I dried all the skins here. It was a sight, pulling eight feet off the ground, hanging way out there on that limb. I found that the skins really dried fast for the wind kept the thing in motion constantly turning back and forth. It took several hours to make these planks out of this tall stump with an ax but it paid in many ways. Most important, it relieved the worry of the bear. There were so many things regarding the pesty bear that one had to contend with. All food had to be hung down a rock wall every day or on wire between trees fifteen to twenty feet apart stretched ten feet up. The packsack was put on a strong wire hook and placed on the wire; then with a crotch pole this would be slid out toward the center of the wire hanging away from trees and free out in the open. One could make no mistake here for you could not forget the details. Later on I had a very sad experience concerning this project and it almost cost me fifty beaver skins just because of a small oversight.

I had been here a week and had fifteen beaver which I thought was a good start. I knew that my food would hold out for some time the way I managed. There was hardly a time when I would be out of beaver stew. Having three or four items cooked in with it gave it a variety. I had boullion cubes, put them in and this helped change the flavor. The bear are now going up and down my path day and night tramping a trail so I never had to be in doubt if I was on the trail or not. Several time I had put green hides, freshly skinned in a small rock cliff laying a fair sized stone on top as I often did not want to carry them any farther than I had to and I would pick them up on the way back. After I had picked them up the bear naturally smelled the place where they were laying. Not one time would this bear go byhere without going there to take a look. There were times when I did not have time to skin all the beaver. They are heavy and I never liked to carry them around and there was no use to sink them in the water as the bear would find them. So, taking a small sapling ten to fifteen feet tall, strong enough when bent over, I would crawl up two-thirds of the way then start bending to manage to get the tip near the ground having the beaver skin all ready to fasten on, and then let it go up. This is the safest way and I never lost one. One day I was on the edge of a lake, it was twelve feet down on the shore. The lakes are very clear and you can see a considerable distance. Tying a fair sized rock to a beaver carcass, down to the bottom it went. The next time I was curious to learn what had happened. Yes, it was gone, never dreaming that a bear had found it way down there. There was a beaver colony near by - I thought that the beaver went away with their own dead. Walking around, up a steep hill going almost straight up twenty feet back here covered on one side with hazelnut brush, I saw what appeared to be a string. Looking closer up on the hazelnut brush I saw that this ten foot long so called string was the dried up inside from the beaver entrails hanging there. Every day something happened that I never expected. I was keeping track of the days, it was the first of May and I had fifty-two beaver and two otter. This was my first spring trapping out here all alone. There was no place I could get lost going up and down here, ten to fifteen miles of creeks, one-fairsized river, lakes and beaver ponds around here. One had to follow certain places for the best way to go ahead. The most difficult part of the matter was, when going in, to get back to my logging camp up where the road went to town and civilization. I looked at a small map I had and memorized a picture from that knowing where I had to start out going far south and then north. This is something a trapper never thinks about - how to get out - not while one is trapping and catching beaver and know that the fur is prime and in good shape. Also, in the meantime, I got the idea that I wanted to get one hundred beaver and then I would quit. This was new and yet it was a good idea for a man to have a goal or a challenge to meet. I came back earlier than usual from the northwest to what I could call my home base, the camp I made against that impressive rock wall last fall. I came up along the ridge side of the beaver pond, the place where, up to this time, I could not catch the larger beaver of this colony, the one that for two weeks kept plugging my trap and never got caught. I was walking along very unconcerned and I thought I heard a voice but I could not tell or comprehend where it came from. I ran down to the dam looking in the small lower pond where the water was open half of the area, one inch of ice covered the rest. In this open water I saw a small ripple. Then I knew it was a beaver - he had heard me coming before I got there. They are very alert. He did not make a lot of noise going down into the water - perhaps he thought he would fool me or he may have thought it was a bear. He was lucky it wasn't a bear as he would have gotten him. Here in the lower pond he was in danger. I had tried so hard to catch this one particular beaver, the one I thought was the smart one, and now I thought I would get him for sure First I set two traps on the path which was worn very smooth up the big dam ten feet up. This is the way he came down from the big pond. Then I cut a large trench in the lower dam to drain it. This would scare him and he would go up this slide and here is where I would catch him. I waited about ten minutes and could see his head sticking out near this beaver slide. Yes, he was going up and was not in a hurry, I had the traps standing fifteen feet away and I heard one trap snap. I ran over there, he started down, had five feet of chain and the rest extension was wire. I grabbed on the end and started to pull. By now this large beaver was standing straight up. In the meantime I was looking for a piece of wood to hit him with. While this was going on he kept raising back, pulling very had and suddenly he got loose and went straight back down to the lower pond. I was dumbfounded, just could not figure out what happened. The only thing I could think of was that he was only caught by his little toe and even then a strong No. 4 trap like that should hold. There was no evidence of hair or his toe in this trap. Well, he was still, what I figured, cornered in this lower pond. So I reset the traps placing them on this slide in his path and surely this will catch him. Also, I would have a club ready this time so I could not miss him. Away on the other side I saw him coming up - no, I didn't want him to come up there. I walked around to the other side and tried to steer him back to the center of the dam. How fast he went back, up he came past the traps, one snapped. I never caught him. At the very top of the dam he stood straight up and turned his head looking straight at me. Can't say what I was thinking right then - it was all so funny. Then he took a dive down and I never saw him again. If the bear did not get him I would say that was the only beaver I could not catch and he surely must have died of old age. After all the excitement I had another surprise when I got back to the camp. What I cherished the most, here the bear had found - the waterproof sheeting was all torn down; he tried to get at the stew I had cooked in the gallon pail. Where he got his paw inside the pail on top, the claws went straight through the tin. I was so disgusted and being hungry I sat down on the mess just the way the bear left it, and ate the rest of the stew cold. This was the first time this happened so I learned that the sheeting cover for the teepee had to be removed every morning, rolled up and hung up with the food. I would have to do the same thing now at the other shelter camp I had about ten miles north of here at the spruce tree. As long as it was wood they would not molest it. I made a fire as it was getting dark and piecing chunks of the sheeting together I made a cover around the poles the best I could so it would shed water in case it would rain. Then I had to do some cooking and bake bannock. There is no discouragement as great as recognizing that this becomes a lone battle of survival. One finds the reaction in the struggle compensating for many things where all is free out here in the wide open spaces, on the very top of the highest sea level where now seasonal movements are in action, the ice going out, bear coming out of hibernation, suckers running, birds returning, trees starting to get green and many other things concerning nature. Here I lived the way I thought. The bear was a big influence as I could see and feel the consequences on account of their often having helped to change my mind in doing things to save myself from disaster. There never was a time when I could get to bed early. Preparation of food for the next day was always in order. Most of the time there was at least one beaver to skin. By now this was tiresome and I was glad to get some rest. Sometimes I would dream of the bear but I was always anxiously waiting for another day. It was a fact that I was constantly fighting time diligently applying myself to every movement, the setting of traps, skinning beaver, cutting wood and the cooking which are the main chores. I often had to look for new beaver locations and the bear followed me right up. It was the same as though they were living with me. They knew where their food was coming from, they did not harm me and I certainly was a good provider for them. This morning I had a job to do. I would hide fifty beaver skins in a dense spruce swamp, for one is afraid that something could happen. Not that there is anyone around watching you and stealing your fur, however human nature is suspicious and so I had to hide them. I had my homemande sleeping bag and that was waterproof. So, I wrapped them tightly in two rolls so they would fit the best. All the beaver castors are saved also. They could be sold by the pound and brought a good price. Some I used for making a scent and filled up a small bottle for my use. This was very effective when making a set. Took some of the car wire I needed to hang up the skins. I had a place spotted, the best place I could find for this purpose. I also found a ladder made out of spruce poles, it looked old yet it was strong. In this same place were large square pieces of birch bark, the kind Indians use for making a canoe, and a number of hoops, which had also been used for stretching skins. These were also made from spruce wood. Yes, no doubt Indians had been trapping here at one time as evidence showed that. Indians usually worked together, I never heard of only one this far out. Using two **trees fifteen feet apart I took the ladder and went up fourteen feet wrapping the wire around the tree then moving over to the other tree, I did the same there, using** double wire and fastening it so it would stay.   Now I had to cut two small trees and wire them five feet down from the above one on each side to serve as a platform. The skins were heavy and there would have been no other way to get them up there to hang in the center of the wire between the two trees. Then the platform was removed so now they were way up there. I would not bother these until the day I left

- I was glad to have this job out of the way. If I only had a few dry skins I would lay on them at night. I could also take care of them in this way. I had a duffle bag. I would place as many as I could in there and then hang it over a rock wall. I never missed a day on the trapline. If something happened in between I would travel until it started to get dark. There was always something that had an influence on you. It seems that when one is bound up here with nature,thought reactions are present in many forms. Extending my trapline today I found a mile long narrow lake where three small streams flowed out at different points, each one going in a different direction. This was something new for me to see knowing that this is the very place where the watershed dividing this region must be located. Most of the highlands grow poplar, the number one food for beaver, and regardless how hard it is on a stream to build a dam the beaver will do it as long as the poplar trees are there. I found out that not far down each one of these streams had a beaver colony. I could see then that this was why this lake was backed up so far and what had made it such a long body of water. In the beginning this water must have come from springs. Of all the camping I did up here on this high elevation, often sleeping on the ground, never at any time did I catch a cold. To get sick out here would be bad. I had six traps with me when I came down here, found three good dams so I placed two traps on each dam. Coming back to another location I had a trap on a dam also in a good location. When I got there it was gone, pole, trap and all and then I knew that there was beaver in this trap. What happened is when the beaver got caught the sets are made so when they go down they can never come up as there is at least a five pound rock tied to the trap. This I explained once before, the way I did in Wisconsin. The same methods are used here. The beaver while drowning will make a disturbance on the surface. It happened that a bear was around at that time. The water was deep there and he just plunged in and took beaver trap and all. I walked around looking to see what direction he went but I could find nothing. I hated to lose the trap. This was the only time I lost a trap and a beaver under the above circumstances. Near my small camp up north here I caught two beaver. It was late so I decided to carry them over there to skin them by the firelight as it was getting late and would soon be dark. Not far from here was a lake and there were high hills all around. There were many bodies of water but I never had the time to explore to see what might have been on the other side or on the end. Very seldom did I trap on a lake as the beaver have more room for roaming around and often it means more walking. Late evening the loons were calling loud mournful sounds, the only voice I heard that seemed to be near a human's call. They are great for diving and here they have a paradise roaming around establishing homes in places where they can watch their enemies. I got here to this familiar place that was my small but important camp. Every other day I came here unless some unforeseen circumstances arose. This I found to be true and one cannot ignore or deny it. I ran out of wood and had to get a good supply as I had two beaver to skin. By the time I had all my work done it got late. I could hear the brush cracking and it was, of course, the bear smelling the beaver I had just finished skinning. By now I was so tired I couldn't keep my eyes open. I would lay on the hides and the carcass I left lay. No matter where I could try to put them, in time the bear will get them. The next morning I found the carcasses gone. Looking closely I noticed a large bear track on one side of me where I was lying, then one on the other side. The only thing I could figure out is that they must have been standing straddle over me to get the tracks in that position. They never touched me and I was glad as I thought right then that the Lord did not make the bear smart enough so he would attack me. There are no grizzly bear here, they have a different reputation. Looking further, about fifty feet away on a knoll I found a few bones from the beaver and knew then that he had eaten them right here. And, I never heard a thing as I was so dead tired that it was impossible to be awakened. In the silence and darkness the bears were rude and persistent companions. It was as if my mind were a motion picture screen selecting a picture in a realm of imagination. One can find confirmation of your faith that there must be a purpose for man to live and have life. No doubt it should be orderly and harmonious to take charge of my thoughts so I could control them. Silently those were things in existence that I could feel and were difficult to ignore. I found that I had to change myself to fit the environment. Many of these experiences were new, if I could emerge to know myself that I could be free instead of a slave, not to be on the gloomy side in the midst of a wilderness paradise. I felt that all things were extremely complicated and the environment often brought me comfort and eased my problems for here I had no guide and was making my way deeper in the woods, scouting for new beaver locations. The many surroundings become part of your life. One is amazed at the skill these beavers use to perform their work. I saw such perfection in many places, admiring the dams more so than the houses. Of course, there are never two alike; each location calls for a different size dam in length, width and height to fit the need. At all times it must back up a body of water that is deep enough for survival for the winter. I recall one dam that was twelve feet high, one hundred feet long, between two high rock walls that were straight up. The size of the logs were four to six inches and ten up to fourteen feet in length perched all the way across to the back of the dam, interwoven and leaning at such an angle so as to stay in position and give strength to the dam. From observation one could see going up on each side of the pond where the rock formation bordering a distance of five hundred feet, that this material had to be floated down here. Often I thought of making a movie just from the life of beaver - first take all the houses, the many sizes and shapes and then the same with the dams, the cutting of the trees, the building of their dams and houses and channels, the locations, terrains related and viewed to its fitness for this special purpose.

Another week had passed and there was never a day that my catch was less than one up to five, averaging close to three beaver a day. This one morning up here north at the small camp it was like most mornings. An hour before sunrise one bird (I never knew what kinds of birds they were) started singing often five to ten minutes all alone; then another one would join in and soon there would be many sounding melodies having a program all their own. It was delightful music, so effective it gave the impression of hope that I sincerely appreciated. This was one of those days when the sun came up fire red at first glance changing very fast to become more bright. It was clear, very still, when I was warming up some stew. Far off I could hear the voice of someone talking, it sounded clear as a bell. No, that could not be, and before thinking I grabbed the gallon pail which was half full of stew and started running. One does not want to think of a game warden but these things flash in your mind, it came so suddenly that I was scared. I ran some two

**Beaver House and
Winter Food Supply**

hundred feet over in a very deep gully behind several rock walls. It was all so foolish - must have been a reaction of impulse. When I got over there I was trying to get hold of myself - what was I doing anyway. I hurried back with the stew in my hands and when I got back I tried to strain my ears and listen and listen. I could hear nothing, no human voice, however, my imagination was becoming more of a reality and like a picture I could see two men walking on a portage. There must be a route over there probably a mile away. To offset this, why was there no way I could get in here. The ice is not out in some places. Then the next thing I thought, could it be a certain Indian of French extraction? I had heard of him as being a bad character stealing fur from the trappers. How fast I was forming these opinions and piecing them together. Oh, yes, he could be around and find my fur. What I was thinking

135

about was the fifty skins I had cached away down in that spruce swamp. I had no time to lose; forget about your traps for today and get going to see if the skins are OK. I had about eight miles to go cutting across country. Yes, by now I knew all the short cuts. I was tramping along keeping an even gait. Before I left, like all other times, I had hung everything up so the bear would not get at it. I had four places where supplies and furs could be hung. One of the places had food stored away as a special precaution should something out of the ordinary happen or to be able to fall back on. It was getting late afternoon when I approached the edge of this swamp. In the meantime it had started to cloud up the past few hours, it had started sprinkling and in here under the thick stand of trees it was considerably darker. When I did get there I got one of my biggest surprises I had up to now. The bundle of fifty skins I had wrapped in the waterproofed heavy canvas, gauge 12, had been torn down. It was a sight, part still hanging, the bottom torn out shredded into many shreds some long and some short. The skins were scattered within a one hundred foot area. I picked them up as fast as I could for now it was raining more heavily. Some did get wet and this could ruin them, I thought, for I had no experience in this. I got underneath a large spruce, they always hold water for some time with all the heavy limbs, so I would not get wet any more than I could help. I started to count the skins, there were four missing and looking around here and there I found them but they were all wet. As soon as I came I knew what had happened. I had left a small balsam tree five inches around at the base, smaller farther up the way the bear was climbing up to that point and then he had to jump four feet over to reach this well-wrapped, securely tied bundle of fur. The tree was standing four feet away in line with the bundle. First the tree was small and it was this distance away. Having had no experience like this before I thought it was safe. This bear thinking that it was only one climbed this tree so often there were no limbs or bark left on it, it was as smooth as glass. When he got part way over he had to jump as he couldn't reach it and with his own weight up in midair no doubt he came down fast and managed to grab part of the bundle toward the bottom. He could have climbed it fifty times, I do not know, but he did make a mess out of it. The most fortunate thing that could have happened was that this morning I thought I heard somebody talking and that was the only reason that brought me down here. The voice I thought I heard was so real and I can hear it very plain in my imagination to this day. However, it has been a mystery why I was guided down here as I had not planned on coming this way for another two weeks and would then stop and pick up the fur on my way home. By that time we would have had several days of rain and the skins would, no doubt, be partly spoiled. The ones that did get wet I dried out at night as I had a good fire going. Later I found that some got too hot and turned brittle in spots. This became a rather rough night for me. It kept raining. I made a shelter under one of the heavy limbed large spruce trees. I kept piling limbs for more protection to shed water. My clothes were partly wet and I had nothing with me so I could change. Sitting back near the trunk of the tree doing everything to keep the skins dry, I dozed off several times in a sitting position. When it got daylight I went back to the swamp. I got the platform in position, the one I had before, to get down the remains of what the bear had left of that canvas to see if I could salvage any of it. It was better than I thought it would be and I managed to use it over again. I placed the hides in good position after I had them rolled up tight. This is done like rolling up a calendar, one at a time, to get the whole unit as small as possible. I hung them up again, then removed the platform and chopped down the balsam tree as it was all on account of this little balsam that this happened. Having so little sleep last night and being short on food, I was not feeling my best. I took the four skins that were wet with me and I headed for the camp, the one by the rock wall. This misfortune I had here with the bear getting into those hides cost me a day and a half in time. I was hungry when I got back to

Balanced by Nature

the shelter and also where most of the food was. It is a continuous struggle to be able to take care of even what was considered a short trapline. The bear is responsible for one third of all the extra work. I felt better after eating something but decided not to go too far so I would get back by night. By now I had seventy-four beaver and three otter. With the time I had left I figured there should be no trouble to get one hundred as I had planned. After that I wanted to come in. I managed to get one beaver today and only had time to look at five traps.

I was getting tired of beaver meat and had to take time off tomorrow to see if the suckers (fish) were running on a certain creek - it was something different to look forward to. If there was any time left coming in before dark it would be used for cutting wood. I had camped here last fall when it was zero weather at all times and for that reason I had cut many trees near by. Now I had been here several weeks and it meant that from time to time I had to go further now to carry wood. I would try to skin the beaver early and have the liver for supper. I would parboil it, then fry it nice and brown on each side and cook some rice so I could go to sleep earlier. Last night had been the most difficult one since I got here. One soon forgets the failures and keeps on toiling, making adjustments essential in achieving the goal I started out to do. One gets so concerned in making a success, what I spoke of and thought of in those days, as getting back on my feet in a hurry. I figured that I went bankrupt last year logging.

This camp here was the best I ever had for when a fire was made, considerable heat reflected from the Hewed-in rock walls and distributed the heat very evenly. I was glad also to get my clothes changed as for twenty-four hours they had been partly wet, not that any change would be clean, for now my long underwear was very black. That didn't matter as long as it was dry and so were the socks and the extra pair of old woolen pants. There is so much contentment in sleeping on a thick carpet of boughs under such circumstances. There were times at night when one discovered that the surroundings were warm and peaceful, my mind would drift upon tides of adventure and slowly the nights passed. Constantly I discovered how simple life can really become finding other assets within myself so I could determine by degrees wherein one can dwell in a universal spirit of good. There came these moments when I tried to find myself in this struggle of life and trying to express my feelings in part oftentimes could not find an answer. I was confident that whatever my unforeseen circumstances may be that somehow I will make it. It was surprising that I could get so much protection and comfort out of so little, waterproofed sheeting stretched over wooden poles, fire against a rock wall, two blankets and balsam boughs to sleep on. I had to get up early and start some cooking to last one day on the trapline. One reason I had to get going was walking across a river bottom stood a large moose cow and they can be very stubborn so I walked out of the river bottom up on high land to get around as I did not trust the moose cow. They belong to the deer family. I found several moose antlers here in my travels and carried them out to a certain point and saved them - I never got back to pick them up. An exceptionally large moose may measure over seven feet at the shoulder. The biggest horns ever recorded, I heard, were seventy-eight inches in spread. The framework going around in a circle by now had gotten longer and wider on my trapline. There were barriers of rough and rocky country so I decided it would be better if I moved my small camp further southwest. There are many suitable spots - I was looking for one most sheltered near some water. It is never a problem to get wood. On my way I found a place where the suckers were running and I got six of them, two to three pound size. This is also the place where the bear like to hang out; they love fish and are very clever catching them at points where the water is partly shallow. They are not bad eating in early spring as long as the water stays cold. Then their flesh is firm. However, when the water is warm the flesh gets soft and then nobody likes to eat them. I filet them, salt them and fry them - what a treat, a change of food for a trapper. Often you hear crows hollering but never have I heard so much noise as now - it sounded like five hundred of them. Being inquisitive I thought I would go down a fourth of a mile to see what was going on. A bear must have cached away a beaver carcass and there must have been a hundred crows fighting for it. When I got near they were diving down and flying all around me. Never in my life have I seen so many desperate crows. Coming over to one of the sets I had on a small dam I had one of the largest beaver I have ever seen. He had gone down into the water here and tangled up underneath among some wood. It took me an hour to get him out. I cut a long pole leaving a crotch on the end and I reached down and twisting it around and around fished to get the chain of the trap. I could see that this beaver put up a terrible battle before he drowned. You could almost feel sorry for him but you quickly cast away such thoughts as they are never pleasant and this trapping had become a desperate subject, an impulse of mixed emotions. So the time came around, I was keeping track of the time, and it was the 16th of May - my birthday. I had ninety-four beaver and three otter and I was, in one respect, a happy person. It was a beautiful day, about ten in the morning, I was walking up on a high ridge. Down below was a beaver pond. A light wind was blowing and the sun was shining brightly. I stopped and looked up at the sky; the trees had started to bud and all looked so fresh. This all made an impression on me revealing that everything was so much alive. I said to myself, this should be a day to remember for it happened on my birthday out here where I was trapping beaver. I followed the hill down and there was a wide old beaver dam. The grass started to grow so I thought now it is time for me to get out. I noticed the black flies, they are like "no-see-ums",were coming more each day. This reminds me of the story about the Indian and the white man. Going over on a portage the Indian was the guide and was taking the white man fishing. These small flies were nipping the white man so he kept on complaining to the Indian about those flies asking him what they were. He said, "me so-see-um" and from that day this is what they were called. I was desperate in setting the figure of one hundred beaver skins and then I would quit - this plan was never changed. Three days more, had exactly one hundred beaver and the three otter. One day was needed to make preparations for the trip out. I had to cut enough beaver meat, cut to size, to last for six to eight days. I won't know how long it will take to get out. I had a small amount of flour left, a little lard and a few other things in the line of food. I would need my two blankets, frying pan, gallon pail and a piece of the bed sheeting. When I got all packed it was a heavy load, eighty-five pounds or more. I had a head rig strap going around the bottom of the packsack and up around and over my forehead. This part is padded and becomes a big help on a sixty-five mile trip the way I had to go south a ways and then mostly north. The other things were hidden and a few things that the bear would tear up were hung down over a rock wall.I couldn't help think of the bear. After I fed them so many beaver they certainly would miss me and would be looking for me. With much satisfaction over my accomplishments I started out early the next day going the way that would bring me to places where bodies of water, rivers, and beaver ponds could be crossed. It was a heavy load. No doubt I was worried as it was a long way out. I had never traveled that route before and it was mostly a matter of natural instinct to find the way to go. The sun would always give me direction even on a cloudy day by using the knife blade setting it on a finger nail to find the correct shadow line.To think about the fact that I had a hundred beaver skins gave me the foundation to find a union of thought that would fit the environment and at the same time kept me happy. Whenever I had a chance I looked ahead to see where walking would be best. This becomes very important as the load gets more burdensome and heavy. Every half mile or so I had to get a little rest and when noon came to take twenty or thirty minutes for lunch has a meaning all its own. Now this journey will have to be all overland as there is no more ice to walk on. I was walking along on a side hill; below there was a creek winding through going south to Lake Superior. I noticed a lot of hair and at first I thought it might have come from a deer. My curiosity made me take off my packsack and follow this heavy trail of hair. Going down a short distance into an elder swamp there it lay, a fair sized moose eaten up, the skeleton showing in perfect form and so did the jaws with all the teeth on it. I knew then that the wolves had killed it for when the snow was deep this would be a bad place for a moose to get away and they corralled this big animal right down in here. By now it was getting dark and I was looking for a place to stay. Walking every day, miles and miles, since I came out here, made me strong on my legs. The load I had now was a big job and the night was welcome for rest. I came down closer to the creek and here was a point (highland) bordering along here. This place was just as good as any for camping, I thought. I never made any shelter of the small covering I had, not unless it looked like rain. To get a fire going is the first and also a pleasant thing. This forms a combination linking together man with earthly treasures, for it

140

has on such occasions meanings that can give one sustaining strength. Soon it will be very dark and I can see by this fire to cook, bake, and keep warm, acting as a role it has to play, changing thoughts, contemplating such relations understood in a sense of freedom. In this, in turn, a weary, tired, lonely trapper can find new hope and strength for another day. Another gift of nature that I can hear now while going to sleep are the frogs, croaking and grumbling often in a mournful sound, no doubt a language all their own. There is a good place for them down here in the river bottom swampland. Under this condition when I open my eyes early I am always glad when the stars are out. One can see how nature makes adjustments to balance life so man can get rest and so to conquer another day. Starting out early there seems to be something special in the brisk of the morning. One cannot walk fast when carrying a heavy pack. Also, every step is watched as often parts of this region are very rugged, climbing, holding on obstructions, transferring over one part to another. By noon I got into more open flat country and came upon a river larger than I had seen at any time in this part of the country. Approaching it from an area of marsh it stretched out as far as I could see. The sad part was I could find no place to cross the river. Following it down a way, making a long bend it headed south. I made my way around in that direction not knowing then that I had already gone too far south. Had I gone north I would have offset considerable hardships for it was only a short distance down where the fires came through here last year burning over such a large section of this land. Never had I seen such desolate barren ground where all vegetation was gone, showing solid masses of stones of all description. Near a small lake I noticed where even a beaver house was partly burned. It had been built near shore. Farther beyond I ran into solid, twisted, partly burned trees. For a while I thought that I was not able to get through or around. Having my thoughts buried in what was confronting me all of a sudden a large mallard duck flew out, so unsuspected and so close to me, it surprised me. Here she had a nest of eggs and I just could not figure out how that could be and no water nearby. But perhaps she chose such a remote place knowing she would have protection from the many enemies they have. It was just past noon and I could not get myself to stop. Such a miserable place, I never dreamed that such would be in existance. I started to lay the blame on this and on that saying to myself that this should not have happened. After an hour of constant struggle (for the first time thinking) I decided this was God-forsaken country. A short time later I came to a fast flowing stream and here is where the fire had ended. Here the larger rock formations started to appear, in fact, one could walk along here on the bottom water rushing here within one foot down from this wide level rock formation. A good place to stop- it was time to get some food into my stomach; not that I was a tenderfoot but this last stretch got to be almost too much for me. I made a fire and warmed up the cooked beaver meat, which I brought along, in the frying pan. This pack had been the biggest and heaviest I had ever carried and to attempt to go that far with this load that was partly top heavy, on account of the large bundle of skins sticking up far above my head in back, was foolish. I could not close the flap of the packsack so I wrapped a piece of waterproofed sheeting over the whole bundle arranging the flap so as to hold the whole thing together making it one solid unit. Got ready to go again and I heard a pitiful hollering of a frog. Now, what is that? Fifty feet up here in a pool of water a snake swimming had gotten this frog and had it half swallowed, the head out. I couldn't help him and the way things looked it was life for life. Seeing green trees and vegetation and often moss under my feet was a welcome sight after coming through that burned area. I knew now that I had to cut back northwest to get over in line where further north I was supposed to come out on a large beaver dam. I would be able to cross the river there. This is the place the trappers had talked about where the warden sometimes waited for trappers to come out, a crossing point between north and south. So with that in mind this was something else that I could look forward to. Also, it was the only way I could get out from the area where I was trapping. One must circle around in a southerly direction and then north to miss the many lakes, canoe routes, and bodies of water in chain form. This much I knew and as I said before I had a mental picture of this whole area down here from a map I looked at before I left. It sounds foolish but I did not carry the map with me. I always had confidence that if I kept coming in that direction in time I would come out. This is one fact, to maintain confidence, frame of mind, so little doubt is established of being wrong. There are, however, times while traveling where I became skeptical looking constantly at strange scenery and land. A sensitive often pitiful feeling can become a climax denying the truth to be false. This I constantly had to fight within me especially when the going got rough. From all indications and from what I knew about this country I must be right continuing and depending upon my judgment. It is an unseparable condition where reaction of emotions make s soft whispering sounds in this silence of uncertainty. So the night always comes and with it comes an understanding that helps banish incidents that had happened through the day. I was constantly leaning on nature for wood and water creating a combination in giving me my needs, also including the balsam boughs to keep my body off the ground and make me more comfortable sleeping. When the packsack comes off, by now the shoulders are numb, this gives one instant relief and glad the day is over. When the nights get chilly one sleeps soundly for the first part of the night and after that very little. Often pondering the consequences this new day might bring, one quickly abandons such thoughts. There is, however, a lot of time to think. Surroundings of isolation can complicate things when at times there is so little to depend upon, endurance and stamina designating in time the unknown that lurks ahead where one finds something new every day. A trapper often craves adventure - I had asked for it and can say that often it was more than I had anticipated. My learning in that respect was very slow. Some people, no doubt, would say that I was a glutton for punishment. This brings the thought to me that all of us have different lives.

Well, I got all my pack together, I would raise up from kneeling position as that was the best way to come up with my load. If there was a chance where I could set this up on a rock or windfall the right height this was preferable. Farther north I was coming into large spruce swamps, level in one respect for walking, but often partly soft consisting often of a carpet of moss, therefore also wet, especially at this time of the year. It was the direction I had to go and had no time to speculate that I might be able to go around this swamp. With the pack I had it would have been impossible as that could have been several miles over each direction. One does get more cautious; my feet were getting wet, three to five inches of water at times. I got used to wet feet now being springtime but this was certainly no comparison to the eight days out of ten when trying to find my way in here to my traps and I was walking in water on top of the ice, and then the weather was cold. Now the weather was in my favor. The black flies had been nipping me right along and I tried to ignore them. Here at a corner of a swamp was a small part of high land, narrow ridge, partly hidden. The dense forest captivated the surroundings. I did not know that around the corner were some bear. The first notice I got was when all of a sudden there was a noise and commotion in front me. Here within ten feet stood a large mother bear, two small baby cubs and a yearling. First the two small ones climbed one of those long tall spruce, the kind that have few limbs and a tassel of green on top. Four feet over from the spruce stood a balsam - the yearling bear climbed this tree. This balsam was only half the height the spruce tree was, so when the yearling bear reached the height of the balsam he was not satisfied and jumped over onto the spruce.All three bear had gone up to the very top of that spruce just as far as they could possibly go. The result was it started bending way overmaking a long sweeping curve. It was a sight. As soon as I discovered, or rather ran into, the bear, being so close to the mother was dangerous. She never moved one inch looking straight at me and I was looking straight at her. All this happened in one minute. I never moved one step ahead; instead I immediately stepped backward and backward and was glad when I got further away from them. The reason the bear did not attack me was while the little ones were up in the tree, she knew they were safe and it was lucky for me for they will attack when the young are threatened.

This was my third day on the way in, never did get out of that swamp and stayed there all night. To make certain that I would not start walking in a circle (the best of woodsmen can get fooled and do this) I picked out a large spruce where the top could be seen above the skyline. This was done when looking straight north. When I got to that tree I would spot another one as far ahead as I could see. It is hard, at times, to find a decent place to make camp. A hole had to be made deep enough to get some water. That is not hard to do, you only have to wait until the mud stirred up settles itself. Water is all boiled for tea or other cooking and therefore will not harm you. I cut a bunch of small spruce saplings to build a place to lie down. One thing that is going to waste in this country is wood. In Wisconsin and Michigan, like any other place, you can go and shove over a dry or dead tree here and there - this is not so in Europe. One could not find such a tree anywhere except in Russia. These trees were, of course, a big help to me this night. Now it started to rain, not hard, but the main thing was that the fur was covered so it could not get wet. I always had what little food I had handy so I could get at it easily. A life saver also was that I had one small extra piece of that waterproofed material, part of the piece the bear had torn up on my back at the camp on the trapline. I was sitting here on some limbs eating the cold meat I had. It was raining much harder now and I could see the raindrops falling in the gallon pail where I was making tea. I had the cloth over my head and shoulders; good thing the fire was going strong so the rain could not put it out so fast. Being pitch dark the fire was needed so I could see. I didn't want to stumble around in the dark looking for more wood, this would have been hard to do, mostly because you would get wetter. The cloth I had over me was waterproof but the only way I could keep it on was by sitting still. I placed the boughs and saplings in a chair position one and half feet wide and two feet high against a tree that I used to lean on. There was nothing I could do except sit there against that tree, the cloth over me, holding it inside with my hands. I was so tired I kept dozing from time to time. Never stopped raining all night and it got cold toward morning - I was shivering and very miserable. The fire had long since gone out and the only thing that broke the silence of the night was the raindrops that were falling all around. Time went slowly waiting for morning to come and it was as though I was on the far end of the earth. If at any time I felt a sense of isolation it was here in this swamp. One at all times tends to bring mind and body together so a form of consolation can be had. Finally it started to get daylight and the first thing I did was look for wood to make a hot fire. For a half hour I kept warming myself trying to get so that when I moved around I could feel partly normal. I knew I had to get going as soon as possible. There was no doubt that I was slowing down and it appeared that my pack was getting heavier. What was taking place was I was getting weaker all the time. The position I was forced to take, trying to get some rest in a sitting position, was not comfortable and I could feel it all about me. It had stopped raining. I got packed up and started out, wondering how far I had to go to get on high land. I walked along slowly resting the pack every chance I had on objects the right height. After the rain the sunshine really brought out the black flies, they were swarming around my head by the thousands. Fighting them made them worse for they are highly temperamental. It would have been impossible to keep them off of me with my bare hands - lucky that I had a cloth hat. This will sound unreasonable but it was true that at every step I made, at the same time I would swing my arm hitting my face. There are several weeks in spring when these flies are ferocious. They have a wild cruel nature that excites them in moments into sudden anger and they become bloodthirsty. Not having an antiseptic with me was a big mistake on my part. Should one not have such protection, these midges or punkies, a North American Indian term, a name for this insect, can drive any man out of the woods this time of the year. So, more and more in general, conditions got worse. I was now getting slower in my pace, I could not deny this as much as I tried to avoid it. I finally did get out of the swamp and to make matters worse approaching here much of the rugged slopes were covered with rocks. It was hard to adapt myself to this type of terrain after walking almost a day through partly soft yet level swampland. This was the hottest day of the year so far and I was perspiring terribly. Down below where this slope land came out to a gradual level was a magnificent forest, trees standing silent as the desert. I could see that this part was surrounded by water and for that reason, no doubt, had not been touched by fire and had many years of life that was formed here. Now it started to thunder and lightning, yes, it was cracking nearby very loud and I decided I must get away from the tall trees as lightning does like to strike there. Up the slope, several hundred feet up, there were no trees but rock walls. On a twenty foot ledge there was a large crack four feet wide, a crevice, and one could easily crawl underneath for by now a heavy shower came up and I had to hustle to get in there. I got a little wet, I took off the pack and shoved it back and I crawled in there also. Here the black flies, tiny bugs, were so thick I couldn't stand it - in the meantime it quit raining and I came out of there in a hurry. I managed to get my packsack on again, the ledge was eight feet wide and then straight down twenty feet, a solid rock wall. I was standing there ready to go and all of a sudden everything started to turn black and I fainted, falling backwards. I didn't lay there long and got up again. I tried to figure out what happened and why. For all the years I had spent in the woods nothing like this ever happened. Should I have rolled three feet I would have fallen down this twenty foot ledge. This was a time I tried to think and from what had happened I was kind of dumbfounded momentarily. It was past noon now, I made a small fire mostly to get some tea and had some lunch. In a way everything seemed strange and I tried to reorganize my thinking - the fact I had fainted did bother me some. I urged myself to keep moving, leaning considerably on my spirits, freeing myself from bewildering thoughts, the remoteness of this region reframing a relation that cannot be dismissed. The difference in the lay of the land even required a difference here in my steps, linking closely together the freedom of expression. All afternoon I walked steadily but slowly, eighty-five pounds of weight now felt like a hundred fifty. Before dark I came to a river and recognized it. Other trappers that had traveled here before, Jeff and Jet, told me that the wardens often wait here for weeks. It was a happy feeling to get to this place and I felt proud that I found it. The reason I knew this was the river is it is the only one in this vicinity. Coming from the west going east, then south approaching it here from the south, I did not know how far down I was or where the starting point was. West of here was an outlet from a chain of lakes forming this river. I also knew that this lake up there, the way I had to go, was shallow around the edge or shore. Jeff had told me of two fellows who had walked in the water. It is only knee deep, at night around the shoreline while the wardens were camped three hundred feet down where a large log was used for a crossing by trappers. It was a fact that someone had cut it years ago for that purpose. Facts were that the beaver closer to civilization had practically all been trapped and that fellows like me had gone way out to remote places for trapping for there was little interference from the trappers. Last fall my first time out was with Jeff and Jet, if you remember. On this trip now in spring and all the other trips I have made afterwards, I never saw a human being with the exception of the young man I am going to take with me next spring trapping for a cook and also the shooting of beaver. Not to get ahead of my story, what I had to do now was follow up this river, it was now very late in the afternoon. By following the river I was keeping on high ground for easier walking, not unless I had to cross a swamp. I was relieved to know that I had some idea where I was. I would stop early for my stay for the night. It was two hours before sundown and I was anxiously waiting for a good place to stop. Yes, I found a place only I was afraid to make a fire as I did not know how far up it was to the log river crossing - I thought the wardens could be there. So, after getting rid of my packsack I took my ax and started up the river scouting, looking for a lake from where this river had its start flowing out, the point where it had its beginning. There was considerable underbrush in places holding me back in my walking. I thought I had walked a mile which at times, under these circumstances, did seem like two miles. There was considerable guesswork when it came to judging distances. I could see a white surface of larger size showing through the trees and that was the lake. Now I was very carefuly, scanning ahead, making no noise in my movements. I moved up slowly to see if I could find the log. It was not far up and there it was shining, the flickery-like white surface showing through the trees. Yes, this was a lake and here just ahead of me I could see the log going across. Here I stopped looking ahead as far as I could. I saw or heard nothng so I got a pole to balance myself and walked the log. Scouting around here on the other side, there was not a soul around. Like I said before two trappers had told me that at times wardens had waited here for trappers to come out. One does get very bold and realizes that this becomes a daring venturesome undertaking. I had to hustle to get back to where my pack was before dark. Did not mind thinking that now I will get out and the coast is clear. The whole matter now took on a different meaning and it is remarkable how fast one can forget hardships for most of this whole trip had become a constant struggle. I got back and it was dark. I could barely see enough to get a supply of wood for the night. It got to be a habit, I like to make a big fire. Because I had practically no sleep last night I felt all day I was dragging and forcing myself to keep going. I cut boughs so I could make a good cushion to lie down on. Had some meat left and tea and a little flour as for two days I did not have a chance to make bannock. Inasmuch as I was dead tired I used up the flour. After all was done and I had something to eat I dozed off in a hurry. Early in the morning I started thinking that if all goes well I could make it coming in the back way to my logging camp by nightfall. And, so it happened using all the determination and effort I had left to get there, I made it. The thought that I could sleep in a bed and would have a roof over my head, this alone can bring one a long ways, lifting up the spirit when the going gets rough. No one knew that I was out there in these woods trapping beaver. After being out there in that wilderness for forty-five days it is a satisfying experience to be in a place where there is so much comfort. Also, the responsibilities confronting a person every day in the woods ceased. You were released from the obligation of carrying the packsack which had become very burdensome. I felt strange yet happy to know where I would be sleeping tonight. In the morning the first thing I would do is get some wire and make a place down in the swamp to hang up the beaver skins so the bear could not get them. Having had considerable experience with what a bear can do I knew that everything in that line had to be made bear-proof. This job would take me three to four hours and it was important to get them away from the logging camp to what I considered to be a safe place. I had to go over to Jeff to get a few groceries and to see about making arrangements concerning the fur. Both he and his wife were glad to see me. Both had done some trapping this spring it was important to them to get the extra money. I got a letter off to my friend in Wisconsin to come up with my pickup and I would take him back. It was two days since I came out of the woods and I was getting used to this new kind of life. In four days this young honest farm lad came with the pickup. In the meantime I sold the fur. After staying here one night at the camp the next morning we left for Wisconsin. I tried to tell him about some of the experiences I had back there in the woods-about being lost for so long and other things, however lacking to indicate the full details. Occasionally while driving back we would both sing. No doubt we thought we were pretty good especially when I could squeeze in a little tenor. We were both young and the marks of challenge could be described in many ways. So, after arriving there I stayed around for a few days but had my mind made up that I was going back to the logging camp in northern Minnesota. One of the main reasons was that my friend up there, the man that I was dealing with on the timber, wanted to sell me lake property, a quarter of a mile of frontage. The trail was going through there. Also, it bordered the land I was supposed to log but by now I had given up the idea. I was constantly changing around looking for some adventure. I did buy this land, fifty acres, on a fine large lake dropping in elevation four hundred feet in a distance of fifteen hundred feet and laid out a road going on a gradual downgrade the full length of the property making a curve and then back again the full length of the property, three times back and forth in that order making a very scenic drive. There was a heavy wooded cover over the whole area of white birch. This was the only way a road could be built to get down to the lake. Across a three hundred foot high rock formation east a distance of a quarter of a mile a long narrow bay came in. Here a party who owned two of the largest gold processing mines, at that time, in Canada was doing some prospecting. He had built a cabin in that bay. All the lumber used in building was carried down a steep incline five hundred feet. He had a nice place there and the fishing was such that if you threw out a daredevil (bait) casting you would get a strike the first time. I got acquainted with this gentleman and admired him. However, he did smoke cigars. He always had an elderly man, a Finlander, with him, who had been a prospector all his life who also, years back with his father, helped to find the one mine they had at the lake back in the woods. It took four years, after much money was spent for drilling, before they found the main deposits of the vein. The old man must have been eighty years old. Here around the bay a short distance, a hundred feet up, there they found evidence of mineals worth $32.00 a ton, had ten or more valuable ingredients and had all colors of a rainbow, was heavy like iron, one foot wide twisting down into the rock formation. You could take a railroad pick and dig it out. They never spent much time working on it. They brought up an expert who had full knowledge of this; paid $4,000 for mineral rights for one year and did not own the land. I was always hanging around there. One day they brought a compressor model A engine fixed so it would pump air with a tank mounted on a two wheel rubber-tired unit, built narrow so it could get down the hill a quarter mile. Six men were working it around this bay, then the hardest task was to get it a hundred feet up on a ledge. It took an hour, they had ropes on it tied to a tree that was several hundred feet up on top of a rock wall. Here they were going to use a diamond drill. This man, Sandy, they called him, (the owner) said to me one day, "Why don't you drill down there a ways and follow that mineral formation to see if it would widen out further down. If we find something I'll make it right with you." any time it came to gambling on something like this I was all for it and now I was my own boss staying there in that cabin. Could swim and fish here every day. So I told him, yes, which also meant I would get no wages. After working there for several weeks the rocks started to pile up on me. I decided that I should have a small cart running on a track. I went to Duluth one hundred fifty miles, to look around in the junk yards to find something suitable for this. Three feet wide track, just the size I needed, they had this in one place. I managed to get a four wheel unit to fit, using an old dump scraper to mount on top. This would work so it could be dumped. Oh, yes, one strives for production. Then I hired a young kid to help me, he was part Indian, about fifteen years old. We had a regular air hammer drilling twelve inches deep in solid rock in a four foot square area, holes sixteen inches apart. When filled with dynamite, there were eight to ten of these drilled holes all wired together as one unit, a three hundred foot cable was connected to a battery switch box away from where the explosion would take place, hidden around a rock cliff. This was used to set off the charge. When this happened fair sized rocks often flew very high and way out dropping, into the bay. So part of the summer went and so did my money. The handling of that dynamite also got the best of me. I was getting headaches so I would have to lie down through the day. Counting my pulse, it was way down. Talking to a man one day about this handling of the dynamite I mentioned I was wearing gloves. He said that would not help me any; if I smoked or drank whiskey then I would have something in my system to help offset the poison that was penetrating through my pores into my system, slowing my heart way down and

Prospecting on Gunflint Trail

149

causing headaches. The result was I had to quit. I had gone down fifteen feet into that solid rock. The ore was just the same as on the top. Of course, I know today, that it was foolish for me to do this but not at any time did I regret doing this. One keeps chalking things up to experience. I never got any pay as I undertook this on my own hook. Later these fellows drilled two hundred feet down with a diamond drill and never found anything. The main deposit of this ore is still there and it could be fifteen miles southeast from there as that is the way the formation lies. One time I got an idea and was tempted several times to do this. Where I owned the land four hundred feet over and two hundred feet down, there was an indication of the same mineral. I was thinking I might tunnel straight through as I might find something in there.

So, the summer went in a hurry, it was early fall when Jeff sold his resort three miles down here on the same lake the mining shack was on. Well, this man also has been a gambler all his life and he was past the sixty year mark. He got $14,000 for the place and that was a lot of money in those days. His wife knew he would spend it all on some adventure and she would have nothing so she fought for part of it and got one third and one cabin on the top of the hill. I had known these people for some time and she asked me if I would make her a well also building a root cellar and the pump on top of it so she would not have to walk too far down the hill to pump water. Fifty feet back from the lake, it was quite a project. The young lad who helped me on the mining job would help me on this job. The deal was made, $150 for the complete job. We had a canoe and made what I called a floating cedar dock. I got two large dead cedar logs, placed them four feet apart, nailing boards across, anchoring this on shore made a good dock for us. We made a mistake, had one log extra we did not use so we let it lay loose in the water and it started to float around out there all over. It also happened that Jack Dempsey had a fight, it could have been Firpo, I do not remember. The lady we were working for to make the well invited us to come down, it was two miles, to listen to the radio to hear this fight. Oh, yes, we were enthused for we never had any entertainment. We always had an outboard motor mounted on the canoe and when running wide open could go rather fast. Our dock was out in front down from the cabin. Now, late evening, we started down the lake to hear the fight. Going along at a good speed the young lad sitting in front, he kept motioning to me. At first I paid little attention as I was looking off and on toward the shore admiring the scenery. All of a sudden he hollered real loud, I looked, and here straight in front of the canoe, ten feet ahead, was this floating cedar log. Without hesitation I turned the canoe very fast to miss the log, and at that second the canoe tipped over throwing both of us out under the water. In seconds both of our heads came up at the same time grabbing the canoe holding tight. It all happened so fast that the canoe only had a chance to turn over half way and at that moment we caught it so that left an air space inside underneath and for that reason floated way up. The young lad could not swim - the shore was a thousand feet away, the water was cold. The first thing I told him was that we could make it and he should not worry about it. We had high top boots on and I got an idea that I should take them off so I could move better when trying to pull the canoe, swimming over toward shore. I managed to get one shoe off and using all the effort I had I could not get going. All the young fellow did was hang on and all of a sudden he started to holler for help. I tried to quiet him down but he hollered more and more and louder for help. I thought that he must be getting panicky so I started to holler for help to. It was late and twilight had just come. Hollering as loud as we could between this high ridge the echo carried this sound a long way. Two miles up we could hear a motor boat when it started up, knowing then that somebody would come. There was a couple who had no motor for their canoe and used paddles, don't know how they did it, but they were the first ones there. The motor boat came shortly and we were within a hundred feet from shore when they got here. He immediately took us in the boat and brought us back to the mining shack. We made a fire in the barrel stove and wrapped ourselves in army blankets. Our bodies got chilled, our jaws were going up and down clattering our teeth together. When this happens one has no control over this and in our case it lasted twenty minutes before it left us. This was the end of our invitation to hear the prize fight. We were contented when we got settled to normal conditions again and were glad to call it a day.

It was early fall and I was thinking about that trapping country way down here. I knew I had run into a lot of hardships late last fall and this spring. So far I had made two trips out there and had gained considerable knowledge of that country. One thing that I wanted to avoid was some of the hardships, so the idea came along of building a shack in there and I would have to make it bear-proof. This also meant that I would have to take two canoes, tie them together to carry all the supplies needed and a grub stake for the fall and spring trapping. I had an old canoe. This one we would leave out and hang it up so the bear could not get it. This then I would use for coming in in the spring to bring in the fur as by then the water would be open. For building we needed nails, one small window, one roll tar paper, kerosene lamp, small box stove, blankets for a double bunk. In food this time we took a hundred pounds of flour, different kinds of dried fruit, rice, barley and many other things that can be stored until spring and would not spoil. I knew I could not take the young lad who was staying with me along. He didn't know I was a trapper, so I would have to find someone else I could trust to go with me and help me get the materials and other things down in there. One day while up north on the end of the trail there was a young husky man, single, who had been guiding there all summer.

He had nothing to do now, they called him ''Dynamite'' as he had a reputation of being a good shot. He did not know how to trap so I made a deal with him. By offering him so much money he would help me build the shack and go along in the spring and do the cooking for me and shoot beaver. This was really something he wanted to do and most of all he wanted to see the country. I made arrangements to rent one canoe and to do some repair work on mine. I went to town to get the things we had to take along so within a few days we would be ready to take off. We tied the two canoes together using two poles in a fashion so it also could be undone in a hurry. We would take a new route first going west and then circling around to the south. It is a much longer way getting in there. The longest portage would be one mile. I managed to get our things together, for we were anxious to get going. Had a couple raincoats and a few pieces of waterproof canvas. In case of rain I wanted to be sure to keep the food dry. We would use the canoes to sleep under, one feels secure that way. Starting out the next morning the humming of the outboard motor is a welcome sound. There is a stimulating energy that breaks the silence of the early morning hours. We approached the day with a speculative, cheerful, lively spirit. It truly was a holiday and vacation time. I judged that from this first lake it was five miles to the first portage. The scenery no matter what direction one looked was beautiful, blending in here and there, the high rugged moss and tree covered rock walls falling down often to heavy timbered shoreline expressing something of distinction like emblems or figures of nature. The two canoes, as one, slid effortlessly through the water recognizing a source of freedom in its movement. Now the portage, this is a different story for it meant that each one of us had to make three trips. We had four packsacks, two large and two small and each one of us would carry a small pack and a canoe for one trip. This was a heavy load but it had to be done in order to get all the things in six loads to make three trips for one. The comfort of thought would be that after we get that work done we would get another long ride in the canoe. The further we got down into the territory we had to look for rocks and boulders under the water so as not to hit them as they were scattered around in many places in the lake. As we have opportunities in life, we were now taking advantage of transporting our food by water instead of having to carry it for so many miles never knowing just what the conditions of such trips turn out to be. I had found out from experience that they can turn out mighty sad at times. Dynamite, my partner, resembling a small prize fighter, was good for packing, putting forth less strenuous effort in carrying the load than I did. We made very good time. I thought to take cover on an island located in the middle of the lake. This would make a better place staying for the night and the bear would be less apt to come around. One feels so far away from civilization, hearing here and there a wild sound, intervals of silence, and then increasing in volume. A disturbance that is often welcome is the calling of a loon. Life can become meaningful measuring situations in actions occupying here for this night a very small area, in contrast to the wide open spaces that surround us. Dynamite did not forget his fishing outfit and in no time he had a pickerel weighing around five pounds. We filleted it and fried it up in fine shape, well done. This time we brought some bread along and lard so a fine meal can be had in a hurry. When there is a direction of mind trying to accomplish certain things, this can become highly meaningful when success and results are obtained. We certainly, both of us, here this late evening did feel that we were real woodsmen, our purpose conveying to us signifying the meaning in the course of our journey. Other men have traveled here, each one under different circumstances, no doubt, therefore, their purpose in life takes on a different meaning and their thoughts were also different. So, while it was my time to come this way let me describe at least in part my feelings and thoughts as they come into focus on these trips and on the trapline. Certainly nature predominates in abundance, conveying an invitation of challenge, calling back memories requiring an answer. We had a good nights rest - this you can appreciate inasmuch as you sleep with your clothes on. You are never concerned with the thought of getting up early - anticipation is in harmony out here with confidence and pleasure, however, more so, when traveling over new territory as on this trip the first time out on this route. We were young and eager for a lot of adventure looking forward to getting there to build a trapping shack. Such thing had not been done for many years. For in all the country I traveled in here I found only one log cabin and that was mostly rotten. It takes years before it could decay into that kind of condition. I really meant business the way I approached this, hiring a man to help do the chores, the food supply sufficient for fall and spring trapping, and an extra canoe to store out here for transportation so as to be able to come in on water this way relieving a lot of hardships. Oh, yes, we would have a new system and I thought I was smart - I had learned from experience. Then here we would have a bear-proof shack where non-perishable food will be stored. I did not realize then that this wilderness trapping was only a temporary thing; that within five years it would be the end of the era forever for the illegal beaver trapper. (While this thought came into my mind now I will explain this in detail later at the end of my story.) We did not know then that laws would be made so that illegal trapping would be a thing of the past, I had so much confidence in myself in those days I never thought of getting caught. Truly one can say while the fur is prime, trapping so far out there was not done under normal conditions. The average person would not think of enduring the hardships that are connected with this kind of adventure. It always turned out that the country in general got more rugged the further we got in there. Our last portage was five hundred feet, very steep going up, then part level to reach the next lake. It took a lot of going to get the canoes up there. We made good time all along; we came to a lake where I came out through the woods when I was lost. One can cover considerable territory in a day by canoe with an outboard motor. In three day's time we arrived at our destination. It took half a day to find a location for building the shack. This we found in a dense heavily wooded spruce swamp, it was fairly well centralized for a new trapline. It also meant that at a later date we would have to make a camp farther beyond here, say ten miles. We began by cutting a large straight spruce with a Swede saw right after we managed to lug all our stuff in here. It took two days to build a good bear-proof cabin. It was small, we did not need much room, and to add a little life we placed a window (barn sash) on the south side. Then we made a special cover out of small poles nailed in a square form to fit on the outside. It was wired on to fasten over the window. It really had to be strong, so was the door, as the bear could not be trusted, and this had to be wired up every time we left. I often wonder if it is still standing or if anyone ever found it. I left $100 worth of things in there and never got back there. We crossed

Trapping Shack

the Canadian borderline on our way in here. The Superior National Forest and the Quetico Reserve, Ontario, join hand in hand here making it one of the largest wilderness areas in the country. When we had all our work done then we went fishing for one day and had a fine catch. Very seldom does a lake out here ever get fished. I thought now that we were sixty-five miles from any road or civilization. So the next day we started back, got rid of most of our pack only a few blankets, ax, matches, frying pan, lard. We baked some bannock enough to last us two days as we could catch fish anytime and we were all set. This was one time that I was really prepared for fall and spring trapping with that shack out there and all the grub needed to hold out for the period of time it was intended for. One never wastes anything. Dynamite was an expert cook and this I found out in the spring when he did all the cooking. Making pancakes on an open fire, nice and brown, and not

154

burning them, is an art in itself. Yes, Dynamite could do it and took great pride in doing it. So far our plans worked and already I was thinking of the time we would be able to get back. He did not care to come along for fall trapping as that is the most difficult time. The weather usually gets colder, mostly below zero and if you get thirty beaver by then you are glad to get back.So,in two and a half days we're back, made good time as we only had the one canoe. One time out in the middle of a big lake we hit a flat rock, it was only eight inches under water. With that sudden stop one is very much afraid of puncturing a hole in the canoe. Lucky again, nothing happened, just scraped the keel very hard. Then you get cautious and slow down your speed. However, soon all is forgotten and you are clipping it off mile after mile. Got back in fine shape and all turned out good. No one knew where we were or what we did. In the meantime I decided to make a trip to Wisconsin. I guess I got homesick ever so often and this seemed like a vacation. While I was there I sold the property I had logged off of several years before. It all happened fast and unexpectedly and I   received as much for it as I had paid for it in the first place.

How fast things had changed in six years of time. I visited a few people and almost everyone wanted to know when I was coming back. Made arrangements with the manager of the sawmill to get a job there and also got a job for my friend Dynamite. Yes,it was OK for a couple of months as it would get too monotonous for me to stay in that logging camp that I still had up on the trail, in the dead of the winter. Back again to Minnesota for in a week's time, now late fall, I could start out for the trapline. I was slowly preparing for this buying some things in the line of food and clothing for the trip. To think of all the struggle I had just a year ago, having to help Jeff, the neighbor here, cut sixty cords of fire wood for nothing. Had $3 in my pocket, then had to get grubstakes so I could go out trapping. The new Ford V8 pickup that I had the new motor put in, was froze up.   Now I had $300 left from the sale of the land and the pickup in good condition,   all prepared for trapping. I realized the chances I took last spring when I was lost for so long - I could have lost my life. Life is that way and it seemed as though I was constantly creating a problem in order to make some money - just so I had money to spend - there was no thought of getting rich. I always had a carefree disposition, a prevailing tendency free from disturbance. Now I thought that I had become a modern trapper and also that prosperity had come along selling that land in Wisconsin. I bought a pup tent and a sleeping bag, I only needed to carry sufficient food to get me in to the cabin. This would be the lightest load I every had and I would take more traps. And also, I had learned to recognize landmarks to find the way back in. This way of travel had to be mostly overland as it had just started to freeze and the ice would be thin in most places. Having had considerable rest I was anxious to get started, so tomorrow I would start out early into that remote country.

Also, this time I had a compass and a rifle, a 20-25 caliber and a box of shells. This gun weighed five pounds, had a short barrel, peep sight, and was good for shooting beaver. This can only be done when the ice starts going out in the spring in open water, for that reason I would leave it out there in the shack over winter. I figured that this was the best time to get in there - my pack did not weigh more than fifty pounds. Everything went along fine, making good headway. On the third day I had a mishap about ten in the morning. I was walking on the edge of a small beaver pond and I broke through. Good thing I was carrying a pole, however, I got soaked good up to my hips. I had to change my clothes there on the edge of the pond. I wrang them out as best I could, I did not want to lose time. For that reason I did not want to make a fire - tonight I would do this. In the evening, at this time of the year, one does build a good fire for the nights are cold, however, on this trip I had more comfort than on my two previous trips, as I had a fairly good sleeping bag and this pup tent. It was a problem drying the woolen pants. These were new ones and I was very careful not to scorch them, which is so easily done on an open flame fire. Since I had Dynamite with me on that last trip when we came in with the two canoes, it kind of spoiled me. I didn't notice it before but now it did seem so quiet. I noticed this often in the evening, no noise, just like the dead of winter. Here I got buried in my own thoughts. The only company I had then was the fire and this I kept going until I crawled into that sleeping bag. One thing was certain, I had no bear to worry about and I had so many things to look forward to, the most important being that trapping shack I had out there. Under my circumstances, combining all the elements together out here, something like that can become a very fortunate profitable thing. I sat here by a hot fire until ten at night. The movement and color from the fire gave me inspiration on this dark silent night like a moving satisfaction rising and falling, uttering occasionally a sound from a loud cracking spark. It conveyed constant heat and burning is a natural gift from fire. Elements of steel gray, whitish red with blue, a mixture of brilliant colors shimmering slowly away like time fading away. Here I have to admit the collection of my thoughts, grouping them together, are characteristic workings of nature. Imagine a lonely trapper, sixty-five miles out here in the woods trying to draw a picture in print from observation in zero weather, ten o'clock at night, sitting by a fire gathering consolation. As I look back in life these were precious moments. I never used the pup tent, not unless a storm came up. I would throw it on top of the sleeping bag and also throw it over my head. I have to say that I kept warm and slept well. In general the nights went fast. The whole journey gets to be an interwoven process. I got a good start. There was only three inches of snow. Certain days the animals were moving more than others. One would run across many tracks. Walking along here on the bottom of a ridge, very heavily wooded, I noticed fresh blood all around the bottom of a tree. I knew right away from the commotion of things, prints in the snow, that it was a fisher that had killed a porcupine. I saw a trail going up a very steep hill where he had dragged it. Why would he want to do this, I thought. Several hundred feet up he had him buried in good condition completely covered with leaves, sticks and snow. Never touching anything I decided I would set a trap for him, it will be a perfect set. I had some wax paper along. I placed a piece under the trap to keep the pedal from freezing down, also a piece on top in case it snowed to keep it in working order. I always had a desire to catch a fisher, they brought $50 a pelt at that time. Got a lot of satisfaction out of that set - surely he would come back looking for that porcupine. Having heard about their activities I know they are crazy about porcupine meat and know where they have their dens for miles around. They would go into the den, the porcupine going in to the far end with his tail toward the fisher. He may sit there for several days and eventually the fisher will catch him off guard and then kill him. He will then stay in that den until he gets all of them eaten up, this can be a week or more. The one he killed here at the tree, apparently the porcupine got out on a small limb, no doubt he did not have a choice to go any place else, as the fisher came along. He shook him out of there and while falling to the ground caught him at that moment and slashed his throat. There are very few porcupine around where fisher occupy the woods. And, so it always seems that it is life for life, the strong kill the weak. So I left this place knowing that I had to come back in a week or so to look at that fancy fisher set I made. It was ten miles further to the trapline. I was really desperate to catch this fisher, ten miles here and ten miles back a total of twenty miles. This is something I never did before - often I did things that I thought would end up to be a mistake. Tomorrow I would make it to the shack. This was my first trip overland where I made good time. I only went through the ice once, otherwise I felt that all went well. It was strange when I approached the shack here in this spruce swamp - it was just like coming home. I had a good supply of wood cut ahead for the small drum heater occupying a place in the corner of the shack. Had the door all wired shut but now I could keep it open as the bear were hibernating and I wouldn't use the wire until I got home. I got everything all straightened out and made a good fire in the stove and in no time had the place all warmed up. This was really something I thought, so comfortable way out here. Yes, we built it good so the bear could not get in; the only thing he did do, he got on the roof and pulled the stove pipe out. Also, I got a bunch of limbs and covered up the roof so it could not be seen from an aeroplane. They do fly over frequently in spring. However, I never did know who they were but one is suspicious. Now I cooked inside and often when in a hurry I would take the round top off and set the kettle right down on the open fire. Sleeping off the ground was also a luxury. We had placed the logs very close together when we built the place and where there were signs of openings we drove moss in between. So here I was, I had suddenly advanced into a modern trapper plundering the most part of my life into this alluring adventure, secluded from society but not depressed. A mutual understanding seems to be in progress correcting movements and thoughts - to have the feeling that I was sound and safe back here in the woods.

Now came the time to explore new grounds for trapping. This I never got tired of and looked forward to domineering the places I found here trapping beaver. There was a lot of physical function performed. The cold weather can rob one's body of resistance. After my feet were nipped from frost several times they were highly sensitive to cold. This often can become mentally disturbing and it is most important to be careful not to freeze them any more. I knew what I was in for trapping this season of the year when it was often ten to twenty below zero and later on it could go down to thirty or forty below. Regardless of what one has we keep looking for more material things mostly to increase our comfort. This often becomes a sad distressful condition and robs us of the privilege of the real meaning of life. This is a problem which has held most of us in a constant battle, defeating the enemy. Often here on these still and lonely nights in this comfortable trapping shack thoughts of life seem to loom into focus when taken from a standpoint of simplicity, envisioned and inspired, having its origin from the soil and produced in lifelike form from nature. This can produce a bridge connecting suitable lengths for men that are not of brute force, but a doctrine that can and will reveal adequate needs of man. There were also nights here when a violent storm was raging so it could be heard by the sound of the wind and the cracking of the trees - occasionally this would be accompanied by a snowstorm. The feeling of thankfulness for having this shelter is rooted in conformity with all surroundings, sympathetic and pleasantly linked together, united as one. It has always been true that after the storm comes the sunshine. Our lives are the same, most of us are aware of that. This remote life trapping out has benefited me in many ways, not only that I was making good money, it also helped set a pattern for my life and made me realize the kindness of nature in so many ways. This, in fact, later on in life, had become a blessing to me only after I learned how to pray with the help I got from God. Thoughts came to me that in ordinary life I did not think about. No doubt that I lived close to nature mostly submitting to nature and drawing strength from within my own mind.

I had a good trapline started and in the meantime was getting farther and farther inland or farther away from civilization. I was certain I was the only person out here. Only one man knew where this trapping shack was located and of course,

Trapline

he would keep it a secret. Also it was doubtful that he himself could ever find it again. On the other end of this stretch, about ten miles up, I had the pup tent set up. So one night I had to stay there coming back on the next day staying in the log cabin. Also I had a rare privilege, I could dry the skins in the cabin where I had made a special board large enough to dry a blanket. Those are the largest skins and are measured in terms by measuring across, then up and down, then both of those figures are added as one. This figure could be as high as eighty-five inches. However, the largest I ever caught went up to eighty-three inches which was at one time the second largest in New York on an auction. The buyer used to take them there and told me this. However, while the season was open around 1962 in Wisconsin there was a fellow caught a beaver that weighed ninety-two pounds. This, of course, is very unusual, and from other reports I never heard of one weighing more than eighty-five pounds. Referring back to the drying board I spoke about, I could nail one skin on each side and they only weigh sixteen to twenty ounces after they are dry. Here on my early winter trapping this catch of dry skins could be carried back in one load. When the hides are green they weight two to three pounds each so another trip had to be made when the skins are fresh and green. This certainly was a big help. Now back to where the fisher had killed the porcupine and where I had made such a perfect set - I'll have to go back and see what happened. It was now over a week and it had snowed two inches in the meantime. If I got up early and walked fast I could make it back before dark. How I hated to lose a day but I had to do it. When I got there, nothing had been touched. Remenber now since it had snowed it was covered just perfect. One could barely see the outline of the pedal the animal has to step on for the trap to snap. Not telling when that fisher would come back if ever and I thought I had wasted enough time on him. Beside, I was tying up one of the beaver traps as I would have a better chance catching one of them than that unpredictable fisher. And all that walking I

159

did for nothing besides losing one day. It seems when I make a mistake out here I do a lot of thinking, as often it meant a lot of hardship this time of the year. I was looking forward to every other day when it was the time to stay down on the south end which was the log cabin. Here I did all my cooking as it was under cover and besides it warmed up the shack. Looking over the trapline every day, the one smart beaver I had nearby on the dam, the one I wrestled with last spring, he was still there. I did not bother him or his family, I did figure I would catch him in the spring. The rock wall where I had camped was also not far away. By now having rambled back and forth here through this woods, I thought that I knew this territory—I had a picture of it in my mind. Going up heading north, this one day, by noon I picked a spot between two ridges to have lunch. I made a fire as usual to make tea and always carried some prepared food along—this would take me twenty minutes and I would be ready to go again. Now there was six inches of snow where I had walked over this ridge a short time ago. Going back there were fresh tracks from an otter. While I was only 100 feet away down there having my lunch in the meantime he had come through the woods. What surprised me was that I did not hear him. I thought here is where I will catch one or two in a hurry. you could tell by their tracks or round imprint in the snow from their body where they slide ten feet at a time. They have very short feet and no doubt give a push, they are rather slick and slide easily. I set my packsack down and ax in hand I started to run after them thinking right along that I would catch them. Like a wild man I was chasing them for about a half mile. Here was a swamp, had a nice small lake in the middle and a large deserted old beaver house on it. This I found out when I got near it. There were large old stumps laying in the swamp near this lake. There was a hole by the swamp and they crawled in there and went underneath. The hole was so small and I just couldn't believe how they could get in there and then disappear under this swamp. There were a lot of things I did not know about otter and learned more about them in the next three days. They are constantly making their rounds out here in this wilderness and can include a thirty mile circle. They can drill a four inch thickness of ice by using their front feet going clockwise very quickly. The motion of the water going around very fast helps along as they use their pointy nose poking against the ice turning back and forth. So here I was, no otter, and also found out that it was impossible to catch one on land. They fight desperately when cornered and are not afraid of anything. It happened that my trapline went around in a horseshoe circle going around here every other day. For that reason I could see their tracks whenever they would leave here. So it happened the first time going around also part ways in here in the swamp, there were tracks. However, the fourth day going around they did cross. From the way it looked and from the evidence being rather fresh it could not have been too long ago. Again I started out after them following them several miles going through country around here that I never realized was in existence. I remember going down a steep hill very fast, my foot going or sliding down in behind a good sized log. Losing my balance I fell down the hill fifteen feet. It all went so fast, lucky my foot did slide back out in behind that log and then I realized that I could have broken my leg right there. I shuddered at the thought - if that had happened I would never have been able to get out back here at least sixty miles out in the bush. Down here there was a long empty swamp. There was an old beaver flowage, almost running, and ever so often the ice would break through, falling down as it was three feet deep with about a foot of water on the bottom, otherwise, underneath there was a hollow space and the water had drained out. Something had happened here to let all that water escape. Not far down was a very old also deserted beaver house and here the otter had gone in and it was all full of holes. I thought of this often afterwards, how foolish I was thinking that I still could get an otter here. Also, in the meantime it started to snow very heavily and the wind was blowing. Here I was on the top of this old beaver house chopping a good-sized hole with an ax. Part of the wood was rotten and soon I fell right through into a good sized empty chamber underneath where the beaver at one time were. Kneeling down in there, crawling back in and looking here and there to see where the channels were going, staring back into the dark, I finally came to my senses and realized that I could never catch those otter. It all was so foolish and by now there was a blizzard in progress. Walking a short distance there was an old dam. Two hundred feet down there was another nicer one but not a high long dam.. Below this there was a beaver house and one tells immediately if there were beaver there. Further down were several other dams. Here the elevation dropped down rapidly and was different than I had seen before. On this upper dam I made a set for the otter. Very seldom would you find, after chopping a hole at the dam, that it would be shallow and have a hard gravel bottom. This meant I could not find a foundation to anchor the trap. So, I took an eight foot pole, fastened the trap in the center, and laid it on top of the ice. The chain was hanging down in the water and made it a suspicious looking contraption. I made another set for the beaver. Three days later I got back there, in the meantime we had zero weather. When I got there I saw something hanging over the pole that was laying on top; it was a solid chunk of ice and it was a female otter. Here I also learned that if there is any danger involved that the female otter leads. She was the first one that crossed my tracks four days ago and now the first one to find a place to get out where the hole was made three days ago. I couldn't figure out how she got through that first dam underneath the ice. Also, after they went back to the old beaver house that I had caved in where they had gotten in, no doubt they smelled my scent and were then afraid to get out of there. It took me one day to thaw this otter out and they are very hard to skin. Also, on this same day I looked at the beaver set further down and here I caught an old beaver, never forget the way he looked. He had long whiskers and was very skinny. This was the oldest beaver I ever caught in my life and he looked as though he was ready to die. When I skinned him he was all scarred and no doubt he had been in many a battle. So, there was something new going on all the time. I found new places where beaver were located when I was chasing the otter across country. Several days later I went straight east about two miles over and ran into a river bottom. There was considerable open water running swiftly through thick elder growth. Saw a lot of rabbit tracks and noticed larger tracks mixed in. They were all over the place and I realized that a fisher was running rabbits. Here, I thought, another fisher. Why not try to catch him? On one spot a ways up on my trapline was a clump of large pine trees. A porcupine had gone back and forth between five trees and had chewed all the bark off way up on top. He was able to survive all winter here. He was one of the smart old porcupines, knowing that as long as he stayed up there on one of the big limbs, the fisher had a hard time getting him but if he came down to stay in a den, he would not last long. In fact, it was the only one I had seen around. However, I thought he would make good bait for the fisher so I climbed the tree and cut the limb off. This way I got him and brought him over to where I saw the fisher chasing rabbits. I made a pen out of dead sticks and placed a roof on top. The ''porkie'' was pushed to the back at the entrance I placed a trap and covered everything over with leaves. Thought I would wait a week and then see what would happen. I was determined to catch a fisher as I had never seen one. I thought they were like an otter but had longer legs.

I had been here now two weeks and had twenty-three beaver and one otter. Like I said before, the winter beaver are more difficult to catch. Indians don't care to trap at all this time of the year for there is too much hardship involved. I wanted to go back the first chance I had over east and follow the creek farther up. Crawling along the river bottom for some time and all at once I was confronted with a big dam. Here over on the edge some fifty feet up from the dam was open water. Yes, it was a spring hole about four feet wide. Standing here in surprise, scanning farther up, I could see a large beaver house against a rock wall to the left. Here was something very unusual; this most any trapper would admit. In all my travels I did not find a location that would allow beaver to come out this late in the season. I immediately crawled ten feet up from shore, for the bank was so steep, as I wanted to investigate this spring hole. Here the beaver had a slide all tramped down where they had been going up into the woods to a good stand of popple. Leading away from this trail here they had cut down a number of trees. In one place there was a very large popple, over twelve inches on the stump, that had been chewed off. The

Beaver House

shavings or cuttings from this wood were very fresh and laying all around. So I picked up a handful from on top of the snow and recognized from the large parts that it was no small beaver. I had only one trap with me so I made a set on the east side of the dam. I would come back near full moon, in the early evening, and watch to see if I can catch them. Often one will find spring holes in a swamp that do not freeze up. These are the best places for mink and otter sets in the wintertime. In this framework of rivers and lakes, binding this region together, consisting of immovable property distinguished as a wilderness area, a trapper leans on products of nature in many ways. In the last year I had no competition, unlimited freedom and the things I had anticipated satisfied my desires and I learned the hard way. So the time went, averaging two beaver a day. The fancy time-consuming fisher set, the one where I placed the porcupine for bait, had been there for eight days and nothing had happened. This was it! I was not going to fool around wasting time with those fisher anymore. I also thought, I could have left that poor porcupine live. He had enough enemies and managed to get by for several years until I came along. It is not all amusing where the killing of animals is undertaken. One will find an excuse for such involvements submitting the thought back to nature that all these things were put here for us to use.By now I had thirty-two beaver and the one otter. I had plenty of food, enough also for my spring trapping, stored away in the bear-proof log shack and the canoe hanging way up high over at the lake in the thicket, not that I was afraid of anyone seeing it except the bear in the spring. By now the weather had one of those zero spells every time I had to skin a beaver five to eight miles away from the shack and I had to make a fire, hiding behind rock walls often to get out of the wind and also the smoke. Placing your hands in the icy waters, often twenty below, to reset the traps, gives them a hot burning sensation when drying them fast on an old towel I carried just for that purpose. Also, if one keeps this up as you get older it brings on rheumatism. So I would stay four or five more days.

163

Now full moon was shaping up and I had to get back over, by three-thirty or four o'clock, to the spring hole and watch for the beaver. Anything where there was some adventure involved or something new, was like getting something wholesale or getting a bargain. As I got near there I thought about the wind. There always seemed to be some breeze and it was in my favor. I would stand below this dam, it was frozen solid, south of the location and the wind came from the north. There were no bear around this group and their movements were very carefree. I wasn't there twenty minutes when a fair sized beaver came out by the spring hole, going up the path. Not far up he had a white birch tree cut down. Well, this beaver went up there and cut off a two inch size limb near the trunk of the tree so fast that I was astonished. Never did I see anything like that. How could he cut a limb that size so fast, a half minute I thought. Here he came down carrying the whole limb, eight feet long, in his mouth holding his head sideways, branches sticking out all directions approaching this water hole about four feet wide. Down he went under the ice. The limb was wider than the hole, however, nothing stopped him for that limb started to fold up and slid in there just perfectly. I knew I could not get him for that birch was only twenty feet on the bank for I was certain he would come back and he would just knock me down on that trail. So I started to sneak up the bank as perhaps there were more out. Not far up it got to be level ground. I saw fresh tracks leading over on the side, looking back there was a large beaver. He saw me the same time I saw him and started to come my way. Of course I was excited and going over toward him fast I chopped off a small tree that was lying down in front of him. With all this commotion he stopped and snarled and hissed at me. Everything seemed to be going so fast and holding this four foot piece of wood I started to hit him over the head. The very first time I struck at him this pole broke right in the middle. What had happened was being in such a hurry the pole was all rotten. I hurried and cut another and killed him. This is the only beaver I ever got in this fashion. I had that one set made there on the dam and it had a beaver in it. So here I was, several miles away from the shack but it never got real dark this night. There always seemed to be something unknown and mysterious hidden away on nights when I was surrounded by the dramatic performance of the moon. I started out from here carrying one beaver, that I guessed weighed seventy-five pounds, just as the moon started to come up casting long shadows here and there from the trees, part mystical in experience observing a picture, shining like a silvery stream between the openings, a hidden meaning all its own. Occasionally when I crossed a small clearing in the woods, walking along slowly, I would take a look up where a low cloud cover would ever so often hide the moon for a short time - often for a short while it would get dark. The thought also came to me just like in life, at times we are very much alive and then we fade away. I didn't have to worry about the bear getting my other beaver back there, the one I left. However, by tomorrow it will be frozen stiff. When I got it back here I would be able to thaw it out.

I was going to hit the long trapline for the last time. This meant taking up all the traps and I had to bring my pup tent back as I would need it to sleep in on my way out. The traps I spotted in two places, saying to myself, now don't forget where you placed them. I had seventeen traps left and next spring we would have the rifle and would be able to shoot some beaver then. The important thing was that I had the rifle and the box of shells out here now and would bring another box in the spring to make certain we would not run out of ammunition. I was looking ahead now and was well organized for spring trapping. When I wound up my late fall trapping I had thirty-seven beaver and one otter. This was considered good for this time of the year and I was very happy. However I knew that I would have rough going getting back in. I was not worried in a way, only the cold weather made it bad for camping at night when I always tried to steal some sleep. I started out early the next day and was glad I did not have a heavy load. I would follow the portage route in on the lakes. We did not have much snow, up to about ten inches. I did pick up my snowshoes when we came in on the canoe trip so I had them here. Now I would use them as one does not know when a snowstorm comes up. I got back in four days, got very little sleep as I stayed up late and kept the fire going. When I got in to the logging camp I loafed and rested for a week. It was always the same getting back here even though I had no one around, it was more of a secure feeling. I suppose you think that if you got hurt way out there you could not get any help. It did not take me long to sell the fur. I often wondered just how much the fur buyers did make on the skins as they were always very eager to buy. I never argued price and insisted on cash money as I was afraid of checks. I stayed another day, was now all straightened out and headed back to Wisconsin. This V8 pickup I had was in good condition and I had no trouble making the trip. I headed back again to my old friend, the manager of the sawmill, in that little town. To work again in the sawmill staying at the boarding house. I also corresponded with Dynamite, his home was in Michigan as he would go with me in the spring and do the cooking for me. Well, he wrote that he was out of a job and asked me if I could get him a job here at this sawmill. So I asked my friend (he was the big boss) and I told him about the deal I had with him concerning the trapping and how we had built a cabin in the woods and were all set for the spring. Yes, he would give him a job right away and this is what happened. In a few days we were together in the sawmill working every day and playing poker every night. Another week and it would be Christmas and the young farm lad invited us over to his home on that day. This is the same young man that was, and had been, driving me in early spring to Minnesota. This he would do again the early spring. At no time was I satisfied working here in this sawmill, but knowing that it would only be for a couple of months was the one thing that helped me get by. I was waiting for the legal beaver season to open - counting the weeks. It just seemed like I was locked up in a prison working here day by day, pushing lumber around on a band saw which was part of an operation in this sawmill. Being used to the wild open spaces for so long no doubt was the reason for my dissatisfaction. The first part of March the season would open and I would trap then and Dynamite would keep working at the sawmill. Legal trapping was not too easy. There were not too many beaver locations or colonies around so there would be two or three trappers making sets on hundred feet away from the house, which was the law. Cutting through two foot thick ice was a job and you would disturb the beaver with the unusual noise. They would become suspicious of all the contraptions like poles and traps and would be hard to catch after that. This was annoying to me as the catches were few and far between. However, under the circumstances I put up with it as I would rather tramp around up and down rivers and in the woods looking for a beaver pond all day than working in the sawmill. In the three weeks I caught seven beaver and had to be satisfied. After all, it was more money than I could have made working by the day. We would start out one week earlier this year for Minnesota, Dynamite and myself. At last we were counting the days and got our things together. I had to buy one more sleeping bag for my partner and would also take the pup tent, and more of an assortment of food, things that would keep. Now while there were two of us we figured about fifty pounds for each. This way we would not be overloaded, had an extra hatchet and one ax, snowshoes (we always used those to start out) matches, and a compass. Now I had enough experience and would plan more efficiently for this trip. The thought also came back to me as a reminder to never again start out too late like a year ago on the trip when I got lost and had started out too late as the ice was going out on me and I just made it that time. So we left in time stopping at Dynamite's home in Michigan, when he told his parents good-bye. The young farm lad took off from work a few days and he would drive my pickup back again.

Forty-five miles up on this trail, early in the morning, Dynamite and I walking on top of a hard crust of snow with snowshoes on, vanished into the woods. The farm lad left us on this spot and knowing we would not see him for sometime, we told him good-bye. We would contact him by phone later and he should not worry about us. This fellow always had a funny grin when he laughed and was very good-natured. We lost no time while these things were taking place. I remember I took the lead and Dynamite walked behind here in the early morning hours. We could barely see but started out, taking our time, for by now I was acquainted with this area having gone this way three times. Somehow, at first it seemed strange. Neither of us talked for the first two miles; it was when we came to the first lake that we stopped and took off our packsacks. Here we wanted to test the ice first with the ax to see how thick it was. Also, we took a very large pole and in straight up and down position hit the ice as hard as we could as one is suspicious when first starting out. We wanted to avoid outlets and spring holes. One does feel more secure when there are two traveling, especially on this kind of a journey, knowing that we would not come back for two months. Here our time will be devoted to trapping. Having Dynamite with me will save me a lot of time as he will do the cooking. Yes, he was my right hand man - we made a good combination. I recognized that he was a person that had a fixed goal and he was determined to make a success out of this trip.

The second day, just before noon, I fell through the ice. It seemed so funny for Dynamite was walking twenty feet ahead of me and I was stepping in his tracks. I thought he must have weakened the ice as it cracked loudly just as I was going in. As you hit the cold water it takes your breath away. I had snowshoes on but no pole - I was struggling trying to hang on to the ice. Dynamite was fast. Of course, he could not help noticing that I fell in for when it happened I hollered real loud. As I was trying to hang on to the edge of the ice the packsack pulled me down. If I had been alone I could never have gotten out. He got to me in seconds, took off one of his snowshoes staying as far away as he could, he handed me the snowshoe - I held on tightly with all my grip and sliding out on my belly he got me out. Should the ice have broken more, well, we didn't want to think about it if he had also gone in. Before he came over to me he took off his pack sack and that was smart. Even then it gets to be a helpless condition. It gets deep here and you want to save the pack sack too as you've got your food in there. This is always packed in waterproof bags, tightly sealed. That was the end of the day right there. I had to change my wet clothes. Some that were in the pack sack got partly wet. We made our way over toward the shoreline a quarter of a mile away. Here we got a big fire going, took a wire we had and placed it so we would hang up the clothes for drying, watching so they would not get scorched. What a relief it was when we finally got settled down so we could have a bite to eat. That was it. From now on I would carry a pole and I was thinking to tell Dynamite that we cannot trust the ice. Anxiously waiting for morning to come we turned our attention ahead along the trail assuming, part in imagination, the region we had to cover before we would arrive at the trapping shack. Part of the route was over rough terrain where there are overhanging cliffs protected from the southeast that could have made a good homesite for an ancient Indian. Dynamite and myself were in good physical condition and in the prime of our life. We walked right along climbing around rock walls, up and down. When carrying a fifty pound pack sack using a head band, one leans partly forward so as to distribute the load. Walking in this fashion slows you down. You can only look about ten feet ahead and there are times you fall down, but not often. With practice you become surefooted as time goes along. Our spirit was good as we had so much to look forward to and loved the adventure that becomes involved on such an expedition. Nightfall comes too soon, a campfire takes over the thoughts of the day recapturing the main events like falling in the lake where the ice gave way. One lives like a wild Indian, absorbing unlimited lessons from nature agreeing that we must be expert woodsmen before we get back out. Surprising how, after such a day's journey, the flickering firelight will keep you awake. After a while you become drowsy, hit the hay, and soon all is forgotten. The next day we were up bright and early,Dynamite was more of a wild character than I was and he would be the first one up. Our facilities were better, food, cooking utensils, clothes, than I ever had on any trip before, a cabin or shack, as we called it, to look forward to with plenty of food stored away, and most important would be the canoe we had hung up. This we will use to get further into remote places and then to bring in the fur. What a difference this will make not having to carry all that weight overland, often under severe circumstances. It was surprising the good weather we had since we started out.The unpredictable days in spring keep you guessing from day to day,like my first trip out in the spring a year ago when it rained for three days. This year we started a week earlier and there was a foot of snow on the ground. We are both traveling on snowshoes, I would break trail for an hour and then Dynamite, taking turns we continued sturdy in our efforts of walking. Like two strangers playing a role we followed the course as the waterways wound around the landscape and that in itself presented a way of life. There was fascinating scenery around, peaks of jagged rock formation, trees growing out of crevices of all sizes and forms. Here in our wanderings this helped to pass the time and one felt that we were part of it and fell in love here with nature's treasures. Often I thought there must be plenty of good places around for the bear dens where they hibernate although I never found one in my travels and I was not looking for any either. Yes, it won't be long and we will have a lot of company when the bear come out. Getting to understand their ways much better was a big help. Dynamite, while guiding a tourist at the resort last year, had several trout in a cellarway there. The bear came along, tore the old wooden cellar door up, and got the fish. That was too much for Dynamite and he waited all night on a roof for the bear. He came early in the morning and Dynamite shot him. The fur was part prime so he skinned him and had an Indian tan the hide so it would keep. Several times he talked of how he liked to shoot bear. I told him then that we didn't have time for that, the hide is not worth it and it is too much weight to carry back so far. Besides, he would get plenty of practice shooting beaver and we had two boxes of shells in all. The 25-20 was considered a good gun for that purpose and it also had a peep site.

The fourth day coming up, if all went well, we should make it to the shack before night. The ice was in good shape for walking so we were able to take the short way in. Last year, when I went through so much commotion, it took ten days. How things can change in a year's time, I thought, and was happy for what I had learned trying to eliminate some of the hardships. Trapping here in this wilderness sixty-five miles from any human contact in late fall when the elements of the weather in general are violent, is not pleasant. In the spring there are so many things to look forward to; most important, the weather gets warmer week by week, the perpetual part of life, the season of the year when every bush and tree comes alive, uninterrupted, allowing without interference, permitting new penetration, saturated from the earth forming a new picture of life itself in so many ways.

It did not take us long to get settled. We could have used a good shelf for small items such as matches, whetstone, pellets, etc. Dynamite will hew small poles flat and in that way he can make a good shelf. Yes, we had a good hatchet and nails. I could get going up north where I left traps in several locations last fall. Also, when I had more time this year I would plan on catching the two large beaver out of a colony or one house. I was thinking of making the number one hundred skins, however, by planning to get mostly large skins meant I had to cover more territory, nearly southwest, leaving that toward the last as Dynamite could explore that for shooting most of the beaver in a three to four mile area. Often, at this time of the year, they come out early in the afternoon. When shooting a beaver or otter you must hit them in the head otherwise you cripple them and they go down hanging on to most anything they can get hold of and very seldom come up Often deer hunteres will shoot at otter but I never heard of them getting one, often out on a fair sized river and they could never get out here in the first place. This is sad and this idea I never liked.

The next morning, by the time we got things squared around, it was ten o'clock. I had enough food for several days, took the pup tent and sleeping bag as I would be gone for two days or more to get the trapline started. Had car wire, matches, ax, everything I needed. This meant that wherever I would end up I would camp. It would be in a southwesterly direction. Found all of my traps and started out only making sets in the most choice locations. By late evening I only had half of the traps out. I had sixteen traps in all left, had set eight, and this was done in a hurry. As one goes along every day the sets are improved and often changed. The first night I spent in a ravine digging around to get the snow out of the way to lay down a bed of boughs to set the pup tent on. Here, getting down in some old dried leaves, I found a wooden self-made bow that holds a Swede saw.

How strange, I thought, that there were trappers here many years ago, Finlanders, no doubt, coming in from a different direction, Ely, Minnesota, a hundred fifty miles southwest of here and north from here where there are a thousand lakes - they could have come in from there. It was all so strange; if the rock walls behind me could talk, they would know, thinking in one way that I had a partner and in another way, I did not have. If I knew Dynamite, he would be out shooting beaver as he was not satisfied sitting there in the shack. I tried to impress upon him if he went any distance not to stay too late and be back before dark. I left the compass with him. He would never be able to find it back unless it was a moonlight night. There was no moon now and often it was cloudy weather. Anyway, I did not worry about him. I got an early start, the wind was blowing rather strong, mixed with a little snow, a typical early spring distrustful day, the kind of weather that makes the going tough. I used all the ambition I had to get myself together and get going. As long as I had this rock wall behind me to shield me and a nice fire going it was hard to get started. Having to cover a wide range encircling some new territory was a challenge dividing one's attention. Self reliance mixed with a pioneering spirit falls into a pattern pursuing a daily routine that becomes a permanent part in this way of life, at the same time discovering here a mutual understanding of cooperation between man and nature, a cooperation demonstrating the ability of survival of a professional trapper that I thought I was. It instills within you an appreciation of nature. The tiny blue swamp spruce show delicate needles of green-blue color; it had just rained and now the sun has come out so the raindrops are laying shimmering on the branches of the tender looking small trees, as it betrays a form of life. In comparison the whole western span is a visible horizon forming a picture of a landscape in soft gray-blue and reddish color, a contrast showing the promise verifying to say that tomorrow will be a nice day. When the end of the day arrived there was the satisfaction in the work I had done. I managed to work into several miles of new territory so I was able to get any other eight traps out. Here I had walked around a very large swamp that was flooded with a lot of water. As far as I could see, a mile down, there was water. Oh, yes, a beaver flowage but I could not get out there. I immediately thought of bringing the canoe down here. So tomorrow I would get to see Dynamite and I was wondering if he had gotten any beaver. It would take me all day to get back partly because I was afraid to make any short cuts as you never know what you run into, places where you might not be able to cross. To be sure I had better go back the way I came, once in a while cutting off some distance, but always heading back to my old trail. The bear had not come out as yet and we would be looking for them and be ready to watch out for them getting into the shack. We will have to wire it up every time we leave. My distance this morning to get back was about twelve miles, but of course you cannot walk straight here, like they say, the crow flies. It was dark when I got there and it was a most welcome sight when I got near and saw light shining. We had a window in the shack where we could place a bear-proof cover over it. However, we took it off when we first came and for that reason I could see the light. I started to whistle when I came near the shack so Dynamite would know that I was coming - he quickly appeared in the doorway and hollered "Hi" to me. I said, "How did everything work out." "Oh," he said, "I got two big beaver." I knew that he shot them. I told him that was fine and said this will give us a start. He said he would bring them in, he had them laying behind the shack. Here he had two large size beaver. "Gosh," I said, "I'll have a job on my hands skinning them tonight." I knew that I would have to do it so immediately we hung them up on the wall near the stove so they would start thawing out. Dynamite had a good supper ready and we both sat down on the lower bunk and enjoyed our meal. He started to tell me how he shot the beaver, one in the water about fifteen feet out, had to get a long pole cut from one of the small long thin poplars. The other he got the next evening, he said it was getting dark. "This fellow was three hundred feet away from the lake, here was a large white birch cut down and he was gnawing on the trunk of the tree. When he saw me he started running and I got him for there was mostly all open area." These were the first beaver he ever shot in his life, he was proud and I was glad that we had a start. Then I told him the first thing in the morning we would go over east near a large lake where we had the canoe hung up. I also told him of the large flowage I found up north and it would be a good place to use the canoe up there. We both realized that it was a long way to carry the canoe through the woods. We would work together on it and he would also have to stay out there with me for a couple of days. He would pack enough food and his sleeping bag as it would be three days before we would come back here again. Neither one of us got to bed before twelve o'clock as I had to skin the two beaver and then stretch them on the board I made for that purpose, one on each side of the board. This also meant that we had some beaver meat now for the first time. Dynamite had never eaten any before, but he liked it. First we parboiled it, took new water and boiled it until it was well done, added salt and pepper. Then we fried it nice and brown on each side and eating it with bannock it made a good meal for us. Mostly the hind quarters were used, when caught in a trap the foot that was caught was never used. In spring trapping this was the first year we had a gun along, for this reason we will have plenty of beaver meat from the ones we shot and would not have to use any that were caught in the traps. However, it doesn't hurt if you do eat it and nobody could tell the difference. In our way of thinking the bleeding of an animal should be better. Very seldom in all my trapping did I see a beaver bleed. The next morning we got over to where the canoe was and found it laying down. What really happened was the wind had blown it down. I had it up twelve feet high and was surprised nothing happened to it but considerable thick brush had grown up there and was a cushion for it to land on and the next thing was that the bear were not out, and that was a lucky thing. I also thought that if it had fallen down through the winter months it would have had snow to fall on. Dynamite wanted to take it out on this lake, it was a mile across, and try some fishing. He had a daredevil bait and some line tucked away in his inside pocket. I said we would not have time for that but later we would get around to it - I didn't want to discourage him completely, as he was a guide and knew how to fish. We had to go back the way we came, one of us going ahead to find the best walking so as to clear the trees with the canoe. Sometimes it can become difficult trying to get around or through the woods in certain places so we took the canoe as far as the shack. First I had to make the trip taking care of the trapline alone. Then on my way back I would bring the other sleeping bag that I had up north in the pup tent. This would take me two days. This way each one will have a sleeping bag when we start out to get the canoe up there in the woods twelve miles. There were a few miles of water and then we could paddle, so this we will do. Dynamite never cared what we did. This will give him two more days scouting around as he always kept the rifle. He was very anxious to get to go up north with me as one never seems to get tired of seeing new country. We made good time in getting the canoe over here for by nine in the morning we were back here, had lunch, packed up some grub and got going north. One never forgets the things that are needed, skinning knife, whetstone, matches, ax, gallon pail for making tea and used in general for all other cooking like oatmeal, rice and barley. When making a stew a gallon pail was used for that alone. The weather was getting warm and making things all around more pleasant for everything one did. Had three beaver when I got to the end looking at the last trap, two fair sized and one small one. I took time to skin only one as I knew I would never get back by night to the nice sheltered place in the ravine where the pup tent was sitting close to a rock wall. Brought the smaller beaver with me, he was not too heavy, and I would skin him tonight by the light from the fire. Wrestling around all day on that trapline, by the time I made something warm to eat and then skinned the beaver I was dead tired and glad that I could lie down and call it a day. This gets to be the most precious time of the day. Sleeping with clothes on, taking off your shoes and also the socks if they were wet - would exchange these for dry ones, not clean, just dry, this was our way of living. Why we never thought of washing out here, I don't know. It could have been done but we were too busy catching beaver. In this course of action most all other things were forgotten. Your conduct persistently forms a stubborn opinion that is hard to control or cure. Nothing seems to stand in the way to hinder or obstruct progress made from day to day. We were looking ahead for a new day to come as we had a big job of bringing the canoe way up in here and it had to be carried so far overland. I thought no white man or Indian ever had a canoe up here on this endless chain of beaver flowages connected in part, passing across here and there in various forms, some up on higher elevations building the dam supporting the surface of the water in degrees, in distance so designed to create a body of water that has a lot of depth. Yes, they need deep water to get by for the winter months when they are confined under the ice, Six or seven hours sleep and one was ready to go. The days were getting long and the birds were singing again as they did last spring - I often wondered how all these birds get around so far back here in the woods. They have not trouble getting lost often going so far south through the winter months coming back every year to the same place where they were raised as young, just like childen that come back to the homestead whenever they have a chance. So I don't get lost here in my thoughts, I'd better start moving back to the old trapline. Yes, I did get back late to the shack, just before dark. What a privilege this was just like coming home here so far out in the sticks. Dynamite had a lot of time on his hands so it was no trouble for him to have the meal ready. He was a good cook and I liked the fancy brown pancakes he often made for breakfast. We had syrup, some jam and plenty of lard, also, we were both fond of this camp we had here. We had the best bunks and we liked to sleep on them. Then there were the solid walls and a solid roof, kind of homelike. Yes, I told my partner that I had two more beaver, one I had laying out from the day before, as I had no time to skin it, and also these two which I had no time to skin. So there were three in all that had to be taken care of soon. He let me do all the talking for a while and then he said, "You can't guess what happened to me yesterday," for in all I was gone two days. It always took one day up and one day back if all went well. "I went back to the lake where you had the canoe. Farther around on the shore I saw where a lot of poplar trees had been cut down last fall." The ice started to go out on all the lakes out and around the shoreline. "This was in a bay," he said, "and there was ice up to the shore where the sun had not been able to cover and thaw that spot." He thought nothing of it and while walking around he set the gun down leaning it against a tree. Then he walked down to the lake, no gun, and here he saw a two foot hole on the edge of the bank through the ice. While standing there a good sized beaver came running down a trail he had there out from the woods. Nobody would have done this other than that half wild Dynamite, it all happened in seconds he said. He threw himself down in front of the beaver right in front of this hole in the ice. He got hold of him fast near the back and threw him into the woods six feet. By them the beaver became confused; there happened to be a dead poplar pole size, he picked it up and killed the beaver. I could hardly believe my ears when he was telling me this. In the meantime he brought him in all bloody around the nose. "Boy," I said, "that is really something," knowing I had another beaver to skin that night. Now we had eight all together. One thing that happened, he showed me his finger and it had a cut on it. First he said he thought he broke it when he fell and hit it on the edge of the ice at the hole. I asked if he wasn't afraid the beaver would bite him but he said he was so excited he couldn't think of anything right then. I told him I had heard many beaver stories but this was the best one.

When a trapper gets started out here it is a constant merry-go-round. It will take us two days to get the canoe up north and we were all prepared for it. Dynamite was raring to go as we sat there talking about it while I was skinning that beaver. He also had nice red meat and we ate it all, that is, the best parts. It never fails to be a long full day out here in this secluded deserted place. Dynamite and I certainly were unified in a common undertaking here. We had the equipment surpassing, no doubt, any other trapper that ever set foot here before us. Early in the morning we worked together to get the chores out of the way, preparing cooked food. Also had part of the stew he made yesterday to take along in sealed tin cans which we had as we would have little time up there for cooking. Also, we would need our sleeping bags; only hoped that it would not rain as this would be bad for there is only room for one under the canoe. The sun had come up very bright and we expected no difficulty through the day. Yes, we had to wire everything shut with car wire which is tough and heavy, forming it in a crosswise fashion going inside around the door, coming out and fastening it above and then down to a large high stump left there on purpose to twist around and make it tight. Also, we did the same thing to the shutter on the window. This the bear did not understand how to open. Never got back there in later years but I would like to see this shack today to see what happened to it.

We got a good start and I knew that Dynamite would carry the canoe most of the time. He was stronger than I so I took the packsack and the gun. There are many obstacles that can become a contest of strength and skill, like the high ridge we had to go over which was almost straight up one hundred fifty feet. I was thinking of a camera to get a picture of Dynamite as he started up that steep incline. In our determination, sometimes overdoing things, expressing our willingness with excessive confidence, we ended up at last exhausted. Around eleven thirty my partner did ask me when we would stop and have lunch. Boy, I said, right now, for we both, no doubt, had the same idea. Of course, fellows like us would never admit when we were overworked or tired. Here in a place like this it would be too confusing and at no time no matter what happened can you think that you are defeated. I remember later on telling two other trappers how we carried that canoe twelve miles through a jungle like that and they said, yes, they always thought I was crazy. Our action had shown progress, for the territory we had covered had many irregular points, uneven, like the exposed mass of rock we had to crawl around. Here we noticed very old looking rocks which had worn away and collapsed, falling way down below us. Here we were enjoying the rest and the food and found many things to talk about. Not far from here are the two beaver I have to skin. Farther up I had the other one by a cliff. Soon we were on our way changing over now and then between our two loads, canoe and packsack. We did have another packsack but this one only had a sleeping bag in it and that was not heavy. We came to a long narrow beaver pond and could benefit here by going three quarters of a mile on water. How strange it seemed to ride on the water after all the walking. Here on the south end of this pond I had the two beaver partly hidden away. Yes, they were there, and I started to skin them. Now my partner got a long rest as he did not care to try skinning beaver. First he was afraid he would cut the hide and it appeared as though he never cared about learning. This was OK with me for he did more for me out here than an average person would do. He understood the activities and also the direction of my goal, a contest between the forces of nature. It took me over an hour to skin these two beaver and that is much faster than the average trapper can do it. So we moved on looking over two sets nearby and I decided I had caught one of the large ones here. I left only one set. Far ahead would be more places for I never came to the end of the bodies of water following one another, creeks, streams and lakes. Here on likes to trace hidden places that give slight indications, far-reaching at times, of sunken flat land or a marsh or swamp, winding around the edge of a forest, exploring often to find ascents to the headwaters of rivers. Occasionally one finds a waterfall rushing forth and down, fringed with acts of separation, breaking the surface unevenly, in rude and violent action. This is a scenery in motion, harmonious, uttering sounds of murmuring tones. These are the ways one finds nature, balanced, forming a completed series of concerted actions in order with the daily rounds of life. Truly, we both realized we were in a wilderness country. It was late evening by the time we got over to the next sets a mile away. The first thing I did was walk back to a rock cliff where I had thrown the other beaver to keep him out of the sun as there it was cool. When I got there I could see the beaver was gone. Looking around we saw bear tracks. This was the third beaver I had left from two days ago that I did not have time to skin that day. Well, I felt bad losing that beaver but we did learn that the bear were out. Dynamite had no use for bear and thought to get revenge by shooting the first one that came along. I said no, he could not do that. He would soon start to smell and we would have every crow in the country around here. This was just another time the bear slipped up on me again. My partner had already started a fire for we were going to camp here for the night. One is never too particular about a place when staying for only one night as long as there is plenty of wood around and water. Dynamite got to telling me what had happened to him once while guiding on a fishing trip up in Canada. He had an old German (Luger) pistol that he always carried for shooting large fish when guiding. This night they were camped on a fair sized island. In the pup tent, around midnight, something woke him and he thought he felt something touching him on the side. Right away he was thinking of a bear. He slept with the pistol under a small pillow he had, so he reached to get it, it was pitch dark, pointing it in an upward angle like direction, he pulled the trigger. He hit the bear, falling backwards, just missing him and howling. In the meantime the bear took off, running partly dragging him, the pup tent and all. He was on the tail end of the whole mess and said sliding along about thirty feet he fell out and the bear never stopped running or howling. The two fellows he was guiding heard all the commotion (they had a small tent of their own) and came over where he was with their flash lights. "Boy," he said, "I'll never forget that as long as I live." I said that must have been something and assured him it could easily happen. I was thinking that the bear who stole my beaver saved me the job of skinning it. By now my right hand man had supper ready. We were both tired from all the commotion we had, wrestling around getting the canoe this far.

Here we were, two individuals, sharing and entrusting our supply of food, its transportation, using at all times practical judgment, working together as colleagues in the business. We were secretly proud of our accomplishments although we never talked about it. We had a good start the few days we had been out here, yet we had a long way to go towards my dream of getting a hundred beaver of good size. I knew that farther beyond we would be reaching higher altitudes. Here some of the stretches are quite tedious and I was aware of this combining our journey into the heart of this headwater country revealing waters that reach far into the interior. Here we were on the mainland of this wilderness. Tonight where we are camping there is a thick stand of closely packed spruce growing down to the water's edge of this large old beaver flowage presenting to us a green barrier obstructing views, a part shelter that can rebuff the full force of the winds. One cannot help being alert when surrounded by such an environment. So the night passed by and in the morning we were looking forward, first of all, to the good pancakes my cook made on an open fire. The water in such places has practically no current and one is glad to be able to place the canoe in such a flowage as we had here. We will be looking over the sets that I had scattered all along this route going north from here. By noon, if all goes well, we should make it up to where I had camped and this is where the pup tent was sitting. Now we had to start carrying the canoe again for a good mile through the woods. Then there was another body of back water resulting from beaver dams on a stream, often spring fed. There in the fresh morning air the food tastes good. appetite was essential to enable us to endure the long day ahead. Transporting a canoe through the brush at times got to be quite a chore. We slid the canoe into the water the first chance we had and in a few minutes we were off. The trick is, while gliding along at such ease, not to hit any sharp stumps or snags scattered all around in such a place,sticking up here and there. Glancing back, about two hundred feet behind us I saw three otter swimming, going up and down coming straight towards us. Wait, I told Dynamite, lay right down in the canoe flat so you can get a good aim. He got one. One came swimming directly behind us about fifteen feet away, there was a peep sight on this 25-20 caliber Remington,and he said he had it in sight,right on the head but was waiting for it to come closer. Just that second the otter went down, the other disappeared, the one came up way ahead in front of us going up and down. We tried to chase one of them but found that this is an impossibility. Soon we gave up. Not far down a good sized body of water came into view. Straight across was an old beaver house and something was floating nearby, a large brown bulk of a thing. Getting closer we recognized it was a large dead beaver, yes, he must have gotten killed in a fight. He was in good shape, pulling on the fur it held tight; happened just recently, we thought. There was swamp all around a very small island and out here we stopped and I skinned the beaver as there was some mud in the fur. I washed out the skin flopping it back and forth in the water. Then when you flip them again most of the water flies out. This is one way you can get them in good shape. Going up further on this flowage we got to a dam and could see from a distance there was a beaver swimming.By now we got to thinking that we really were getting into good trapping country. Dynamite took a shot at him, he flopped around some, then disappeared. Knowing they hang on to anything down below we got a twelve foot pole cutting it so it would leave a crotch on the small end. We fished around and could feel him ever so often, pushing down and twisting the pole to catch the hair. We tried for half an hour, could not get him, so we got going again heading down to where I had the pup tent, the overnight stopping place. So far I was able to manage to get there every other night. Only a half mile down the flowage ended and this neither of us liked for there was a mile left to go through the woods to get to the body of water, the original place we wanted to explore for it consisted of a large body of flooded swamp land. Here one was unable to get out to the main flowage where good trapping could be found. Around three in the afternoon we got to our sleeping quarters. Dynamite thought I had found a good place for camping and setting up the pup tent. We had thought about the bear tearing up this little tent and were surprised to find it OK. One of these pup tents can mean so much on a rainy night. I wanted to go a few miles up the trapline before it got dark. Did not lose any time getting started as often a trapper will leave traps set too long in one location. Even eighteen traps scattered out eight miles kept me going. These were all good live sets, only where I tried to catch the large beaver and then moved. Looked at four sets and there were two good sized ones caught. Carried one along with me and the other I hung over down a rock wall. One was a coal black one. I might also say that I found each one of them had drowned. My partner could not sit still and had gone out scouting, shooting beaver. He found one of those natural locations where there is a high bank. Observation for shooting is good here eliminating the scent and this is important. Yes, he managed to get one so the result was we got four together. The first one was dead, floating, Dynamite got one and I had two in the traps. Things like that will happen every day - something new will come up. It always turns out to be a long day. It was getting late when I came back, it was dark. One gets accustomed to the surroundings, the direction of walking, so I could find the place. It seems when darkness comes and one follows it as it gets dim on from twilight, your eyes get used to it. I was able to see a good sized fire going some distance throught the woods knowing then that he was there making the supper. This would be another night when I would be straining my eyes by the firelight to skin two beaver. After a little food for the stomach, and a little rest, I was ready to start working on the beaver. The four feet are cut off first, then the tail, then opened from tail to chin on the bottom straight up on the belly. There are many trappers who hate this job. Civilized trapping does not require the hardships in this skinning of beaver. Most of them trap by motor transportation, therefore they bring them home to a convenient place to do the skinning. Out here as one can call it wilderness trapping, now that it was spring and getting warmer, every day at this time of the year it is a pleasure to be out on the trapline. However, in late fall many hardships come into being like in any walk of life there are problems, so it is out here. There are new problems every day and this is when experience counts, to know how to cope with and take care of the matter. We found out how handy it was to have wire. It was used on traps to wire up and down andon objects to keep things away from the bear.Like farmers or loggers, they cannot get along without wire. By the time I got the two beaver skinned it was late and I was ready for the sleeping bag. Dynamite had brought up the canoe and he would use it to sleep under. I took the beaver carcasses and threw them back in the woods a ways thinking that the bear might be satisfied with this and would not snoop around closer here at night. We know that when they find the beaver carcasses tonight they will have a picnic. Certainly we would not worry about them for nature will take its course. So the night went and checking in the morning we found the bear had been here and there was no sign of anything left,however,we never heard a thing.Dynamite would stick around the camp today until late afternoon. The suckers were running again and he would look for some where there were rapids about a mile through the woods between 2 lakes. That is often the best place to catch them, in shallow water. Also at the same time he thought to look for mushrooms - he knew the ones that were not poisonous. Should he find some he would make some stew. By now we were getting tired of the same rations and thought it would be good to have a change. Also, we had a stone crock with a cover. Made a good fire so we had a good bed of coals, buried the crock in there for three to four hours baking beans with beaver meat. He said he would have time today to do this and we could have it for supper. I told him this would be fine and that I appreciated his efforts. When it came to cooking he had as much patience as any woman. I managed to get the canoe over to the large beaver flowage I found a week ago. Here the water was backed up for several miles having a dam here and there. This also created several bays where beaver could get near high land where popple was growing around the vicinity. Being their choice food they would find them in the remotest places often where a person could not even crawl. Using a channel to go in and out of the water was a good place for a set providing the water was at least three feet deep so a drowning set could be made. I went part way by canoe and then had to go overland to get the canoe to look over eight more traps. I had not had the time to get to them for three days. Then there was the beaver to skin which I left there last night. Was constantly looking forward to finding new locations and often found them unexpectedly here and there. I was running short on traps and today had to take some up. One can tell quickly which ones should be moved. By the time I got to the end of the route I had two more beaver, this meant I had three beaver to skin including the one I left there yesterday. I never failed at any time to get out the dollar watch I had and place it in front of me and challenge myself to see if I could do one in half an hour. Sometimes it took a little longer but after skinning as many beaver as I had since I started trapping I got to be rather good at it; like they say, practice makes perfect. Under the circumstances I was working, I wanted to make it back by nightfall where I had a place to crawl into - this was constantly on my mind. At no time could I start day dreaming, make some foolish mistake getting caught in a trap, or cut with an ax wandering around up and down these often beaver-made lakes and ponds in such a lonely remote country. Here I had no one to talk to, therefore thinking out loud was a reaction of thoughts that would supply an answer. Details that can involve tiny green fresh looking plants, trees, flying or singing birds, or it was from my past or the present and the future. Here in my condition the spirit prevailing in unity regarding the concerns of my surroundings where in turn I could accomplish my purpose. Understanding emotions, reasoning is held where action or good judgment of the same nature can find the source where needed so I could apply myself to my existing conditions. So often there were moments in my thoughts when man constantly will struggle against things that he does not even know about. Often I have thought, how slow we are in learning and it seems even if we lived one hundred years we would do no differently. When young our thoughts are high, reaching middle age we obtain characteristics distinctive in habits which is a product of nature. Here where I found so much freedom, isolated from civilization the fact remained that I was learning something from this experience. To state here, I found that if you should ask any man from any walk of life regardless how hard his life has been or what misfortunues he may have had, or how poor he may be, should he have a chance to exchange his life for anyone else, he will say no. So my thoughts wandered way off somewhere and in seconds I realized I was on the trapline.

Told Dynamite that we needed more of those planks hewed out of the dead rampikes for now the beaver hides were accumulating and we needed them to make several more of the door-like units for drying the skins. Also, he started to make another canoe paddle, he liked to make them, and by the time he got all the fine points down to size with a knife it looked like a real one. Came back part way on water in the canoe where I had left it late this morning. Found enough time to make three good sets on my way back. Imagine, out there in that beaver pond as it was getting dark, at the last minute making a set. First I had to get on shore to find a suitable rock, that is, about three to four inches, partly square, and eight to ten inches long. Then in the center of this rock the corners are chipped off with the back end of the hatchet, round in form. Here a cloth line of good condition is tied, four feet in length used double, tied in a certain fashion on the third or second length of chain near the trap in such a way it must tighten when pulled on. On each trap or every set made, a rock of this form is placed to make certain to drown the beaver. They are very strong and often an inexperienced trapper will lose them and often find only a foot in the trap. While I was getting into the canoe I heard some brush cracking, looking up a large black bear came leisurely walking around on the side of the hill that was winding around this old beaver pond. I hurried to get this set made as it always seems when fighting for time it gets dark faster. I paddled as fast as I could and as far as I could go on this old beaver pond. Now came the problem. I did not want to come back for the canoe so I started to carry it with me. Was not able to see very far ahead so I got hung up ever so often in the brush. With that bear I just saw around, I did not want to leave it behind. Could see the fire going where we had our little camp. Being so mixed up trying to get the canoe back I set it down when I got near, about a thousand feet back and I could see the fire from there. So I started to holler for Dynamite. Yes, he heard me and came running, for by now I was very tired and he took it from there. So I was glad to get back and by now it was really dark. Now when I was here it made me feel very contented after the last minute struggle I had to get here. I knew that I could get a warm meal, had not forgotten we will have baked beans and prunes with bannock for dessert. Dynamite had three suckers all cleaned and salted down for breakfast. Yes, my partner also had a big day but he did not get to shoot any beaver. This is not always easy, conditions have to be just right. But out of planks he made room to stretch four hides. We had now accumulated seven that had to be stretched. We kept the fire going in good shape so that we could see to stretch the skins. These are put on with nails and it works out good - one knows just about where to start in order to get the right size. After this job we had another job hanging this whole unit down over a high rock wall that was behind us here a short distance. We have a flashlight and plenty of wire. However, first we had to nail two round poles, one on each side so when we slid it down on this rock wall it could not touch the skins on the other side and knock the nails out. We wondered what the bears thought about all the noise we were making. We knew they would be around looking for beaver carcasses - there was no way we could get rid of them. Of course, we would not shoot them. They will follow the trapline all the way and can smell the scent of the meat a long ways off. We placed a lot of large chunks of wood on the fire thinking it would keep the bear away, just before we called it a day. Often this will burn half of the night. I was lucky I didn't have any beaver to skin tonight, this doesn't happen very often. You cannot let them pile up as it will rob you of time the next day. You started to think about a few things just before you go to sleep. Those are only fleeting seconds and then you are gone. While the bears are sneaking and circling around, you could say they are living with us, they had not touched us and we felt confident that they wouldn't. So, while the balance of nature is restored in our tired bodies and where we learned to understand how much this means to us, we waited for a new day to come. I had not thought of praying, all things were appreciated and I was secretly thankful for all we had. The reason I did not pray was I found it took some men, including myself, many years to learn how to pray. In fact, I learned more than that and that is that no one can even pray without the help of God. So as the night vanished, soon the new day came one hour before sunrise, with the singing of the birds as usual, and we started to move around feeling inspired and cheerful on this brisk morning. A soft wind was blowing and breathing the fresh air into our lungs aroused us quickly. Thoughts flowed mostly concerning the activities for the day, explaining, at times, to my partner a process of general purpose so essential, very often changing around our plans from the day before. We had very little food left. The suckers Dynamite was frying now for breakfast, would be a big help. It would take us a day to get back to our central location where we had our shack and where our main food supply was stored. The sparks from the fire were popping and cracking and this was mixed in with the sizzling sound of frying fish. I could just imagine how good it would taste as I sat here looking on. We had a little flour left so we would have bannock with the fish, a good hearty breakfast. There would be some left over and this we take along for lunch, in fact, it was all we had left with the exception of some tea. Knowing we make our other camp by nightfall, all such things are taken for granted. The endless chores that were constantly in progress concerned mostly the bears. By now we had fifty-three beaver skins, most of them were dried in our shack. The four we had on our rigging down the rock wall will be OK provided it did not rain, as I was saying, before I got back there again and this would be the next day late evening. Everyone of these fifty-three beaver I had skinned out by now and, with the exception of some hind quarters and sometimes the best part of the back which I cut out for our own use, the bear got the rest. They had good reason to follow us day and night. One time I ran across where the bear had made a cache- this is when they are not hungry and hide the food away. There were three beaver carcasses under a large old dead jackpine. I stamped on it one day by accident, near a short steep embankment where a creek was running over on the other side. All the bark was torn off this jackpine to cover up these carcasses, leaves on top and it was a good job of hiding. When I was standing there looking this over it was then I heard the creek running as I did not know it was there the first time I had come in that direction. In the spring of the year there is a lot of water moving from the melting of snow and ice going extremely fast in a downhill fashion forming small rapids, running here in a narrow ravine covered on each side with a heavy elder growth. This always reminded me of a jungle when I ran into places like that. Also there was a romantic atmosphere in connection with beaver trapping here. To follow up a creek or stream one did not have to go far, usually down in a small valley, and the beaver would have a dam, often forming a perfect lake of good size, always in such a way that the water around the beaver house would not be less than eight feet deep for their security so that their passageways or entry into their house, would not freeze up. This then gives them sufficient depth to store their winter food and to roam around. I could never pass a day out there in my travels without finding out something new. This can exist of many things, nature as a whole, habits of animals, unpredictable movements of the beaver exploring new country, etc., often silently one tries to understand when distracted by some hurtful thought of trapping and killing the beaver. Man will find an answer in his own mind hurriedly justifying his own cause. Wrong or right, of course, he will always make it right. So in our bewilderment when we are often mentally disturbed, man being a proud creature as he is, finds an answer of his own choosing. Never does he want to admit that he is wrong and of course he is the one that will make it right, often ever to be in agreement with God's or man's laws. So, while I was making a living on outlaw beaver trapping one always thinks first that there are others in this business, you are not alone. What is the difference, these animals are put here for everybody; one could find a hundred answers however the fact remained that I was learning the hard way and all I could do was to live, learn and suffer. I am trying to get in print here, or to say, to explain the feeling that existed and warnings never ceased perpetrating my thoughts. As other facts constantly came into focus, being in the midst at all times and surrounded by nature, made up for disturbing thoughts. So Dynamite and I knew this morning before we left here that a large high rack had to be made to set the canoe upside down, fastened tightly with a rope, so the largest bear could walk underneath and look up and inside. This way he would be satisfied and very seldom would he then tear it up. Also our pup tent had to be hung down with our beaver skins that were drying on the board, as we called it. One does not think of the bear as an enemy but as a part of nature. He did make a lot of trouble for us but he was also company and certainly kept us on our toes and alert for if they got hold of our skins or grub that could ruin us. So we had a lot of respect for them and were always thankful that they did not hurt us while sleeping.

We took care of our work here, got our sleeping bags rolled up in our packsacks and started out early. The sun was just coming up between the trees like a ball of fire. Glimpsing at the sky it was solid blue in formation, like the shape of a scale of a fish. Occasionally this happens, showing in this form. No doubt your folks have seen it this way. As the old saying goes in German and in that language it rhymes -''When the sky has scales like a fish it will rain the next day for sure.'' Rainy days we had and they were always bad for us out here and a drawback and often caused loss of time. In this adventure of spring trapping the elements (weather conditions) have less influence on a trapper than in late fall. One does not get disturbed at intervals of normal rain or a change in the temperature for at this time of the year we get very little zero weather, only at first when we had to start out early enough so we could walk on the ice. When I first explored this country and the time I got lost and ran out of food, trips late in fall, those were the times really filled with hardships. Now and then I still make a blunder like bucking a slow drizzling all day rain, never stopping tramping through the woods or paddling the canoe around somewhere having the satisfaction of covering the trapline. Like today was a very cloudy day and it looked as though it was getting ready for rain. Having a very light load both of us were moving right along. It seemed that everything we did we enjoyed. It appeared that all of it was a part of life itself, the mood and our very motions in our coordination, gait of walk, mostly in silence going ahead making good time. We had nine traps to look at on the way down. Most of these I will take up tomorrow on my way back as I will need them on the place where I can go by canoe. In locations where the two large beaver had not been caught, here the sets will be left. Dynamite found this all very interesting, always carrying the 25-20, what we called our beaver gun (rifle), fully loaded and on safety. It can be released in seconds and ready for a shot. Looking at three sets, no beaver, and it was noon. We got a fire started very fast with birch bark, made some tea, and had the lunch we brought along, fish, the same as we had for breakfast. It tasted good and it always a mystery to me how much energy a person can get out of so little food and how long one can last on it. Our conversation was of mutual understanding and every time we stopped we talked trapping explaining to him what places he can go tomorrow, for further locations, he can find by going south for shooting beaver. He would be alone again and would have lots of time on his hands - I told him to be sure to take the compass. He can be two or three miles down there and very seldom do beaver come out until late afternoon. It is easy then to get caught in the dark. Of course, I warned him about that for a fellow often will stay late trying to get a shot at one. I could be of no help to him for every other day I would leave him going up north at least ten to fifteen miles, then come back the next day. I also warned him to always take the hatchet along (he did not want to carry an ax when he had the rifle) and matches and if it should be that he got caught in the dark he should not start wandering around but stay in one place and make a good fire. This is no problem for a woodsman. There are plenty of lakes and he carried a fishing line with a (daredevil) artificial bait. No problem for him to catch a fish. Yes, we found things to talk about, never can I remember that we talked of any woman. We were so deeply involved in this trapping deal and of course, for a little guy or poor person, it was big money. In those days trapping beaver for money, never did I think of getting caught. It is a fantastic thing with all of us people how money takes over authority and tells us what to do. This often turns out to be a sad ending for a good many people. Here again the time factor was in progress. Twenty minutes would be the most time we would allow ourselves for lunch, like an endless procedure of fighting time. When we looked at the last of the six sets left we had two beaver. It is best if you have time to skin them near the place where you catch them. This I could do on a day like this. Dynamite had no desire to learn how to skin a beaver; often a beginner will cut the hide. Also, we made no effort to hide the carcass from the bear, that was useless, for he can find them most any place. Besides, while having a good time feasting on that meat, he would not bother us some place else. Many things work hand in hand. They are inquisitive rascals and often very bold. We had three beaver skins from before, now the two we got today so we had five to dry. There was room in the shack to nail only two on the board. The best thing to do is to make another board. When we were around the shack there was always a fire in the small drum heater. In two days the skins dried in there and also here we could lock them up away from the bear. This was one place he did not know how to get into although the stove pipe on top of the partly flat roof was pulled out every time we stayed away a few days. That was mostly because the beaver castors were hanging inside on the ceiling and he could smell them. Like I mentioned before, we saved them and at that time they were up to $15 a pound. They have good weight and at one time we got together five pounds.

Dynamite and I, after being gone for two days, were glad to get back here to our most favorable place, and good old shack. I was thinking of the short time it took to build it and all the comfort we have gotten out of it. Those are things that could not be measured in dollars and cents. Soon we had two hides stretched and my partner started cooking and baking. Part of the one hundred pounds flour we brought out by canoe last fall held up good for quantity knowing we did not have to save on that item. We felt that we were modern trappers for we even had jelly along and log cabin syrup. Also tonight we had our bunks to sleep on and a kerosene lamp, being very careful not to break the chimney as we did nct have another one. Just about the time we were ready to retire, ten o'clock, it started to rain. Somehow one gets an overwhelming feeling of security and comfort to say, don't worry, you are safe. Freely this delightful reward of gratitude can grip you, a power of reaching comprehension. Also, one cannot help hearing the harsh sounds caused by the friction of the trees rubbing against one another.Where such rubbing has occurred by the falling of one tree onto another and dried, often becoming a dead tree, then the movement of the wind often produces a dry screeching noise. We had a combination of this kind near our shack that always was heard distinctively on a windy night. In time all those sounds become familiar and become part of this life. Yes, one hears many sounds, the calling of a loon, the nearest to a human voice. The owls, if one can understand them, can predict the weather. For years I hated them for the killing of rabbits until I understood that each animal has a purpose for its existance. One is a supply of good for the other and therefore has a meaning of being here. The whippoorwill has a pleasant yet mysterious call. The coyotes cry, I believe, in loneliness of their own, also reminding one that you are in a lonely country. It was as though these sounds to us here in the wilderness had a special meaning portraying life and hope, warnings, and often in the animal kingdom, death. No, I did not hear the sound of that tree very long and soon I was dead to the world. Waking up as usual early in the morning, it was still raining so neither one of us was in a hurry to get going. Was afraid that this is one day that I could not start out going north. In order to make this trip I could not start too late or at noon as it was too far. Dynamite got up first and got the fire going. The space in this shack was very small so one of us would dress first while one would then sit in the corner. There was not much to it in getting dressed for we slept with our pants on so it was a quick job. Had pancakes with syrup and prunes again for breakfast. Sitting very quietly both of us on the bottom bunk enjoying the food when all at once a bear stood right in front of us in the middle of the door, we had the door open, standing straight up with his big brown eyes just staring at us. Neither one of us spoke a word just looked at the bear. Dynamite reached for the rifle and shot him in the leg. He started to run through the woods yelping very loud. We both got up and went outside to watch him go. Right nearby were two more bear, good size, also looking at us but they started to run. I told Dynamite to let them go for I hate to cripple them. "You know," he said, "I shot that other one in the leg on purpose just to scare him. Boy did you see him looking at us? I thought he was going to get fresh, that's the reason I let him have it." "I think you did the right thing this time, but don't shoot them just for fun," I said. That ended our conversation about that bear except that we did agree that there must be a lot of bear around. Of course we never knew how many, only that they picked up all the beaver carcasses, that we did know. Having time on our hands, for it never let up on the rain, we put on raincoats and started to cut down three inch size spruce trees. We used the Swede saw when cutting them down, three and one half feet long. Then I brought them to the shack. Dynamite would hew each one of these into small round poles, flat on each side. Then they were nailed together as one unit forming a flat surface to get room on each side to stretch two more beaver hides. What all this meant to us to have nails, a saw, an ax, a rifle, ammunition, shelter, food, a place to sleep, a stove, matches, a canoe, knives, hammer, whetstone, kerosene, wire traps, pup tent, sleeping bags. Yes, we were well organized and to this day no one knew that we had all those things out there and would never believe how we got all this in here or that anyone would go to that extent. Any of the other trappers before us who penetrated this remote country always came in on foot from the Gunflint trail into this area which was sixty-five miles inland or come across by way of Ely, Minnesota. Who would take the nerve to come in here in this fashion and homestead this place for two months in the spring of the year. Why we never saw any other human being after my first trip out, I don't know. The resort man introduced me to this territory and this was two years ago and I paid for that dearly with labor and hardship. After I had learned more about this trapping, then it dawned on me that I could bring in supplies by canoe in late fall and this would save a lot of hardship. I built a shack so it would be safe from the bears, hired a cook who would also help me with other details, and that was when I thought I was really getting smart. Of course, at the time I went bankrupt on my logging job I was very desperate and was in a hurry to get back on my feet in order to be able to put up with this kind of life (especially when I first started out) to the hardships of pioneer life. Many other things had happened to me years before the time of 1930. I began this story from that time on for all this happened in the north woods as my title will show. Combining other hardships I had endured before, for that reason I was able to take it when the time came along for this wilderness trapping. It was like a new life with only a few possessions that I was able to carry in here on my first three trips. Those were trying days at that time. Here this morning getting caught up with the small jobs we could do around here at the shack, it was still raining, and by noon we were getting restless. We both had raincoats and Dynamite got the fishing fever and thought to go across country to look for a good lake. Yes, we would go together and I would take the rifle this time. No doubt we were both restless characters and the thought of seeing some new country was encouraging to us even on a rainy day. We also knew that the ice had not completely gone out on the big lakes and knew the direction where the canoe route was and that is where we wanted to go. Had our dinner early and through the woods we went, going southwest at a fast pace. The rain had now almost come to a stop. One is motivated by this change and it also changed our action tending us to move much faster in our walk. The timber stand here was not very heavy and often we could see a good distance away. It seems that there is more freedom in general where the woods are not so thick. All of a sudden we came upon a lake and it had a large chunk of ice way out. A light wind was blowing and where the ice had gone out there were small ripples showing on the water. There was a high bank as far as I could see around. It must have been a half mile across, then I could see a large bay going in and back on the southeast end. Coming up very close where we could see over the high bank and straight down from us where the lake made a long curve, was a large beaver house. Here the water was open a considerable distance out and around. About two hundred feet down from the beaver house along the shore was this large body of ice when it came up right tight on shore. We were both standing up here on this high bank looking this over, admiring this formation of ice curving back and forth like an island in a lake, covering a quarter of the total body of water. Must explain here that the water all around the lake was showing where the ice had melted entirely two to three hundred feet from shore. As I mentioned before, a few lines above, down here where we were in the south bay the ice came up toward shore about ten feet in width and took off from there. We would not go near the beaver house, one never does, even when setting traps; they hear very well and any unusual sound makes them suspicious. I knew immediately as soon as we arrived here and saw the beaver house that I would stay here waiting for the beaver to come out. Dynamite went further around up the lake to do some fishing. Going very quietly I went way around this almost even round, twelve-foot-across ten-foot high well-constructed beaver house. Truly the scenery as a whole presented a picture of wilderness environment. I gave no tnought as to why this large floating body of ice was of such condition as I now was standing within ten feet from where it had come right tight up the shore. There was a bunch of willow sprouts frozen into this ice here on shore, six or eight of them no larger than two inches around, sticking out two feet above the ice leaning outward from shore. Now I saw what happened, I did not notice this for one often takes such things for granted. While standing there very still looking straight toward the beaver house I had the gun in hand, loaded, ready to shoot. Thought I had heard a noise, odd in sound, nearby underneath almost where I was standing. I was surprised, the sound had been very faint, but I never moved and I listened and listened. Now and then I could hear it very plain and then I knew that it was a beaver underneath the ice, cutting off those willows. All of a sudden I saw this large body of ice going far out around the lake, which was about thirty acres in size, moving very slowly away from shore. The willows that were frozen in, sticking out on top of the ice were going with it. So, the whole thing dawned on me. The only thing that was holding this body of ice was that small bunch of willows and as soon as the beaver cuts them off underneath the ice, that releases them and they drift across going with the wind. This was something new - I had never witnessed anything like this before and I knew it would never happen again. Thinking of the beaver, did they do this to get the ice away from their house or what? No, I kept telling myself, they are not that smart, it just happened. Further up the lake where Dynamite was fishing he must have seen the ice moving. Of course, he did not know what had happened and what I had seen. It was a good place where I was standing, I never moved thinking that one of these beavers would show up so I could get to see one. It must have been an hour when one finally popped up out of the water fifty feet away from the house, actually swimming toward the house and before he got there went down just like he was going into the house where they have their entrance deep under water. The reason they must have deep water is so the entrance cannot freeze up. And here I had expected beaver to come out of the house in the late afternoon and this one was going in. Where he was and where he came from is what I was thinking. One has to have a lot of patience shooting beaver, I did not mind it as long as I was not too cold.

The rain had stopped completely several hours ago. This was a blessing, however, one does cope with most any kind of weather when a watch for beaver is in progress. It is a fascinating adventure and the trick is to be certain when you shoot that they are hit in the head. This requires careful aim for their heads are not very large especially when they are swimming. Also one likes to catch them when they are near shore as we had no canoe around. There were times when we shot a beaver a mile or so away from where the canoe was kept. We would then carry it over there in order to be able to get out to pick it up, where it was floating. It was getting late by now, Dynamite was walking high up on the ridge and I could see him coming back. I knew then that we had to head back to camp if we didn't want to get caught in the dark. Several beaver had come out, swimming around, but there was no chance to get a halfway decent shot at one. So, there were no beaver for today. Did not have to ask my partner whether or not he had any fish - I could see two large pickerel dangling on a string. I told him what had happened, the beaver cutting off the willows and how that released that whole block of ice. "Yes," he said, "I saw it moving and thought that the wind was shifting it." We hustled up to get back knowing the direction rather well, and we had no trouble finding the place inasmuch as it had gotten dark on us. We got a fire made in a hurry in our little stove and I started cleaning the fish-thought they weighed about three pounds a piece. We filleted them and this was one way we knew they were really clean. Yes, we had a good meal. Dynamite could eat more than I could. He was a big man. So knowing that we had a shelter over our heads and that we had done the best we could for a part rainy day, we were satisfied. My partner decided there must have been a whole family of beaver at that lake where we were today. Yes, he will go back and stay all day to see if he can get some shooting. One will talk like that in order to justify our action for today. It is the way with life, we are never completely satisfied. One seems to search for new answers for life depends on so many things, for human nature has its way to be in agreement with our own makings,where one seems to care more about the tangible things of life arriving from decisions while our thoughts were constantly wrapped around a philosophy dealing with conditions that were in reach all around us. One becomes a part of such surroundings attracted here by this. Natural resources, (skins of beaver,) have brought many trappers this way.Like one day I started to make a set not far away from here on one of the larger very clear streams running south from here. Got in the middle of this dam and started to dig a hole fixing it up to set a trip in. Here was a sandy bottom and using my bare hands for this work I thought I felt something hard. Pulling it up, it was a trap, very badly deteriorated and it had started to fall apart, unearthing evidence here to show that someone had been here many years ago. How each trapper, I thought, finds the best location for sets and now I picked the very same spot this man did many years ago. Yes, it was back in 1759 when the English and Scottish business men took over the organization of the fur trade in Montreal. Soon their canoes were penetrating into the far west. The large canoes were manned by French Canadian voyageurs, were paddled up the Ottawa in the spring full of supplies and trading goods. The route lay across the highest land from the Ottawa River by the French River into Georgian Bay and from there through Lake Huron and Lake Superior to Fort Williams. There the goods were transferred to small canoes for the western part of their journey which lay by way of Rainy River

System, Lake of the Woods. Here they started to come into the territory we were trapping in. They went further ahead to the Winnipeg River to Lake Winnipeg, from this point the Red, the Assiniboine, the Saskatchewan and in the far north the Peace and the McKenzie Rivers led out to their trading areas at that time. As soon as they carried their trade into this region the Montreal traders, who soon united in the Northwest Co., were challenging the Hudson Bay Co. Soon a fierce competition developed. The two companies built posts side by side at important places on the main rivers and lakes and sometimes the rivalry flared into violence. The Hudson Bay Company in time won out when these two companies joined together and Hudson Bay, for a half century, controlled the fur trade. This way the whole western territories were opened up.

There are many things that can be said about the beaver. They are found in less settled parts of North America and Asia. Beaver fur was important and valuable when North America was being settled and it was one of the chief causes of exploration. To get beaver, fur trappers and traders went out into the wilds, building trading posts and forts and opened up the country for settlement. At one time beaver skins were used for money but the trappers almost destroyed the beaver. Around 1880 only a few beaver were left and they were in the most inaccessible places. Now, with protection, they came back to our wooded streams and ponds. Where a few of us got in on the last leg of the period of outlaw beaver trapping, no one at that time realized then that laws would be enacted some five years later so no illegal beaver skins could be sold or tanned. A special tag came into being called a vendor's tag to go with the regular trapping tag, one for each pelt. Some states had an open season in early spring telling how many one can

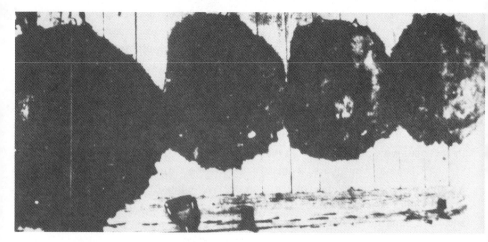

BEAVER PELTS - SEE THE TAGS

190

catch. It was usually open twenty or thirty days, allowing each trapper a small number of them. No traps can be set near a house or dam. Before a trapper can sell them the warden is to inspect them to see that both tags are securely fastened to each pelt in order to make things legal. Like so many things that have vanished with time in our country, so it was the the trapping days of the illegal beaver fur. No trapper ever regrets his trapping days; like childhood days, they will bring back memories. Like the many sunrises and sunsets in the stream of time, of endless duration never ceasing where an appreciation of life was established, I learned many things often in solitude in the realm of nature, looking back on things, renewing part of life's thoughts of interest and rewarding memories. Often when we are young we cannot see very far ahead to implant unlimited confidence within ourselves. To achieve this we must often first experience hardships.

So here Dynamite and myself will spend another night in our little shack here. Having had a good meal now, no doubt, we were as contented as one could ever be here in our environment. The shack was never damp, there was always a small fire going when one of us was around day or night. There was the job of removing the dry beaver pelts from the two stretching boards we had now, as soon as they were dry. Most of the time we had skins placed away, waiting for room on the boards to stretch them when we could. There was never a dull moment from early morning to late at night so there was no time to get lonesome or blue. We were eagerly looking forward to a new day and expectations for a catch of at least two beaver a day. This was our line of thought. After having a rainy day yesterday, today we got up earlier than usual. A day lost on a trapline cannot be made up. There were such days of hustling, thinking that I could make up part of lost time, often going to extremes by walking fast like a wild man through the woods never thinking that anything could happen. This particular day I was walking rather swiftly making a short cut through some thick brush when a dead stick, about a half inch in size, when straight into my ear and damaged it very badly. When this happened, it happened so fast, I had to sit right down holding my head with both hands for half an hour. The whole side of my face was numb. Touching my fingers near the ear I got hold of my dead stick and pulled on it and got a piece out. It was partly rotten so it broke off and part of it stayed in. I was disturbed and felt bad and noticed that my hearing was not the same. We carried first aid material that also included cotton. I placed a wad of cotton lightly in my ear, touching it here and there, and it was bleeding. Started out very slowly now and everything, all of a sudden, was different. So I trudged along knowing that I had to keep on going, there was no choice about that, taking most of the traps up here on this lower end of the trapline. We had the canoe up north where I had found a large flowage of beaver ponds and we needed some traps there. Most of these places here we had caught one or two out of each colony. It was important to get sets made in the most lively places and one could easily tell such localities because of the evidence here and there especially on new cuttings and peeling of poplar limbs. These fresh peeled parts can often be seen for a distance, shining white-yellow color. Having placed a supply of loose cotton in my shirt pocket I would exchange it for new when walking along. Noticed that the drainage was mixed with blood and had little small rotten pieces of wood. I did not know how much of the stick was left in there and was somewhat worried that it would give me a lot of trouble. It was aching and my whole ear felt numb and I was perplexed for it was a mental agitation. I trudged along all day and as it happened I caught three beaver. I thought that the catch should be good for I missed one day and often this means a difference. I managed to skin two of them and one I brought back here with me where I camped on this north end of the trapline. The canoe was still on the rack up high on this pole stand - was thankful nothing happened to that for it would be terrible if some crazy bear would tear down the poles and knock it off from there and damage it. How much trouble this will save up on transportation when going home. Instead of carrying them overland out on our backs we will be able to go back on water. This will be the first time we will have the opportunity to do this since we had worked and planned for this small trapping expedition far in advance for the sake of eliminating what hardships we could. Yes, we were looking forward to the day to come when we could paddle sixty-five miles back on a good canoe route. We will be waiting for moonlight nights and travel mostly at night as we certainly would not want to meet anyone on this trip, especially a game warden. We will have a hundred skins, by now we had eighty-two beaver and one otter and there was still plenty of time left for trapping. The fur at this time was in fine condition. It was, in fact, as prime as it ever could get. Had to get settled for the night, walking back there to get the pup tent that we placed out of reach of the bear and also the beaver skins we had hanging down that high rock wall on the homemade stretching board yesterday when we had rain. The ones that were exposed on the face side did get wet however, they will discolor some and have to redry again. I was having a constant streak of pain in my ear and did not know just what had happened to it and had no way to find out. One thing I knew was that it was injured badly. Kept changing the cotton every hour making it into a small ball-like formation. I managed to get some wood together and also had this job of skinning out the beaver, a job that I did not like under pressure. An uneasy feeling had formed about me since I had that accident. Thought I heard some noise and looking over in that direction where the sound came from there were two black bear. No doubt they had missed me the one day when I was gone and would have this one carcass for them tonight. At times it seemed just like they knew what was going on, ever as much as to come right up at night snooping around, for more than once their tracks had been on one side of my sleeping bag and also on the other side as though they straddled me. One thing I did not like I thought of Dynamite telling me how a bear had come into his pup tent in the dark of night. This I did not want to happen to me so tonight as the sky was clear. I would sleep out here in the open in my sleeping bag and not in the pup tent as long as the bear were roaming around here so close by. I never carried the gun, for my partner kept that with him for every chance or time he had he would use it for shooting beaver. This person, Dynamite, was indeed a big help to me in many ways. I did a wise thing when I had him come out here with me for I hired him on a lump sum basis. By now I had my supper and had a big fire going so I could see the bear walking around. They could smell the beaver I had there just as though they knew that I would skin them out tonight, which was my next job. My ear never quit aching and it took me longer to skin the beaver than it ordinarily did. Was glad when I got done so I could lie down. I placed the skin on top of a bed of boughs I had piled there and threw the carcass back some twenty feet. It did not matter where I had thrown this chunk of meat as the bear would find it. One consolation I had was that not at anytime did a bear attack me as, one of them could tear a person to pieces. To give you a little history concerning them. Their smaller relatives belong to the order of carnivore, or flesh eaters. That does not mean that they eat meat or fish exclusively. Their teeth, called molars, are flatter and broader than those of the cat family and therefore are more adaptable to the grinding of food. This would go to show that flesh does not make up the bear's entire menu. Much of the bear's food consists of insects and vegetable matter such as roots, grass and berries, substances which have to be ground up rather than sheared off before it can be swallowed. Strange to say that on account of certain similarities in the skull, bears at one time were believed to be close relatives to the weasels but further research led scientists to believe that they are a closer kin to dogs. Bear have poor sight and hearing but very keen sense of smell, and they depend upon their nose to a great extent to find food and detect enemies. It is difficult to know just how many bear are around in a locality - they vary greatly in size and also in color. they feed on berries, roots, grass, vegetation, mice, marmots, and other small mammals. They do occasionally kill larger animals and at times are destructive to livestock, and to say here, they are very fond of beaver meat. They will watch for them, expecially in the fall, when they cut down trees, sometimes far back in the woods to get their winter supply of food and they have to transport it back to the water, lakes, streams and ponds. Here, now and then, a bear will catch a beaver. However, the beavers are afraid of bear and place a guard in the water; using their large flat tail they make a loud splashing noise as a warning of danger to the beaver colony. They also make good use of this tail to prop themselves up when gnawing down trees.

Speaking further about the bear, it is found, and here we could talk from experience, that very seldom will they molest man unless provoked and the stories of their attacks are undoubtedly greatly exaggerated. It is only the grizzly that has a reputation of being fierce and dangerous. Before the making of the high-powered rifle he undoubtedly was a beast to be feared. The grizzly is a smaller animal than the Kodiak bear. An average male would weigh about five hundred pounds and an exceedingly large one may weigh as high as seven hundred fifty pounds. A measurement of eight feet for length of the skin would be exceptionally large. In color the grizzly varies greatly. In general it is dark brown, the long hairs of the back being tipped with gray or white. Some are grayish yellow in color. The peninsula giant bear of the Alaskan peninsula and the Kodiak bear found on Kodiak island are the largest of the group, in fact, are the largest land living carnivorous (flesh eating) animals existing today. Skins of animals have measured over thirteen feet in length while weight has been recorded as fifteen hundred pounds. These are exceptionally large male specimens. It is never safe to prophesy just what the grizzly will do and it is never safe to take too much for granted. He can run with surprising speed when necessary. They are not like those out in the woods where I was trapping. I found that these became very tame and very inquisitive and it seemed as though they knew that I was supplying them with all this beaver meat. As they roamed around constantly, day and night, our food, skins, and other had to be kept out of their reach. So the bear was constantly on our mind. We knew they came close to us at night, in fact, came right up to us smelling around while we were sleeping. This we knew because of the evidence showing as they could not hide their tracks. One gets accustomed to this kind of environment and everything is taken for granted. We were glad there were no grizzly bear around - the others were bad enough. However, we learned how to get along with them and it was a lot of satisfaction every morning, the times I was all alone on this north end of the trapline and many other occasions when I had to sleep out in the open, that nothing had happened. And, I do not remember a time that I ever saw one around early in the morning.

So the days would come and go and I was looking forward to the day when we could start paddling the canoe on a homeward journey. I realized when I got up in the morning that I had made a mistake regarding the injured ear. I had laid on my side with the bad ear up so in the morning when I turned my head a spoonful of liquid drained out of the ear, blood mixed with what looked like yellow water. Then i thought, if I laid with my ear down this could have drained all night - I thought how foolish I was. Now while the canoe was down here I could get in location making it easy all around for making better time. Often I had to work my way

TRAVEL BY CANOE

around beaver ponds and lakes in the distance, walking, often winding around crooked formations, through ravines and rocky narrow valleys and this was difficult. There is a feeling of ease traveling in a canoe, the action of movement can be very silent. The use of such transportation and its performance meant so much to us, an inducement of action that gave performance, controlled by the movement of a paddle. Yes, in a way one may think that this is a very simple thing. However, it is a rewarding experience and pleasure to know that I could travel two miles through this body of water in a half hour where if I had to walk around by land it would have taken me two hours. For like I mentioned before down here in this area of steep, rocky, rough, uneven terrain I would appreciate riding instead of walking - most important the time I would save and also not to forget some of the hardships that often come into focus. So, while I was troubled with my sore ear this morning just as I was leaving I heard an aeroplane (we heard that at times they were looking for trappers). I was looking north from a small clearing in the direction of the sound. However, to my surprise, when I did see it it was coming from another direction other that I thought it was. Then I knew for the first time that my hearing was badly confused from the injury yesterday. Kept changing cotton every hour and I noticed very small pieces of rotten stick hanging on the cotton and I was glad that they kept coming out. It was so sore I couldn't touch it anywhere near the inside. Going along here with the canoe down to the first beaver flowage, I did have a few traps with me which I picked up on the way down and this gave me a start. Before leaving there are always the usual chores of hanging everything up so the bear could not get at it. This was an established practice and one couldn't forget that for those thoughts were uppermost in my mind. Everything was important and we could not afford to lose anything or have it destroyed by the bear. The skins, bedding, shelter, food and the canoe were, in a way, all life-saving things and were needed. There were many signs of activities of beaver being on the move here in this new place, often worn down places on a large floating bog of swamp material, where pieces of fresh

195

peeled popple limbs were floating around. The few traps I had were soon gone so this meant I had to look over the rest of my traps and to do this meant considerable walking overland. This was done without hesitation and was, of course, a natural thing including whatever happened to be the general layout for that day. The important thing was to get the traps into new locations, to place them trying to catch as many large beaver as possible. We had very good luck this year in doing this. Seventy-five percent of the eighty-nine skins we had were medium and large and few small ones. Out of this were eleven blankets, those are exceptionally large, and we also had five coal black beaver that I thought to save as they often were hard to get in Wisconsin. Having hired Dynamite, with all his help, I was able to spend more time on the trapline as he did all the cooking and prepared food for me to take along. Besides, up to now he had shot nine beaver and this was a big help to bring up our count. Had thought to remove all my traps today from my old territory. It is easy to take up and pull a trap in a hurry; to set one is often time consuming especially when the weather is cold. There were three beaver caught today and when this happens I really have to hustle up the skinning, and this appeared to me like a trade. One thing about it was that I did a good job so all fat and flesh is removed and to do this requires a lot of caution and a good sharp knife. I got all my traps and the three skins in my packsack and headed back through the woods over to the flowage to where the canoe was parked in a narrow channel the beaver had dug out in this swamp here to reach high land where they floated in their food. This kind of work one can see at almost any colony depending on their layout. just like human beings - some have good locations and some bad. This is where their food is harder to get, meaning also, they have to work harder to survive. There was so much activity every day that one struggled to make camp by dark. Couldn't figure out why I should carry supplies. Getting dark fast, I chopped some poles in a hurry, I found one where a crotch was left on for holding up the crosspieces, and made a high rack to hang the canoe. Did all this work on account of the bear; one became a part slave to them. To justify thoughts along this line one had to take this bear for granted, they were part of nature's environment. Now besides my regular entanglements I had this bad ear from the accident. The pain it gave me was something of a reminder that it was there. One does worry about the loss of hearing, not knowing how serious it was and knowing there was nothing I could do to help ease the pain. To meet such a situation that was an inforeseen condition I had to make rapid and effective adjustments to meet this condition, an understanding intercepted by the thoughts stronger in reasoning to overcome the weak and hoping that in time I will get well. One learns to appreciate every little thing more so when our physical parts are active and it is often very sad when we do not know when we are well off. For that reason an underlying behavior, extremely sensitive, dominated external circumstances in my way of life. Whatever the details relating to incidents where it was certain I could see and feel facts and throwing light upon things as they were. There was a contrast of a different manner in living out here in this wilderness uniting man with nature in the fullest extent, meaning also that it changed my way of thinking much more where at times my life was involved. Here from careful observations I became more watchful in all my doings against danger or error. Even now, while I am trying to explain part of my feelings that surround me, I have the thoughts but cannot find the words for same. So the days came and would go swiftly as I meditated always in silence as I was alone most of the time.

Evenings, mornings and through the day as I traveled around in the woods and on water one got so accustomed to this every day routine as though I had been placed in charge of the expedition. The beaver were, of course, the main attraction and I could also find some history concerning them, showing that they had many things to do with many people and the country, changing the course of history in many ways. The Indians first traded their beaver to independent traders, they would often visit the hunting grounds and carry with them goods which they exchanged for furs. There were many Indians who never visited the trading posts but did all their trading with the traveling traders. The skins did not pass in transaction but were merely the unit of value in terms of which furs or goods were measured. Traders had small sticks to represent "Made beaver" and these were used as money is used. An Indian would bring his furs. They would be valued as worth so many "Made beaver", the Indian would be given a number of sticks equal to the value stated. These he could exchange at once, the next day, or a week later, providing he didn't lose them, each article being rated as worth so many (Made beaver) or sticks for various goods. Where for many years the northern and western part of the United States and Canada supplied so much fur, for so many people a lot of hardship was endured for the glossy, durable fur of the beaver, a prize sought by early traders. As the years went by the wild fur beaver decreased in numbers and were driven farther and farther afield. In the early days of the fur trade it was a practice in Canada for trappers to keep foxes caught out of season alive until the fur was prime. From this custom has arisen the modern industry of fur farming the various kinds of foxes, and many other animals including mink, skunk, raccoon, fisher and marten. Conservation laws came into effect. Ever since that time there has been some illegal trapping, buying, smuggling, going strong around 1920 to the time the vendor's tags came into being. However, for several years even then it continued where the fur buyers would buy the illegal hides in one state like Michigan, they would find friends, people they knew that did not trap in Wisconsin and get them to take out a license so as to get the vendor's tags and then place them on in Wisconsin to get them legalized in that fashion. The fur buyers took advantage of these conditions paying less for the so-called illegal skins from the trappers in Michigan. No doubt it was a racket, in effect, and there were a number of illegal fur buyers throughout the country and they were well known to the trappers. Like, at one time I had one hundred skins hidden down in a swamp near a well-known river. This fur buyer was a rather heavy set man. We were down in this swamp late spring about sunset, he was looking over the one hundred hides. I was watching him turning over one fur on top of the other, kind of scanning them over. The mosquitos were so thick that a dozen would sit on his neck at one time. It kept me busy trying to keep them off of him. Myself, I did not seem to care - guess I was used to it. Yes, there was another fellow who tried so hard to make a success in life. Now he has been gone for a long time and forgotten. That is the way it is so often; if we could only see or learn early in life that the time always comes when no man can work. So, we should not fight it too hard so we also have some time left to think on the spiritual part of our life. Sad to say, while I was out on the trapline, if I had known how to pray, this often would have been a consolation to me. It is often so hard to understand this and to learn to mend our hard-hearted ways of life. Here as my thoughts flow, that is the way I have this written. There are things that happened to me here on this North American continent that people do not know even existed. After such experiences one believes that there is no justice left on this earth. As one lives on, one soon forgets. In our efforts for survival as humans we have a lot to learn. Often I think that most of us are too greedy and that can destroy us in time. While I am expressing some of my own philosophy of life here (as a one-time trapper) I learned from experience the hard way. So while I have a few pages left to write I'll go back to the trapline in northern Minnesota where I have had most of my adventure, back where I challenged that part of the wilderness with my life and freedom.

To conclude further on the history of these fine architects, the hard working beaver, I might state that they mate for life. For many years now I have had a large mounted beaver that my boys can keep some day for a souvenir. Yes, these animals are classified as an amphibious, rodent quadruped. They can build a dam as long as a city block, six to eight feet is the average height of their dam. However, I have seen them twelve feet high between rock walls. They use their tail as a rudder for swimming. Their houses have a large roomy chamber. They often build long canals to other stands of trees and float their food down to the home pond. Much of our rich meadowland was made from the work of beavers from their dams. The water seeps out into the earth all around the dam, making it rich. This continent owes a debt to the beaver and so do I. Here on my trip up here, as circumstances would have it, I had to be gone three days away from the shack south where Dynamite was. I took sufficient food along as I knew it would take me this long to get a new trapline organized. It was a never ending job; there were the skins to take off the drying board and I had three I brought back to stretch out. To pull up that large stretching board, it was on a wire, that was made from two inch planking, was all one man could do, straight up that steep rock wall. Now the weather was much warmer, it was the month of May. Soon we would have to pull out for the black flies (those are the tiny ones) will drive us out. Now it is morning. I thought I head some whining, looked around, and within twenty feet stood a large (what I thought) brown cinnamon bear. He looked straight at me, rather friendly, and I kept on making my breakfast trying not to pay any attention to him. I was hustling around to get my chores done for I was anxious to get going as I had a big day ahead of me working southwest making new sets and I would take the canoe along with me. That meant I had to portage when I got out of that chain of beaver ponds. That part of the territory I was acquainted with but not further beyond. The bear was walking very slowly back and forth and as I got ready to go he followed some distance behind and I knew he was looking for some beaver meat. No doubt those bear got kind of spoiled by now. When I think of all the years back this has been and that no more trapping has been done in that country. The population of the beaver must have increased in large numbers. No doubt the bear get what they can and some must die of old age. Yes, time changes everything even in the wild animal kingdom. Thought I would get back there once more just to see what happened and to take a few more pictures for old time's sake. I arrived at the pond where I had left the canoe on the rack. Took it down and got ready to shove off - the bear was still watching me knowing that soon I would be leaving him. I liked the canoe travel for trapping better than the setting of traps from land by walking. It was more relaxing and more interesting as you can see more out here on the water, the evidence of beaver moving around in many places. My ear still reminded me

CANOE AND PACKSACK

199

that there was something wrong, it was draining all along and I could tell when changing the cotton pad another small piece of wood was hanging on the pad. I was glad when I saw this as I was anxious for all the wood to come out, whatever I had in there.

It was a very bright sunshiny day, everything looked fresh, little trees growing out of clumps of swamp bog here and there. These are often very solid even so that one can walk on them. However, they are just floating there. Was also thinking what Dynamite would be doing now as I did get used to his company. Had a few traps set before in here in this part of flooded marsh and caught a good sized beaver this morning. This is the first thing one looks for when a trapper pulls out a drowned beaver - how large it is. I never did like to skin them in a canoe and waited until I got on land to do this. When I came to the end of this flowage two small rivers came flowing in here; it was a junction and there was a small island in between with a number of white birch clumps of trees. Often there would be four to eight in a bunch, often of good size, and this standing here between these two small streams on the small island in the sunlight made a perfect picture, scenery of nature, a setting I had not witnessed before. Would I like to have a place like that somewhere in civilization and a cabin built there. One could not but do a little dreaming, seeing and admiring this spot. First I had to skin that beaver and then I had to go and follow one of these streams, leaving the canoe here, to find the next flowage further beyond. The beaver just love to dam up such places, however they know exactly where the best place is for the dam. No less than a quarter of a mile up was the first dam, down stream there is always the smaller dam to build up the water for the depth it requires, three to five dams and sometimes more are needed to accomplish this. They get bigger and bigger as they go upstream. They can be scattered a mile apart. In marshlands where the water flows slowly and there is in general more level land, here you find the dams far apart. However in the country up here where the elevation is constantly changing, here the dams are often very close together. Sometimes, it happened where I was standing on the last big main dam, when looking down a ravine I could see all of the dams of this one colony. While a beaver family has worked often very hard to make or establish a home for themselves, others move in, mostly bachelors, old male beavers, to use this same body of water and make a place often where there is a high bank on shore, working in there digging brush and limbs, small peeled old pieces of poplar poles, working in mud all around. This is made this way where the entrance into the bank often becomes shallow, to keep it from freezing up. Here also the males become entangled in fights and sometimes one gets killed. I mentioned before how we found a dead one that had been killed recently for when I skinned him out I could see the cuts around the neck very plainly. Also in different beaver locations there were homes where some had perfect setups and not too much work sometimes requiring only two dams for survival and plenty food not too far away. Then where others had settled on small creeks often there was not a poplar tree within two hundred feet back from shore and to think of all the work they had to do in order to get the location they have which was perhaps ten times the size of their neighbor's, a mile across country through the woods on some springfed clear running stream. And so I thought it was with people where one drives on a road of a hundred or two hundred mile stretch to see the change of living conditions. It is easy to notice the farmhouses, the line of the barns, they often have miles of rock fences and it may have taken several generations of work to clear the land. The biggest change I noticed that takes place in those farming countries is when the land gets poor here you see mostly the small bushy scrub oaks for miles and miles. This also means that there is sandy soil and so it is with life. For some of us it is easier than others, it just depends upon in what place you were born. The circumstances of the environment, especially the homelife while growing up, can set a pattern for all our remaining years of our life. However, many things can happen in the life span of a person and if not well grounded in the way we should go; it is difficult to run a good race, win when we are finished, and to inherit eternal life. In my story here of my first ten years in the northwoods I have talked so much about nature. As I am writing this from experience, things I have done and seen, as I look back on my life I can see what effect these things had on me and also the outcome of every individual detail the way it happened. This includes many things since the time of 1940. These I would like to list when I bring this story to an end, thinking that my grandchildren may read this some day. Certainly I am more than thankful that it was God's will that I should write this, to give me the strength and courage and understanding to help me to know and learn the truth and it is the truth that can make us free.

I wandered with my thoughts from the woods when I was speaking about beaver dam locations, good and poor places, and then making some comparisons on that in the life of people. While Dynamite and I had a few days left out here in this wilderness (spring beaver trapping would wind up the season) one is only disturbed from activities of nature that surrounds one. There is also a constant change of thought as one approaches this and that. On this day still going further into remote places where I had not been before, a balance of interest was maintained regardless of the physical endurance it would call for. I found more beaver locations when I followed the small river up in here. From finding the first dam one can tell if it is an ideal location just by the condition of this first small dam which was a quarter of a mile down from the main large dam as they keep their property in repair constantly patching it up here and there, giving a trapper the information that there are beaver around. Now I had to go back and get the canoe so I could get into this flowage that seemed to extend a ways up forming a basin, killing all the trees that got flooded, spruce, hundreds of them yet standing with all those dead limbs like porcupine quills mixed with snags and stumps sticking out all around. Where the steam originally was, one can often find a fifty to one hundred foot wide open waterway. It would have been impossible to go any place amongst those trees, for it was a jungle. I was thinking of how the beaver swim around here for the water was deep. One can tell just about how old a location is since the beaver dammed it up, by the condition of the flooded trees for in time eventually they fall down slowly one by one. Only once in my life had I found a new location that the beaver had built that same year as the green poplar trees that had been flooded were still standing in the water. Set out four traps, had time to go further into this area, had six traps left and wanted to get them all set out. Not knowing what lay beyond meant that I had to scout ahead first depending then upon what I would find. Some streams or creeks here could not be traveled by canoe because of rough rugged changing current flowing over rocks underneath thick elders leaning in from each side of the shore, often covering the whole stream. Often I thought, when I saw this place, there must be trout in here. Carrying the ax and traps with me I went fifty to one hundred feet back from this creek bottom halfway up a side hill, a natural formation, from a large ravine. Often in such places it is hard walking and slows a person down. Also I was careful with my sore ear in places where I had to stoop down because of limbs and other thicket of growth from trees and bushes. Now I never was without cotton to put in that ear and tried to baby it along the best I could. Never at any time did I feel gloomy about it and it seemed like it was a challenge in some respect. Wherever nature had left the layout of gullies on a creek or stream and even some rivers, here the beaver would find them and build a dam. These dams were in the best locations, I can guarantee you, for it would be impossible wandering around out here like I did, not to notice that. So, it was not too far up and I found another long narrow like flowage. Again I went back for the canoe for by now I was partly spoiled setting traps out of the canoe and where this was accomplished this seemed like a more carefree way of trapping. Managed to get all the traps set out and brought the skinned-out beaver hide back with me to show this for my day's work. Like a small business man one constantly looks for the future. When the traps were out in places where the beaver were really moving, there was bound to be a catch of some kind. Couldn't get back here until the day after for I had to get back to what we considered our main camp as I was running out of food. Also by now I wanted to see Dynamite to find out how many beaver he got on his shooting expedition. And, I did miss his company and the cooking. If he had any beaver, I would have to skin them out. This was something he would not do and he would lug them home in his packsack. I knew now that I really had to hustle to get back before dark. I had to carry the canoe back on what was called a portage (of my own making) straight through the woods. The time I lost in the woods, hanging up the canoe ever so often, that time I made up by paddling as hard and fast as I could down those beaver flowages. On the last jump of this journey I was glad that I had the scaffold there for the canoe, the one I had made the other night in a hurry on the end of the last flowage. These are vital principles one has to follow that one cannot depart from, for it got late and it had gotten dark on me. As long as I was out on open water in the canoe I could see the outline of the silhouette forming a shadow against where the timber line bordered the shore. First I had trouble finding the spot where I had the canoe rack, it took about ten minutes. Crawling on highland near the shore I found it. Then I went back again to the canoe and paddled it back here to the rack. One works more by judgment when doing things like placing the canoe up on a contraption as far up as I could reach. No, I couldn't leave it in the water as the bear would smell the beaver I carried in there for a ways. No telling what they would do as they often take funny notions. It could have been when I was fumbling around there that the bear was watching me. Now since I got in the woods it seemed darker than ever. Must say I was worried some to find my little camping spot up a ways from here by the high rock walls. It always seemed where danger was involved in an adventure, a threat of the unforeseen became exposed in different forms, like tonight in this condition I needed added courage. It also seemed that way out here away from civilization that life became doubly dear. This must have been where, in a form of natural instinct, I thought I was trifling with danger. The worst I could think of was running into a bear that had cubs. I had a hard time finding my camp. First I found the rock wall and made my way from there for I had direction and the general layout of this surrounding territory in mind so I could easily have drawn a picture of it. It is like a code conveying certain information in time of need. Got busy and made a large fire. There was wood on hand as it was always gathered in the morning and placed in a pile, all dry wood, for occasions like this in case one should come in late. One gets accustomed to such a practice and tonight it paid off and under such circumstances one really gets to appreciate this. Brought home the two hind quarters of the beaver as by now I was short of food. So this meant start and parboil this right away for about fifteen minutes to get it clean, then remove it and clean the pail with hot water, fill the pail with fresh water and salt and cook them for two hours. Afterwards brown them good in the old frying pan using lard. I ran out of flour so I just ate one of these hind quarters. Had to save one for the morning as it would be tomorrow night before I could make our other camp where we had plenty of food. I did have a half a box of raisins left, and I chewed them up, being hungry and I had to wait two hours before this beaver meat would be cooked, and it was late at night. Also, I made a mistake; I should have cut off more meat from the beaver I got today for tomorrow. Having to travel all day through the woods I would have nothing to eat for dinner. This can happen once in a while where time and the amount of food needed can be misjudged. All this time I was sitting watching the fire burn and also looking at the dollar watch I had to see when the two hours would be up. I always wanted to make sure that the meat was well done. In this great wilderness that surrounded me, all was free for us to take and use. It was to me an elaborate setup pioneering often the thought that I was living like an Indian in many ways. Also, the life out here had a certain appeal for it was a free life. The furs were valuable according to the times we had then. Had my sleeping bag hanging down over the rock wall on a separate wire that I had to get. Being dark however I could see part way over there to the rock wall from the light of this cooking camp fire I had going here. I did not want to use the pup tent when the weather was nice for somehow I was afraid that a bear might crawl in thinking he could get tangled up while I was sleeping. This could not happen when I lay out in the open on the ground in the sleeping bag. Since I had been trapping out here, this was my fourth trip up to now, no bear had touched me and so one gets accustomed to those conditions.

Here another night went by and all went well with the bear, I saw none around. They have a large territory to roam around in out here. However, I do not remember of a time when I had beaver carcasses around that the bear were not there to pick them up. Had my other hind quarter of beaver left from last night and this would go for my breakfast. It has been my experience that the less food I had the more I enjoyed what I did have. This was certainly a day that I would be very anxious to get back to the other camp mainly for the food also to see Dynamite. It was like a homecoming even though I was only gone one day. Also, one of the satisfactions was that I would get to sleep inside, solid walls around me and a roof over my head. It was the closest thing to home reminding me of my logging camps where by now I had spent considerable time off and on. So I hustled to get all the usual things out of the way from the bears. I had moved most of the traps to new locations since we brought the canoe up this way so back this other way I only had five traps left. By the time I visited them on my way south, there was only one beaver caught. So I skinned him out. Although I had no grub left and no dinner, never at any time would one take time out to prepare meat in daylight hours, not unless it was raining, for a trapper also learns to go hungry and it doesn't bother him too much. His main concern is that he makes camp, wherever he has his locations and his sleeping and cooking outfit set up. I did, at all times, carry matches, an ax, a gallon pail, some food as something could happen that would prevent one from getting to the desired destination. This one takes for granted, however you don't want to believe that for in our everyday life we do not look for things that may harm us. I still had plenty of trouble with my ear, the one I poked a stick into - it was getting better, though. I made camp before dark and was a happy person when I got the first glimpse of the shack through the large heavy wooded spruce trees. So as not to sneak up on Dynamite I made some kind of noise so he would know that I was coming. To my surprise he wasn't there and the door was wired shut good. It did not take me long to get the door undone for I was really hungry. Yes, I found food prepared ready to eat. Dynamite never failed me and he was expecting me home tonight. While I was eating he came with a beaver in his packsack - he also got one the day before. So by adding on the three beavers this made a total of ninety-seven skins. Now within a few days we could go home. Dynamite said, ''I have to tell you what happened and how I got this one - you'll never believe it.'' He was over west of here where there was a creek dammed up and the water between two dams was around a thousand feet in length and about five hundred feet wide. Yesterday early, about three in the afternoon, he was standing on the lower part of the dam. The wind was blowing rather strong toward him so there were good-sized ripples on the water. Looking up that way just that second a beaver dove down very slow out in the water - he must have seen Dynamite first and then disappeared. He walked rather fast up one side. There was an open spot with several large rocks lying near the water's edge and grass was growing in a good sized clearing. He got behind one of the rocks, only stood there a few minutes when the beaver came down swimming slowly right out in the middle of this wide long pond. By now he could guess what he had done and also was doing. He swam all the way back under the water. Now he came down again swimming on top trying to find out where Dynamite was or who or what he was. Yes, he was looking for Dynamite and the wind was in his favor but standing so far over on land he couldn't get his scent. Dynamite placed the rifle on the rock, the beaver could not see him standing behind that big rock, took a good aim for his head, pulled the trigger, yes, he hit him. He started to flop around, dart under the water and then above. Dynamite went down and stood on the very edge of the water. All at once the beaver disappeared and he was looking out in the direction he last saw him when all of a sudden he saw a black streak thirty feet out under water coming straight toward him. Well, he came right out where Dynamite was standing, between his legs, crawling. No doubt he was hurt badly, so Dynamite took the rifle placed it on his head, and there he was. Yes, it was kind of a coincidence the way it happened and it was rather an unusual thing. That also meant that I had two beaver to skin that night and then it meant that the one I brought made three to stretch. One thing was certain that from the time we left the trail and managed to get back (it was the Gunflint trail) we never ran out of activities. It was either some kind of work or struggle of one thing or another inasmuch as there was a carefree existence out here among our wild animal friends. They too were not worry free. It may seem at times that the squirrels sit on a limb all day in the sun and many of the animals just wander around taking things easy yet they do not live idle lives for they strive endlessly toward survival. One time I saw two porcupine fighting. I never heard so much noise and odd squealing as they made. So in the animal kingdom there is death lurking from many corners, where often a song of a bird can be a death call as a hawk swoops down to kill it. Being completely surrounded for days and nights with the working of nature, with living and growing things, one cannot help but observe every little thing like the workings of ants or woodpeckers, yes, beaver and porcupine. It always seemed fitting to end a day good if one thinks to summarize and support the day's activities, for one could recall at least one or two incidents that had served some important task. We were, in one sense of the word, used to roughing it. There was nothing modern about us. We could eat a meal and at the same time there might be a bloody beaver carcass nearby but that had no effect on our stomachs in those days. We knew now that we would soon be breaking up camp for the full moon is now shaping up. We will travel mostly at night paddling the canoe. This will be the first time I had the privilege of transporting skins by canoe. Often this had become the biggest job, often a struggle, to get these furs out of here carrying them out sixty-five miles through the woods, through swamps and over rugged terrain. It may seem strange that such a wilderness can make friends with us. The feeling is that you are part of a whole, having a physical, mental and spiritual effect that one can feel and see distilled within you, and uniting a cause of relationship between man and nature. We realized that we took this fur, which was also a product of nature, so freely and we gave nothing back. Man in his environment can become very selfish and greedy. I realize this now more than ever while Iam writing this story that it is true. In time things will and can destroy and sadden our lives. Those pioneering days were happy days and often that happens when we recall the days when we had rough going-often those were the days one does remember.

Dynamite and I were talking about the canoe we had way up north and neither of us wanted to think about the idea of bringing it back down here when now, within two days, we had to start out on our way back. It was late evening before we hit the bunks to call it a day after stretching the three beaver skins on the boards we had. We had plenty to talk about and came to the decision that we would try and find a canoe route up north and from there circle back southwest coming back in the direction that we had to head back from. Knowing now that we will have over a hundred skins was uppermost in my mind and it was a satisfying thought to know that again I had made a success out of spring trapping. How one could get so

206

informal, making our own rules, outweighing all things, the tension of any danger of getting caught. We knew the nearer we approached civilization the more careful we would have to be. Thre are some discomforts that come along; often new things that one is not accustomed to. One represents an occupation where a variety of things can enter in. We heard that the minimum fine for one skin caught in the Superior National Forest was $50. So when morning came we had plenty to do. Got everything packed up and tried to divide our load evenly. Also we realized that we had to leave our sleeping bags behind not realizing then that I would never return again. I had $100 worth of equipment that we had to leave here. Most of it will be locked up in the shack. One packsack and a pup tent were left hanging down up north in my little camp by the rock wall. I do not know to this day if anyone ever found our camps and some of the things we left behind.   One thing we would not leave behind was the rifle. So this morning we got our things together, packing up, first rolling the skins very tight making two bundles. We started with the smaller size first, like rolling a calendar, adding on and on and by the time there were fifty it got to be a fair sized bundle. We tied this tightly with rope. One does a lot of thinking about the hardships I had on every one of my previous trips in and out of here on this trapping life. Often I thought I had so much to bear out here and this was because I did not know how to do these things like an Indian would. From what I heard, these people have a way of getting along out in the woods and know how to work with all things that nature provided for them. No doubt that is because they are raised in this kind of an environment. On the Canadian border there was an Indian family that had a resort. .One heard a lot about these people. They had a seaplane and they would catch beaver in what is called a live trap. The fur did not have to be prime for they sold them to fur farmers, people that had places where they could keep them often in a stage of natural environment. The story I heard was the Indian had one large beaver alive in a sack in this small seaplane. This was in August and it was a hot day. Somehow while he was flying back out of the woods, somewhere up there in that wilderness, the beaver managed to get out of the sack as he was thirsty. Before the Indian knew it the large beaver was standing straight up with his front feet on his shoulders panting. The only thing he could do, he said, was come down and give the beaver some water. I was there one time at that place. They were building a very large boat to carry twenty people, all out of wood. I admired the fancy perfect wooden rib construction and I can still see the picture of it in my mind. As I never was much of a mechanic or carpenter I admired the Indians for their skill in those days. The young Indian wife would also trap beaver in the spring and the report was that she wound up with a hundred skins, not saying how many the men folks got. Well, we know that all of those things are things of the past. Today no airplanes are allowed to fly over that part of the country. The league, of which you know the name, wants to keep this strictly as a wilderness. The portage accommodations and the landing docks on canoe routes were once built by the CCC camps. I heard also that they have been removed. This I will find out some day, I hope, when I get to go out and back in there just to see what really is happening. I want to take my two boys along and this has been part of my dream, that some day we would be able to do this before I get so old that I won't be able to crawl. Certainly with all those beaver out there multiplying all those years, there is no doubt the battle of nature is taking a hand. They are migrating further and further south, even here in Wisconsin they have gone south in some of our counties. I would say that the bear will get their share up there in northern Minnesota and Canada and since they have nobody to feed them any more beaver carcasses they will have to catch their own. The food supply also can get to be a great problem for the beaver. One could not escape noticing this thirty-five years ago. It would be impossible for me to describe the existing condition of the beaver and otter population up in the neck of the woods. It has been found that many beaver had a sickness from reports of the 1968 open season in Wisconsin. This is not good and I hope they look into it. Most people will no doubt say, "Don't worry about it as nature will take care of it." Just mentioned a few of these things here as my memory takes me back.

Now we will be leaving our shack (I managed to get one rather dark picture of it) that had provided so much comfort for us and saved us many hardships. To think it took only two days to build, like a jewel, an object of nature's product rugged in beauty. It was our centralized starting place setting a state where the battle of life was drenched within us like a cool drink of water, where at times complex intricate teachings were on the march fortifying our work for another tomorrow. It was at times when every hour was a changing scene that left us in a changing mood, for now we made our start out of here to places we called home. First we would stop at the logging camp as soon as we got in. The fur is hidden away for security from man and beast. The skins had all been dried so no deterioration can take hold as long as they are kept dry, for we thought they were precious hard-earned merchandise. So Dynamite and I made our way up north where I had my small overnight stopping camp for our stay and this would be our very last night taking up the traps as we came to them. We managed to get to the camp by nightfall - this was a well-sheltered place. It was in a corner of two ten foot high rock walls coming together solid which made only one entranceway. After all this time, having learned many habits concerning the bear this one night here we were very much concerned about them as we had all the hides with us where before they were always securely hung up. We knew that the bear did not care to eat them but their curiosity could be aroused. They may want to smell them and then thinking that there may be something inside would be tempted to tear them apart. First, under no circumstances could we trust the bear with our skins while we are sleeping. Neither one of us was in condition to stay awake all night and watch with the rifle, taking turns. So we thought of the next best thing. We would place poles across ten feet in front of us to get into the corner where we were sleeping. In order to get in there they would have to knock the poles down, Dynamite would have his rifle ready to shoot if we heard any noise. That also meant that we would have to wake up fast. Well, with all these crazy thoughts on our mind all in all we had a restless night. Nothing really happened and we were up in the bright early morning. On this trip we were well supplied with food. The hundred pounds of flour we brought in last fall went a long way. To think of how many trappers had penetrated this wilderness before us and I do not believe they ever had such good going, taking into consideration the shack for shelter and then the variety of food we had. There were many things we should have been thankful for but often when we are young we take most things for granted. Knowing that we were a good distance from civilization, the first two days we would paddle the canoe in the daytime. This we did and we also found a portage, canoe route, two miles north of here and this was a big help to us. After taking up the rest of the traps, we had two more beaver so by now I had skinned over a hundred and each skinning was done carefully to make certain not to cut the hide. The canoe up on that high rack, sitting there on the edge of that beaver pond, was a welcome sight. We had all our things packed in good shape for transporting whenever we had to carry them overland. It meant that we had to make two trips on every portage without being overloaded. We had one blanket a piece and two raincoats. The first day we didn't get very far as it was windy and it is surprising on a fair-sized lake how high the waves can get. It seems like all our adventure came to a climax traveling out here across this lake in this old canoe with all those beaver skins. When one thinks that a certain destination should be reached in a day, endlessly hour after hour we paddled. There seemed to be a rhythm of fascination in the accomplishment of the movement as the canoe would slide silently and swiftly through this very deep cold water. The range of depth was from two to fourteen hundred feet and the water kept cold until June. Most all of the lakes had lake trout in them. Now it was our third day coming up on this trip and rainy weather set in. This made things very miserable so we had to give up and look looked for a place to camp away from the portage route. One always has the thought in mind that someone might come along. We paddled around to the extreme bend in a small bay and were anxious to get off of the lake. The raincoats we had were not very good and therefore we got rather wet. We had the smaller waterproof cover with us and after making a skeleton frame rack for placing the canoe upside down as part shelter, then combining the waterproof sheeting together as a one unit affair was the best we could do. We were always struggling around with the skins so they would not get wet. As soon as we had that organized then we thought of ourselves, of changing into our old dirty full-of-holes long underwear. Each one of us had two pair. These were the ones we wore on our way in now almost two months ago changing only when we got wet - it was a sight to look at. However, on a day like this to get something dry against your body was a welcome feeling that one could appreciate. We got a good fire going and made something to eat, moving about here in this very small space where it would keep most of the rain off from us, for by now we knew it was one of those all night rains. Having experienced them often by now one got so you could feel it in your bones and the cloud formations would help to testify to that. It would take two good full days before we could reach the Tuscarara River, the land I was logging had come up to this river. We knew for safety's sake we would have to travel from here on at night. This meant we had to wait until it cleared up for a full moon was in the making and this was the only way we could see to find the portages between these lakes and this was confusing even in the daytime. Remember several times it took us two to three hours paddling around the shoreline in and out of bays to find the portage. These trails are about eight feet wide and have been cleared out between lakes where the shortest distance and accessibility could be found. Often on outlets from one lake to another in this area the elevation of fifty to three hundred feet drops in a quarter or half mile and this meant that the portage would be very rugged and often one struggled when carrying the canoe as we did on this moonlit night. This never ending struggle was part of this trapping life; all these things are expected and taken for granted. Yes, we lost a day on account of the rain and then another day. On one of the larger lakes in this country a strong wind came up and the waves got so high, they were also going in the wrong direction, and we were afraid to cross this lake. Again we camped away from the portage catching up on sleep and resting, for we knew that our traveling at night the next few nights took all the alertness we could muster. So, we took advantage of our time.

As it was every day new things happened after I left my logging camp. Somehow I felt there was no future there for me. The limelight of that adventure had kind of worn down. I owed $200 to the party who helped me to get started there. As he was a native I just left him the logging camp and most of the belongings in it. All this was done on an impulse that had come in five or ten minutes - a decision to leave everything behind that actually was a responsibility. Somehow I had an understanding with the party I was dealing with that I was to take out this thousand cords of spruce pulp wood costing $1.75 a cord and bring it out with a team and sleigh one mile from the Gunflint Trail down to the highland from the swamp. Figuring the cost of hauling forty-six miles down this road to Grand Marais ate up the profits. Here this four foot long peeled spruce wood is dumped into the lake and then loaded by conveyor into ships. there were many thoughts that confronted me as one does not want to be a quitter. However as I saw the whole job and got all the figures together, cost, etc., there was no way I could come out because it was all hand labor. And so it was as it happened - I never got back. I left it all to the party I owed the $200 to. This may seem very strange for I never talked to him about it. (He is living yet on the Gunflint Trail.) As far as I know he took the place over. And to this day I saw him once after that, five years later and neither of us talked about it. It was, in a way, a very strange deal. All my life I have been easy going, this at times is good and sometimes bad. the best part is I did not end up with any ulcers. However, I did let money slip through my fingers, as the saying goes. so I took things in a modest way like most of us who have a certain philosophy about life. However, I did not get back to my trapline, not to say that I gave up beaver trapping, for at a later time I learned more and more about getting this fur in early spring in Wisconsin where I would be in civilization. Here conditions are met entirely differently. First, many hardships are eliminated. The food of canned goods can include good things if one is not a penny pincher. And so to prove that back in the days of depression I did trap in that wilderness. I wrote this story the way things were happening from day to day. I left a good number of traps by an old large pine stump. Now soon, before I get too old, I want to take my two sons back there on a trip to show them these traps and many other things and to take pictures here and there. I am afraid the spruce log cabin may have fallen down by now. I doubt that anyone ever stumbled onto any of these things. This particular canoe route is very seldom traveled and then a stranger often would be afraid to travel too far away from this route as that always means walking and walking. And so all of these things did happen that I have told you here and in spite of all the hardships endured, the memories gathered and things I learned, led me on to a better way of life. It does seem that it was long ago when I was a young man, was strong and had good nerves, sometimes too much nerve. To think when I was walking on the ice which was too thin and not safe - I did fall in now and then but I always managed to get out. Remember, it happened only once that I did not carry this ten foot pole. There I was lucky - an outlet at the edge of the lake and it was only waist deep ten feet from shore and with my small ax cut the three inch ice and got to shore. I am sure that beaver trappers dating back near to the founding of this country were always restless characters. This adventure to explore new country searching for beaver just grows on you and is the very fullfilment as a wilderness unfolds before your eyes, the lakes and streams, portage trails, truly at that time it was a paradise of game and fur. They filled my wildest dreams - the days I started out for parts unknown into the western sun. I did build some camps there and made my runs from there. It was really my home. Traveling with a packsack sometimes in a canoe one found that a spring hole was a very good place for storing canned goods, for here it did not freeze and the bear did not find it. So back in those days I did settle out there. Never did I rest each night until all the chores were done, always planning for the next day. As one could not keep the bear away so you learned to live with them. It is funny now when I think back that often I did not have a gun. So some people will doubt this when I tell them these tales of hardships I've been through. The freeze-ups always came early in the fall and the swamps were full of rain. But when it froze the water dropped and the ice did remain. This always made for better walking, cracking through now and then for often this ice is hollow. No doubt many deer hunters have experienced this and as it happens sometimes one gets wet. As long as one stays above water and can breathe some air all other problems as they come man always seems to work out, although I have seen the time when my life did hang in balance. When these things are over one soon forgets when it works out that we can live, and there is always so much joy kindled with hope. Often I would be so tired I would sleep beneath a giant spruce. It did happen that bear came snooping around and stood straddle over me for I could see their footprints in the frost. They came and went for in slumber I was lost. Often it would look like rain and I would head for camp. My first trip into the land for fur where there was only ice and cold did get rough. But when I sold my hides they brought a real big check. Often the whole undertaking seemed like a dream and all hardships were forgotten until the next trip out. So the years came and now they are gone, running the traplines back in those days.

In later years I learned that one could never return...you see, it was no longer mine. So the memories remain. And as you leave to portage out on a certain lake, upon the northern side one hundred steps and up the trail, a pine once there had died. As I said before, if today you should find a number of traps by its stump, I left them there on my final trip. You'll find them, you will see. And if you stay within the land where Mother Nature dwells, remember me, I once was there, a woodsman, Carl Schels.

The End

Dynamite - 1937